the

soft

edge

the
soft
edge

**a natural history and future
of the information revolution**

PAUL LEVINSON

LONDON AND NEW YORK

First published 1997
by Routledge
11 New Fetter Lane, London EC4P 4EE

Simultaneously published in the USA and Canada
by Routledge
29 West 35th Street, New York, NY 10001

© 1997 Paul Levinson

Typeset in Perpetua by Keystroke, Jacaranda Lodge, Wolverhampton
Printed and bound in Great Britain by T.J. International Ltd, Padstow, Cornwall

British Library Cataloguing in Publication Data
A catalogue record for this book is available from the British Library

Library of Congress Cataloging in Publication Data
Levinson, Paul.
The Soft Edge: A natural history and future of the information
revolution / Paul Levinson.
Includes bibliographical references and index.
1. Information technology—History. 2. Information technology—
Forecasting. I. Title.
T58.5.L385   1997
302.23—dc21   97–7248

ISBN 0–415–15785–4

To Donald T. Campbell,
1916–1996

CONTENTS

PREFACE

The Soft Edge is about the difference that communications media make in our lives. The edge is soft because information is intangible. But it is pervasive and advantageous inasmuch as we cannot do without information, and because those who possess certain kinds of information — and more effective means of processing it — usually have an upper hand. For those unaware of this power of media, the edge can also be a precipice.

All life, indeed, operates on information. What characterizes human life is that we presumably are aware of information and its various modes of conveyance — yet so ubiquitous is this information, like the very air around us, that we often take no notice of its most profound consequences, the ones that arise when the currents of conveyance change. This book is thus a voyage of discovery, of a history and present we already know and a future under way, with an eye toward explaining how information technology helped bring them all into being.

We begin in Chapter 1 with some general principles. To say that the printing press engendered the modern world, radio the totalitarian audience, computers a new hybrid of author and reader, is not to claim that the media created and imposed these ways of living upon us, but rather that they provided crucial conditions in which new worlds could and did emerge, pathways in which human penchants long in quiet residence could now find larger expression. Part of this process is out of our control, since inventions so often have unintended consequences. But, as we'll also see, media have impact because we select them for survival over their competitors, as we did with the alphabet over hieroglyphics, talkies over silent movies, computers over typewriters. And we frequently invent and deliberately apply media to specific remedial tasks, as with the home video recorder, which gives television the means of recall and anticipation.

Stocked with these and related navigational guides, we start our tour of history. Our first stop, in Chapter 2, is the ancient world. Here we find the Egyptian heretic Pharaoh, Ikhnaton, who more than three millennia ago decreed a new monotheistic religion — whose practice in Egypt barely survived his lifetime. In contrast, the monotheism of Moses just a century later took permanent root and went on in its Christian and Islamic transformations to convert most of the world. Could the difference have been that Moses used an alphabet, in effect a digital medium whose capacity to easily describe an omnipotent, omnipresent but essentially invisible deity was lacking in the Pharaoh's picture-based, "analogic" hieroglyphics?

Our next port of call, the Europe of Gutenberg in the late fifteenth century, picks up the story of media and religion, with the proposition that the printing press made the Protestant Reformation possible by making available the Bibles that Luther said people should read for themselves. But Chapter 3 also explores the mutually catalytic relationship of the Reformation, the Scientific Revolution, the rise of national states, public education, and capitalism — each running to some extent on print, each also coaxing the others into action. The information revolution as an elicitor of human patterns already present can be seen nowhere more clearly than in the Age of Discovery, one of the prime engines of the rise of national states. The Vikings reached the New World some five hundred years before Columbus; what made Columbus different is that word of his discovery was printed and distributed throughout Europe.

Chapters 4–10 introduce us to the photochemical–electronic rounds of the revolution with photography and telegraphy in the first half of the nineteenth century, and follow their development and surprising results through the telephone, electric lighting, radio, and television to the doorstep of the computer age just a little more than a decade ago. The phonograph and motion pictures of course also figure in this recent natural history, but in this rendition they play supporting rather than leading roles, appearing within and between, rather than on top of, chapters in starring title credits. This brings to the fore an important point about our narrative from here on in: the pace of invention became so quick in the nineteenth and twentieth centuries that I have focused only on those media whose presence was clearly decisive in shaping our world prior to computers. Indeed, they still shape our world today, as do the alphabet and printing press. These selective dispatches from the information revolution describe critical junctures, some often remarked upon, others less obvious, sometimes arising from the same invention. Electricity serves not only as a distraction from reading when powering television but as the book's nighttime accomplice when providing light.

Radio not only convened the world's first simultaneous mass audiences but has flourished in an age of television because it is an incomplete medium that gives us sounds with no images, allowing us to do other things while we hear it.

The personal computer and its extensions is a medium *par excellence* for facilitating both reading and multi-tasking, or doing many things at once. Chapters 11–15 consider five aspects of this revolution before our eyes: word processing, online publishing, hypertext, its implementation on the Web, and the role of icons and images in these processes. An advantage of looking at such innovations so close at hand is that their emergence is in abundant evidence all around us, and often subject to our direct, personal experience. I have no hesitation about citing my own pleasure with word processing, and the freedom it gives from frustrating negotiations with the typewritten pages that once were required for every correction – or the lessons I have found about online communication in Connected Education, which has been offering university courses through personal computer and modem under the supervision of my wife and me for more than a decade. Of course, a drawback to studying a transformation newly in progress is that we cannot be as clear about its outcome as we can about inventions and consequences that first appeared three thousand, five hundred, or even a few years ago. As recently as 1994, surveys estimated that the average American watched 1,560 hours per year of television and spent 3 hours on the Internet and other online services; by the middle of 1996, a different kind of measurement shows television still reaching more than 250 million Americans in contrast to estimates ranging from 9 to more than 40 million Americans on the Internet (see Dizard, 1997, and Kantor and Neubarth, 1996, for details); all that we know for sure about the extent of online patronage is that it is growing rapidly, yet is still a fraction of that enjoyed by older media.

In the concluding four chapters of the book, we embark almost entirely into the future, the hard evidence of which is in even shorter supply. In Chapter 16, we weigh the prospects of a medium to which we and our words have been remarkably attached since the printing press: paper. In Chapter 17, which may be the most important practical section of this book, I argue for stronger, not weaker, provisions for intellectual property in the digital age, and make an explicit proposal for a new kind of "smart" patent number, an electronic watermark embedded in every technology, which would provide people with a ready listing of its inventors, and therein heighten the profile of authorship and the products of intellectual labor. I offer this proposal in the hope that it will be seriously considered and then implemented.

Chapter 18 shifts from the practical to the ethical, and indeed more than any other stage of this excursion enters the "what if?" realm of science fiction. What if we developed computers that were more than adjuncts and auxiliaries of our intelligence – the extensions and enhancements of cognition that they are today and will continue to be, at least in part, in the future – and were truly autonomous intelligences? The very posing of the question presumes that we do not yet have anything like that, and I elaborate at length as to why I think that is the case, yet need not always be. Our popular culture has worried that such AI entities might destroy us – but if we did develop machines with intelligence that truly rivalled our own, would we be right to treat them like slaves?

We round out the voyage in Chapter 19 – in a sense return home – with a look at what is, in effect, the other side of the AI question: are there some aspects of being human which, absent a modification of our genome which would make us a different species, can never be satisfied by any information technology? Investigation of this issue brings into play the fundamental contrasts of information versus physical reality, remote robotic versus in-person acquisitions of knowledge, representations versus originals that reside in the very heart of all information technology, and its continuing evolution which is the subject of this book. The ultimate limits of what can be done in cyberspace, or by any conceivable medium of communication, are the limits of the information revolution, and of *The Soft Edge*.

In addition to the expectations about the evolution of media with which we began, we will encounter throughout our journey a recurring set of characters, issues, and theories waiting to greet us almost each time we step ashore.

The first is what I call the Greek chorus of critics. Actually, only one, Socrates – and/or Plato – is Greek. And in most ways the chorus is not at all uniform, ranging from Socrates to Hitler in benefit and damage its members have other-wise bequeathed to the world. But both were vehement in their denunciation of the written word (Socrates in *Phaedrus*, Hitler in *Mein Kampf*), as are Karl Jaspers and Jacques Ellul in their attacks on the technological enterprise itself, Lewis Mumford and Neil Postman on electronic media, Gore Vidal and others on personal computers. What makes such criticism worthy of special attention is not that it is criticism – like Karl Popper, I believe that criticism is the essential operating system of knowledge – but that it targets certain media, or fundamental human activities like technology itself, as the root of all evil in a given society, or as lethally incompatible with certain modes of thought and discourse. We will find in this volume that the first is never the case, and the second very rarely. Moreover, inasmuch as many in the scholarly world apparently take such media pessimism as obligatory (see, for example, the brief summary by Lohr, 1995), and assume that any optimism about media can only arise in people ignorant of such critiques, I make a point of highlighting its refutation by reality throughout this book, and the optimism that stands not ignorant of but after its defeated arguments. Socrates' claim that writing is incompatible with dialogue was battered by the printing press, and thoroughly put to rest by the advent of electronic text — a development that similarly contradicts Postman's contention that electronic media are incompatible with rational discourse, unwarranted even when first lodged against television.

Second, there is what might be called, in its best light, a political expression of the above concern about the negative impact of media. In its worst light, it is plainly an abrogation of the First Amendment to the US Constitution, and its guarantee that "Congress shall make no law . . . abridging the freedom of speech, or of the press." That fundamental safeguard of free expression received a grievous blow in the 1934 Federal Telecommunication Act, its establishment of the Federal Communications Commission in America, and subsequent legislation and Supreme Court rulings which held that broadcast media are a special kind of press whose speech can be abridged, to the point of censorship, by government. Print media also have been put under government pressure in this century — the worst instance being Richard Nixon's attempt to prevent *The New York Times* and *The Washington Post* from publishing the "Pentagon Papers" in 1971 — but they generally stayed clear of legislated interference, until the new Telecommunication Act of 1996 and its prohibition of "indecent" written material on the Internet was passed by Congress and signed into law by Bill Clinton. Against these and frequent other occasions in history for government attempts to control the flow of information, I argue along with Milton, Jefferson, and Mill for the inherent rationality of people, our capacity to separate truth from falsity, identify garbage and teach our children about its dangers. We perform these tasks imperfectly, but far less so than government, which not only always fails in its high-minded intentions, but in the trying runs the risk of impairing the vehicles of free expression which are the best hope for improvement. This, indeed, is the real threat, not only to rational discourse and freedom, but to the process of media evolution itself. If this book does nothing else, I hope it calls attention to the uselessness and peril of the Communications Decency Act (the section of the Telecom Act that applies to the Internet; see Chapter 13 in this volume). It not only deserves to be found unconstitutional; it never should have been enacted in the first place.

And, speaking of the evolution of media, this narrative comes woven with a theory of media evolution that I developed some two decades ago in my doctoral dissertation, "Human replay" (1979). As that title may suggest, the theory is simply this: All media eventually become more human in their performance – that is, they facilitate communication that is increasingly like the ways humans process information "naturally," or prior to the advent of given media. Voices on the telephone replace the dots-and-dashes of telegraph; color photography replaces black-and-white; and the fluid online written dialogue, more like speech in some respects than print, now is beginning to compete with older, paper media. That the older forms – telegraph, black-and-white photography, print on paper – were developed in the first place was due to the enormous extension across space and/or time, beyond our biological means of perception, that they provided. We were willing to put up with their tradeoffs, with their sacrifice of essential components of human communication, as long as we had no other way of communicating across such vast reaches. But the pressure remained for media that extended beyond biological barriers without dispensing with the voices and colors and immediacy of the natural world, and slowly the best of both is being obtained. This, of course, flies in the face of critics of the technological age in yet another way, by showing that "artificiality" is but a waning, early, condition of media. The reader will find this "anthropotropic" theory – evolution of media towards human performance – and its applications cropping up throughout our natural history of information technology, especially in Chapter 9, where we use it to explain why some media survive and others fail in their competition for human attention.

Like all works, this one makes use of the work of many others. Rather than thanking all of their authors here, I list them in the Bibliography.

But there are four people whose work has made a preeminent contribution to this volume – whom, moreover, I have personally known – and I therefore want to say a few words about each of them.

Marshall McLuhan (1911–1980), more than any other writer in history, created the very field of study of "media effects" and how they make a difference. His observations and speculations light up nearly every chapter of this book – even those concerning personal computers, which came of age after his death – and who knows how many insights I picked up from him in the wonderful conversations we had around his home in Wychwood Park in 1977.

Donald T. Campbell (1916–1996) wrote articles rather than books, but they were more than enough to establish the discipline of "evolutionary epistemology" – the continuities and analogies between the evolution of biological organisms and the evolution of human knowledge that are the sails and sea winds of this voyage.

I wrote "Human replay" and its Darwinian theory of media evolution just prior to reading Campbell's work, but I remember how thrilled I was to come upon Campbell's much larger, stronger, schema, and how pleased I was, sixteen years later in 1995, when he wrote of my then-new book, *Learning Cyberspace*, about "Levinson's career as an evolutionary epistemologist and exponent of Karl Popper's philosophy. Alone among us, he has extrapolated this philosophic framework to display the implications of the new information technologies." *The Soft Edge* is an attempt to further fulfill the challenge of that blurb.

The philosophy of Karl Popper (1902–1992) indeed plays a central role in this natural history too. More than any other thinker in the twentieth century, he systematically argued that our response to dogmatism need not be an anything-goes relativism, but rather a recognition of both the fallibility of our knowledge and its capacity for improvement via criticism and testing in reality. As a champion of reason in an alternately fanatical and cynical age, Popper's political contribution puts him in a league with Jefferson and Mill. As an epistemologist, he worked the same evolutionary fields as Campbell and laid the groundwork for my own extension of this approach to media, since technologies survive only to the degree that they embody some accurate knowledge of reality. In fact, I first came upon Campbell's work when researching *In Pursuit of Truth*, the *Festschrift* for Popper I edited in 1982.

The Foreword that I commissioned from Isaac Asimov (1920–1992) for *In Pursuit of Truth* constitutes the main evidence of our intersection prior to this book, but I have known his work far longer than any of the others, ever since I read his science fiction about robots when I was 10 years old. If this voyage were just one of history, Asimov would still be a relevant guide, since he is throughout his work a staunch advocate of human reason and its application in technology as the best means of our improvement. But when we turn to the future, Asimov's science fiction becomes an indispensable preamble. More so than any formal philosopher of artificial intelligence, his stories about robots bring to life the hypothetical question of what we might do with these ultimate information technologies – and, indeed, after our history of what media have done, what remains in *The Soft Edge* and after is what that edge might do, which in turn is mostly a question of how we decide to use it.

Professors routinely thank their students, but in this case the tour of history and the future conducted here has been in motion since the "Intro to Mass Media" courses I taught at Fairleigh Dickinson University in the 1970s and 1980s, and indeed in the "History and Development of Mass Media" course I currently teach at Hofstra University. In between, courses in "Artificial Intelligence and Real Life" and "Popular Culture and the Media" I developed and taught at the New School for Social Research provided many occasions for refinement of some of the ideas presented in this book. Discussion of theories in classrooms and seminars provides uniquely useful clues for improvement, and I am grateful to all of my students over the years for helping in that process.

Special thanks go to my Editor, Adrian Driscoll, and the top-notch staff at Routledge.

The three people in this world with whom I have no doubt discussed the ideas in this book more than with any others are my wife, Tina, and our children, Simon and Molly. Innumerable dinners, breakfasts, walks on the beach, around the block, trips in the car, sprawlings in front of the television have been punctuated by some thought about media raised by me, or one of my family, and the conversations that ensued. If, in addition to the soft edge of the information revolution, there is a soft edge – a human awareness and dimension – in the way this book has been written, the credit belongs to my family.

Paul Levinson
White Plains, NY
May 1997

1

INTRODUCTION

"Natural histories" abound in scholarship and popular treatments of human affairs — a recently re-issued, not entirely inapt, example being Tabori's *The Natural History of Stupidity* (1993).

So why risk the danger of adding to Tabori's volume with a natural history of information technology?

The association is more than attractive, provocative packaging. Information and the structures that disseminate, preserve, and thus shape it are, in their very origin, natural: what else is DNA, and the living structures that it both shapes and is shaped by, if not a system of information technology *par excellence*? As the pioneer cyberneticist Norbert Wiener recognized – and clearly articulated (1948) – a half-century ago, biological and technological systems both run on patterns of information dispersal, including feedback, which was Wiener's greatest interest.

We should not be surprised, then, to find in the history of information technology, and in its current configurations and future projections as well, an evolutionary dynamic in many respects very much like that of the literally natural, organic world. This complex process of media evolution, of course different from as well as similar to the evolution of living things, will be the backdrop against which we will consider each of the episodes of information technology and its impact on the world in this book. Each of the episodes will be probed, in other words, not only in terms of its influence in its immediate human environment, but as an expression, clarification, on occasion refutation, of a larger theory of technological evolution also being developed in this book.

We begin, in this Introduction, with a brief description of some of the evolutionary dynamics of information technology.

INFORMATION TECHNOLOGIES COUNT

In the natural world, information not only counts on the genetic level in the ordering of proteins to form living structures, but on the environmental level, where living organisms daily face life-and-death encounters with all that surrounds them. Information about those surrounds is clearly crucial: the amoeba that lacks information about a noxious element in its vicinity may well embrace it and die.

Donald T. Campbell (e.g., 1974a) has shown how various modes of perception that have arisen in the organic world – touch, taste, smell, hearing, and vision – each provide a means of vicarious interaction with the environment, a knowledge which in some way allows the organism to encounter the environment from a distance, to embrace it without the possible payoff of immediate death. Two cardinal characteristics of this vicariousness, which will be considered extensively in our discussion of information technology in this volume, are that (1) it always entails some loss in accuracy of information, some potential for error, in comparison to the mere total embracing of any object in the environment (amoebas do not suffer from optical illusions), and (2) the particular sensory modes favored by the specific perceptual apparatus of any organism are crucial determinants of what the organism is, and how it functions in the world (sightless organisms live in a very different realm from those with vision, and indeed look very different, as well as differently).

In human beings, the vicarious mechanism of abstract thought and language works in all of the above ways. We, its possessors, have a palpable survival advantage over similar organisms that do not. To tell a group of hominids that there may be a lion a few hills away gives that group an edge not enjoyed by an otherwise equivalent group of chimps, whose only information about the possible lion comes from a member of its troupe frantically pointing and gesturing. Of course, abstract thought and language – facilitating the capacity to communicate about things not immediately present – also opens up large possibilities for lying. And these two consequences, the amplification of our survival as well as our capacity for error, are a fair shorthand for what we are as a species.

No information technology developed by humans since our emergence as thinking–speaking beings has come close to equalling, let alone exceeding or in any way replacing, the centrality of language as the essence of our species. But these technologies have had nonetheless, in more limited ways, a profound impact on our existence. We turn now to one useful means of categorizing that impact.

MEDIA DETERMINISM: HARD AND SOFT

The origins of speech and thought are so deeply entwined with our very emergence as a species that questions of which came first — abstract words or abstract thought — are very difficult to settle, as are issues of to what extent we were meaningfully human prior to our capacity for abstract language in its external and internal ramifications. I have argued for years (e.g., Levinson, 1979, 1988) that abstract thought at very least presupposes a capacity for its communication via abstract speech. Absent an ability to communicate abstractions, they provide limited evolutionary advantage: thinking a lion may be over the next hill the next day is hardly as effective, in terms of group/species survival, as speaking that thought to neighbors who can understand it.

The question of what role the powerful co-evolutionary combination of abstract speech and abstract thought may have played in determining our human existence is probably a bit easier to answer, though by no means uncomplicated. Clearly, abstract language (comprising speech and thought) is a necessary condition of our humanity: we could not be human without it. Whether language is a sufficient condition — meaning that its emergence made our humanity inevitable — is not as clear. Certainly other aspects, including bipedality and digital opposability, played crucial roles.

To the extent that an information system has an inevitable, irresistible social (or other) effect, media theorists refer to that relationship as "hard" media determinism. The relationship of abstract language to humanity comes closest to that extreme or ideal; the fact that it does not fully achieve it highlights a very profound point about information technologies and their impact on human beings, to wit, that media rarely, if ever, have absolute, unavoidable social consequences. Rather, they make events possible — events whose shape and impact are the result of factors other than the information technology at hand. Media theorists refer to this type of determinism as "soft."

To appreciate the difference between hard and soft determinism, consider the operation of information technology in creating organic structures and systems on the genetic level. Here the relationship of genotype to phenotype is not close to 100 per cent either — other factors like catalysts for the operation of DNA are significant — but there are clear pathways of cause-and-effect between DNA and organisms lacking (other than in metaphor) in the relationship of information technologies and social structures. Genes determine the colors of eyes in far less soft a manner than telescopes and microscopes applied to those eyes determine the scientific revolutions that may ensue. Indeed, though neither relationship is absolute, or "hard," which means that each is actually a variant of soft determinism, we may reasonably call the genetic hard and the social soft.

Soft determinism, then, will be the *modus operandi* of all the social consequences of information technology we will be considering in this book. It is a system of making things possible – of the result not being able to occur without the technology – rather than the technology inevitably and unalterably creating that result. It is a system that operates synergistically in its power, meaning that other crucial factors played a role in the result. The elevator made the skyscraper possible. Clearly, tall buildings would never have been constructed were there not a way to get up and down them in a few steps. But equally clearly, architecture competent to construct tall buildings was also necessary. What good is a tall building with an elevator or escalator inside, if it crumbles in the first strong wind that comes along?

Provocative assertions of media theorists may appear to be claims of hard determinism, and have been derided as such, when in fact they are assertions of soft determinism, dressed to kill as hard. When McLuhan, for example, observes that "Had TV come first there would have been no Hitler at all" (1964, p. 261), he is claiming that the substance and style of Hitler's message found essential support in the intensely personal but faceless mass delivery of radio – an intimacy between speaker and audience shattered in the more arm's-length, antiseptic images of television. Such an assertion is provocative enough, but it is hardly an insistence that radio alone or inevitably brought Hitler or the Nazis into being. McLuhan's critics (see, e.g., *McLuhan: Hot and Cool*, edited by Stearn, 1967) often miss this. Obviously, Hitler was also the result of other factors and human choices – though, as we will explore in more detail in Chapter 8, the simultaneous mass acoustic audience created by radio resulted, even in open societies, in the two most powerful democratic leaders of the century: FDR and Churchill.

Soft determinism, then, entails an interplay between the information technology making something possible, and human beings turning that possibility into a reality. Human choice – the capacity for rational, deliberate decision and planning regarding media – is an ever-present factor in our consideration of the impact of media.

In the next two sections, we will briefly consider how human rational control of media has been and can be manifested, and then how media nonetheless seem to teem with unintended consequences.

HUMAN DIRECTION

Before we address the question of human control of media, we first must consider the larger issue of human control over any events at all. Do we have free will, or is everything we do determined (in a "hard" way) by our genetic programming, environmental influences, over-arching currents of fate in the cosmos, or whatever?

I have always found the most persuasive reason for rejecting such blanket determinism, and therein keeping the possibilities of free will in play, to reside in the recognition that were everything indeed so predetermined, so would this very text, so would your and my and everyone's consideration of this very issue be a complete sham or illusion. And since I believe with every fiber of my being that I most certainly have a choice in everything I write, not to mention a healthy suspicion for any argument that inherently undermines itself (to argue for total determinism, i.e., no free will, is to argue against the efficacy of argument itself, which plays no role in the predetermined outcome), I feel comfortable rejecting any doctrine of total determinism – scientific, religious, or otherwise. At the same time, I readily admit that this choice is one of emotion as well as reason – for my brief that argument counts may indeed be a self-reflective illusion – just as beliefs that the world is real, not my dream, or rationality is preferable to irrationality, are pre-rational, or choices which cannot be unparadoxically defended by reason alone (see Levinson, 1988, for more). As someone who believes that critical rationality is the best path toward progress, I'm not particularly happy about this; but as a critical rationalist, I have no choice but to admit it.

The invocation of free will as a fundamental principle, however, is no writ for a free ride in a universe in which anything goes. Free will comes with all manner of strings attached. For example, as I frequently point out to colleague devotees of science fiction (e.g., Levinson, 1994c), free will is incompatible with time travel to the future (unless we also claim an existence of cascading ever-emerging alternate realities), for if someone could travel to a time five minutes from when I was first sitting down to write at my computer, and look over my shoulder to see what I had written, then I would have no choice but to write just and only what the time traveler had seen.

And free will, of course, also entails responsibility: for to have control is to have responsibility about how we control. In a world in which free will operates, in which the impacts of media are possible outcomes among which we may select and discard, mitigate and enhance, what control have we exhibited over our information technologies?

Unsurprisingly, as we will see in the very next section, the instances of human intention proceeding unimpeded from inception to invention to implementation are few in the realm of information technology. Indeed, unintended consequences of invention abound: Edison first thought his phonograph would be most used as a device for recording conversations on the telephone, which was in turn invented by Bell in pursuit of a hearing aid for his wife.

But there is an indirect, after-the-fact exercise of human rationality in media which is equally ubiquitous, and best captured in what I call the phenomenon of remedial media and the parable of the window shade:

Once upon a time, the only way we could look out of walls, necessary for our protection from climate and people alike, was to make holes in the walls. But these small holes resulted in our being rained on every time we used them in inclement weather. So, we invented the window. This information technology allowed us the protection of the wall from rainy, cold conditions even as we looked outside: the window was a wall, or a piece of a wall, that acted, informationally but not physically, like a hole. And therein was its great advantage.

But the advantage – like the advantage of all things evolutionary, and all things technological – was not without drawback. For as the window greatly enhanced comfortable perception from the inside out, it also enhanced easy perception from the outside in. The window brought into being the Peeping Tom. It increased our protection from climate outside the wall – for it replaced holes – but as it did this it decreased our protection from *people* outside the wall, at least insofar as they had increased informational access to the inside of our homes.

One very significant lesson we can derive from this is that all technological evolution – indeed, all evolution – entails tradeoffs. We who have vision and abstract language can be victims of optical illusions and lies which, as indicated above, are unknown to the lowly amoeba. So the window, like the vision it was designed to enhance, and the rationality that helped bring it into being, is a tradeoff.

But that same rationality allows us to do something more about tradeoffs than just accept them. Unlike the amoeba – and, indeed, all other living organisms, as far as we know – we can evaluate the tradeoff, and perhaps invent and bring to bear new technologies, remedial media, which improve the balance, if ever so slightly, in our favor.

And that is indeed what we did with the window. Rather than acquiescing to the Peeping Tom, or reverting back to holes in the wall, we invented a battery of remedial media to give us the advantages of the window without its informational disadvantages: we invented window shades, Venetian blinds, all manner of curtains. Of course, these media do not bestow perfection – a window covered with a shade can still be broken into, whereas a wall cannot – but they do increase the ratio of benefits to drawbacks in this environment.

And we can see the operation of remedial media analogous to the window shade in diverse other media systems. Television once was criticized for its ephemerality, for the incapacity of its programming to be browsed before viewing, or captured for viewing or re-viewing in the future. These drawbacks were significant indeed, for they made television on a very basic structural level less amenable to human control than the book. Indeed, some of the more extreme critics of television (e.g., Mander, 1978) urged that it be abandoned entirely, if possible, in favor of the book. Fortunately, this advice, on a par with going back to walls in response to the problem of naked new-born windows, was not followed. Instead, we invented video-taping devices, which endow television with a reviewable past and a programmable future *vis-à-vis* the viewing audience. We might say that the VCR is to TV as the window shade is to the window.

As we will see in subsequent chapters (especially 10–13), the personal computer and its impact on writing can be seen as a remedial medium that addresses the inadequacies of writing lamented as far back as Socrates, who yearned for an "intelligent writing" which could respond to questions put to it, as in a dialogue, rather than preserving a "solemn silence" (Plato, secs 275–276). Of course, not all remedial media are invented for the corrective role they may come to play – computers certainly were not invented, in the first instance, as a way to improve upon the shortcomings of text wedded to paper.

Unintended consequences thus are pervasive, even in the deliberate application of human reason in the development of remedial media. We now take a closer look at this essential Darwinian process.

THE REVOLUTION OF UNINTENDED CONSEQUENCES

A fundamental tenet of Darwinian theory is that the generation of organic characteristics and organisms occurs independently of environmental influences – that is, the environment exerts its influence, makes its selection, after the organic characteristics have been generated. In this way, the environment's influence is expressed subsequent to its encounter with an organism, which, if it survives and procreates, conveys genes that give rise to traits in some way compatible with the original environment.

This means that the gene pool and thus the generative process is far from random – the message in its code is rather at very least a blueprint for some kind of organic victory, or non-defeat, of the past. Moths, after all, do not come in all possible colors. The difference between all possible colors and the actual colors of moths is one measure of the non-random component of Darwinian generation.

But of the limited range of moth colors that are generated, those that survive at any given time do so because the color confers an advantage in a current environment. Moths whose wings are mottled in black-and-white, to use a famous example from England, once had an advantage over dark-colored moths in an environment in which lichen flourished on silver birch trees, and the resultant coloring rendered the mottled moths less visible to predatory birds. Soot from the Industrial Revolution reversed that advantage, killing the lichen and giving dark-colored moths the edge. Recently, however, we humans have cleaned up the air – a move healthy for us, but not for dark moths, which in the latest reversal of shades and fortunes find themselves easy prey against the lighter bark (see Yoon, 1996, for a parallel example in Detroit, Michigan).

In no case was the winning moth color the result of a plan or design; rather, the moth genotype generated a limited range of colors, and the color that prevailed was an unintended consequence of that color happening to be the same as the bark of the trees at a given time. In this sense, the survival of any organism is an unintended consequence of its characteristics – more precisely, the consonance of those characteristics with the current environment. And this capacity for any organic characteristic to suddenly fall in – or out – of favor relative to its environment makes evolution continuously surprising, or revolutionary.

Human technologies are of course the embodiments of their inventors' intentions. We might consider these intentions equivalent to the blueprints for past non-failure – the limited possible colors of moths – that comprise biological genomes. But as in organic evolution, the performance, impact, and survival of inventions in human society may not be in accordance with their inventors' intentions. The social environment in which the selections are made may change, like the lichen on the tree; the invention may wind up performing in an environment in which there are no trees at all, only shrubs and flowers. Bell's initial intention for his invention that became the telephone, as mentioned above, was a hearing aid. From the point of view of the telephone, and its enormous impact on society, Bell's intention was as irrelevant as if the telephone had emerged as an unintended product of biological natural selection. Since the inventor's sphere of control by and large extends only to the embodiment of an intention in an invention – not to the marketplace of ideas, finance, and custom that will determine how the invention will be used, and how successful it will be in this use in satisfaction of human needs — technologies traffic in unintended consequences every bit as profoundly as biological organisms.

Certainly the most long-lasting and significant impacts of information technology throughout history were unintended consequences of their invention. When Gutenberg began printing Bibles in the mid-1400s, he had no idea that some fifty years later these Bibles would put teeth in Luther's thesis that people should read the Bible for themselves, rather than depending on Church interpretation — a dictum that was academic and unenforceable in a world in which every Bible had to be copied by hand. Thus, as we shall see in Chapter 3, was the Protestant Reformation made possible by the press. Its success, the first successful heresy against the Church in more than a thousand years, is a classic example of an unintended consequence.

Nor could Gutenberg have realized that the spread of reliable information by the press would stimulate the Scientific Revolution; the Age of Discovery via its printed descriptions of Columbus' voyage to the New World (his was certainly not the first — the Norse were there before Columbus — only the first after the presses were rolling); the rise of national states via the printing of vernaculars; and the rise of public education as a response to the urgent need to learn how to read engendered by the new availability of books. And, indeed, only with the wisdom of hindsight can we see how each of these threads stimulated and made possible the others — how the Church, weakened by the Protestant Reformation, was less able to oppose the gathering Scientific Revolution, whose success in turn further weakened the Church, which in turn allowed the fires of nationalism to arise and go forth in a bonfire of unintended consequences, a potent molten determinism that brought our modern world into being. Ultimately, this world would overtake in many ways the Chinese culture that had invented the very first printing devices, in perhaps the longest-range boomerang unintended consequence of all.

Of course, we have no such wisdom of hindsight regarding the impact of the computer and information technology in our own age. But after discussing the above and related impacts of the alphabet and the printing press, and the new world of electronic and photo-chemical media — the telegraph, photography, motion pictures, radio, and television — that typified our informational lives until the past decade, we will turn our attention to the more speculative consideration of today's and tomorrow's media. To the degree that the consequences of these, like all technologies, are unintended, we can expect little guidance from their inventors and purveyors. Nonetheless, the mediation of human rationality in the fine tuning of information technologies can perhaps provide some grounds for reasonable expectations and predictions.

This constant assertion of human rationality is in the end what makes the information revolution different from the biological revolution of natural selection. At every turn, the impact of every medium is subject to an audience of human appraisal, expressed not only in ideas but in the behavior of utilizing a medium or not. Thus, unlike in the natural world, the selecting environment in technological evolution is a sentient one — imperfect in its capacity to learn, guided as often or more by emotion than reason, to be sure, but capable of learning and reason nonetheless.

With these two balancing factors in mind — the profoundly unintended consequences of any information technology, coupled with our capacity to appraise and perhaps adjust for its effects — we embark on our tour of the history and future of the information revolution, a tour of how this revolution has made our world possible, a tour of what worlds this revolution may make possible in the future.

2

THE FIRST DIGITAL MEDIUM

The alphabet and the rise of monotheism

Sometimes an idea can be too big for a medium to convey.

Consider, for example, the notion of a monotheistic deity, omnipotent, omnipresent, and − invisible. Difficult as it is for such an idea to be thought, spoken, and discussed, how would one draw a picture, even a stylized rendering, of it? How can visual representation be given to that which is everywhere and nowhere at the same time?

In ancient Egypt, the stylized visual representation of hieroglyphics was the dominant medium. Indeed, it was the only mode, other than the natural device of memory, for preserving the spoken word beyond its immediate and total physical decay. But unlike our alphabet, in which visual symbols represent sounds rather than images, the components of each hieroglyph were usually rooted in some visual depiction of the world. A stick figure of course is a poor rendering of a human being, but it is physically and literally derived from the human form in a way that the words "human being" − or any words, alphabetically written or spoken − are not.

One hundred and fifty years before Moses, Amenhotep IV (reigned *c*. 1372–1354 BC) had an idea about an all-powerful, ubiquitous, essentially formless monotheistic deity. As Pharaoh of Egypt, Amenhotep IV was the most powerful person in his realm. Who better than he to convey this revolutionary notion to his priests, his people, and their descendants? Moreover, Amenhotep IV seized upon a literally brilliant icon to portray this all-powerful, all-present deity that had no animal or vegetable form: the sun.

Amenhotep's glorious sun reformation − which also brought him the name of Akhenaton or Ikhnaton, after Aton, the disc-sun god − succeeded to the extent of his own reign (see Redford, 1984, for details). It ended with the death of his son-in-law, Tutankhamen, forgotten until uncovered by modern archeologists. The failure of such an idea to take hold after such a politically potent send-off, coupled with the success of more or less the same idea in the hands of the politically powerless Hebrews a few years later, serves as one of the most important demonstrations in all of history of the power of media to make or break the ideas they carry.

For other than the extraordinary disproportion of temporal power in favor of the Pharaoh, the other significant difference between the two cultures is that the Hebrews sought to convey their monotheistic notion via an abstract alphabet – the origin of our alphabet – whose letters had no visual connection to anything on or off Earth.

Such letters, then, were far better repositories of an idea about a deity whose centers were everywhere – far better than even the sun, which, for all its inchoate, globally dispersed energy, is after all easily discernible as being located somewhere.

The Pharaoh's hieroglyphic failure and the Hebrews' alphabetic success in conveying the monotheistic idea is the story of this chapter, the first stop in our history of the information revolution.

MONOPOLIES OF KNOWLEDGE, AND THEIR JEALOUS GUARDIANS

Harold Adams Innis – Canadian economist, pioneer in media theory, and acknowledged mentor-from-afar of Marshall McLuhan – coined the phrase "monopolies of knowledge" (1950, 1951) to describe the way those in possession of scarce information technology hoard and wield the advantages it provides. Nowadays, we find such monopolies in limited linguistic areas, like the professional jargons that doctors and lawyers use to differentiate their special caches of knowledge from that of the lay public. Much is made of computer elites, and the monopolies of knowledge of those who have access to the Internet and Web (see, e.g., Rifkin, 1995, and Sale, 1995, summarized in Lohr, 1995; also Ohmann, 1985); but as we will see in detail later in this book, computer elites are in practice self-eliminating, because computers are getting both cheaper and easier to use.

Literacy probably constitutes the most significant monopoly of knowledge in human history. Our public education system is in effect predicated on breaking that monopoly of knowledge, or making sure it does not arise in the first place. Our open democratic society believes, quite rightly, that having access to knowledge of the day – not only via broadcast media available in this century, but to older, printed modes of communication that still provide the most depth of detail and analysis – is a cornerstone of healthy political existence.

Interestingly, as Jacques Ellul (1962/1965) pointed out, many totalitarian societies share this emphasis on literacy, as a valuable conduit of their propaganda. Hitler and Goebbels, however, apparently thought otherwise, and burned more than 20,000 books one night in Berlin in 1933 (see Manguel, 1996, pp. 279–289). Richard Brodie (1996, p. 169) offers a view of reading that accommodates its facilitation of both open and closed societies, but most of all the uncontrollability of its consequences, observing that "journalism is rife with mind viruses that have spread certain biases – certain memes" (see Dawkins, 1976, for more on "memes," the cultural equivalent of genes; see also Lynch, 1996). This unpredictability likely makes literacy a more reliable ally of democracy than its adversaries.

Learning how to read and write is in any case no easy thing. Unlike spoken language, which quite literally comes naturally, the rules of our alphabet and grammar, always arbitrary in terms of the alphabet and sometimes inconsistent in terms of the grammar, take years to master. And that's for a system – our system – comprised of twenty-six different letters.

Ikhnaton's written medium, in contrast, was a hieroglyphic system with an indeterminate number of characters – the current Chinese ideographic system has more than 20,000 – because each object or concept required its own hieroglyph. Some had phonetic components (such as the rebus method, in which the word "belief" – to use a hypothetical example in English – could be written via depiction of a bee upon a leaf); others were more purely pictographic. But each hieroglyph was nonetheless an attempt to represent a referent via a mode that was burdened by far more than the limited number of abstract, interchangeable components – the twenty-six letters – of our alphabet.

Who, in such a demanding communication environment, could possibly have time and wherewithal to learn how to read and write – to master such a system? Mostly the priests, the guardians of all sacred knowledge.

It was to these priests that Ikhnaton had no choice but to entrust his revolutionary monotheistic sun religion for future generations. The priests so entrusted must have realized that they were being given an agonizing choice: the religion which they had been schooled in, which the Pharaoh's reform was seeking to sweep aside, held that the Pharaoh was the chief deity on Earth. Does a Pharaoh-God have the right to renounce the very religion which holds him to be a God – does the religion which makes him a God therein give him the authority to renounce it? And what accord should be given the Pharaoh's pronouncements if his renouncement of the religion that brought him god-like power is taken seriously? Ought a new religion promulgated by a God of a replaced religion command obedience and respect? Ikhnaton was in this self-eradicating exercise of power not unlike Mikhail Gorbachev in our time, who used his dictatorial powers in the Soviet Union to undermine that dictatorship, which led to a democracy that removed Gorbachev's source of power – and, eventually, Gorbachev as well.

We know that at least some of Ikhnaton's priests indeed recorded, in detailed hieroglyphs, the substance of his new religion. If not so, we would know nothing about that religion today. But we also know that within a mere generation of Ikhnaton's death, the priests reestablished the old religion, seeking (unsuccessfully) to wipe out all mention of Aton, the universal, monotheistic sun-force. Archeologists think Tutankhamen (*fl. c.* 1350 BC) – Ikhnaton's son-in-law – may have fallen victim to this priestly plot.

So, in the end, even the Pharaoh whose power the priestly monopoly of knowledge was supposed to protect was not enough to surmount those who believed their monopoly was being undermined by the Pharaoh, whose new religion scarcely survived his death. Perhaps the Pharaoh's apparent success while he was alive flowed from his verbal ability (Redford, 1984, p. 234, deduces that Ikhnaton "possessed unusual ability as a poet"), and the similar ability of some of his priests, to convey what his religion was really about – a capacity that hieroglyphs lack. Perhaps the only reason that we can think we understand something of Ikhnaton's reform is that we are indeed an alphabetic culture, well versed in the monotheistic religions that alphabets support.

We turn now to the first known success of monotheism – by a group whose temporal power was practically nil, but whose informational technology was infinite in the magnitude of the ideas it could convey.

THE ALPHABET AS SCEPTER

The monotheism of Moses (*c.* 1250 BC) of course began long before him. Indeed, for all we know, there were non-Jewish monotheisms prior to Moses which fared worse than even Ikhnaton's – whose practitioners lacked not only an alphabet but also the monument-erecting capabilities of the Pharaoh, and thus left no trace at all. For all we know, Ikhnaton's sun religion was itself an offshoot of pre-Mosaic Jewish monotheism. Perhaps Rameses II persecuted the Jews with special zeal because their monotheism was too reminiscent of Ikhnaton's and its usurpation of the traditional Egyptian god Amon, fully restored by the time of Rameses and his conflict with Moses.

We do know that Jewish monotheism took an extraordinary turn under the leadership of Moses. The political manifestation of this was at the time modest – the exodus of a small group of people from Egypt, and their eventual establishment of a state which survived just a few hundred years. The cultural manifestation, however, has survived against all odds continuously to the present, resulting not only in the re-establishment of a Jewish political state in our own century, but the development and global dissemination of Christianity and Islam to account for well over a majority of the world's religious beliefs. Christianity has just under two billion faithful, Islam just under one billion, and all others including Hinduism and non-religions comprise the remaining two-and-a-half billion forms of belief on this Earth (Jews number just under eighteen million; statistics from *Information Please Almanac*, 1994, p. 412).

What so distinguished Mosaic monotheism from its predecessors – Jewish and Pharaonic – to have such impact? Moses not only led his people out of bondage, to the Promised Land, but along the way delivered to them the Ten Command- ments, and the Five Books of Moses. He delivered to them, in other words, an expression of monotheism and its meaning which, unlike the Pharaoh's, could and did amply survive his oral and political capacity – indeed, has survived his death by more than three millennia.

By the thirteenth century BC, when Moses led his people from Egypt, and shortly crafted or received the Ten Commandments and the Torah (or Pentateuch – first five books of the Bible – the Books of Moses), the Phoenicians and pre- decessor "sea peoples" had already established a vigorous and far-ranging maritime civilization. That culture not only made the Mediterranean into a lake long before the Romans, but would travel as far as Britain to mine tin, and give rise to Carthage, Rome's most serious rival in its ascension to temporal power. But no doubt the most significant Phoenician contribution was the alphabet – the phonetic alphabet – which nearly bears its name. That device would go on to revolutionize all subsequent culture via its impact on Greek philosophy, political theory, and science, as we will see below, as well as via its influence on religion. Since the Phoenician inventors of the alphabet likely had no knowledge of Moses and surely none of Plato, the use of the alphabet by Moses to present the Ten Commandments and the Torah – and later by Plato and his successors to present their abstract notions of truth, beauty, and moral excellence – constitutes perhaps the most explosive unintended consequence of an information technology in (recorded) history. (As to the unrecorded – or the recorded that did not survive – who can say?)

But why did the Phoenicians design a system of recording which radically departed from the pictographic form and its insistence on a different symbol for each word or concept? Cyrus Gordon (1971) hypothesizes that the pressure of numerous commercial exchanges with diverse cultures connected by sea and ocean created a need in each Phoenician ship for someone with the capacity to make a quick but accurate record of these transactions. A hieroglyphic system provides neither sufficient personnel (it takes too long to learn) nor speed (it takes too long to write). The alphabet, in contrast, has the requisite rapidity on both accounts.

The Phoenician phonetic alphabet was of course not invented out of whole cloth. Egyptian hieroglyphics had phonetic elements such as the rebus method mentioned above, and other, more abstract, renderings of spoken syllables. But these did little if anything to reduce the number of different hieroglyphs that had to be learned, and the continued role of pictographic symbols rendered hieroglyphics even with a few phonetic elements no less cumbersome. The overall efficiency of any communication system – the "throughput" of the communication it allows – is always hostage to the efficiency of its weakest link.

The genius of the phonetic alphabet is that it had no such weak pictographic link at all. Indeed, it takes the opposite tack of breaking communication up into such tiny bits – letters – that they correspond to nothing complete and recognizable in the world, or even in our language. With the exception of a few vowels added later by the Greeks, the individual letters of the alphabet lack correspondence even to the syllables that we speak – they have loyalty only to smaller bites of sound, which have meaning in our language only in combination with other sounds. The advantage of this atomization, as in instant coffee and digitized information in the twentieth century, is an enormous boost in transportability and preservability. By parsing speech into four or five handfuls of minimal, mixable components, meaningless individually but therein capable of meaning anything in proper conjunction, the navigator's shorthand that is the alphabet revolutionized ancient communication – just as rendering of diverse forms into one binary digital code would transform society at the end of the twentieth century. When we consider that the brain itself operates via some kind of neuro-chemical process not yet fully known, but apparently as yet unknown, but common for all its inputs, and as literally unrelated to the events it describes (and contemplates) as the alphabet and binary code are to their referents, the success of the alphabet (and digital communication) should come as no surprise: they all partake of a same, highly powerful, underlying natural strategy of communication. Indeed, DNA itself operates in this way, looking nothing like the complex protein structures it commands into being.

Whether Moses realized this or not, the phonetic alphabet proved to be a perfect device for the representation of that which was not representable. The Phoenicians had found that by breaking down descriptions of their commercial transactions into a small set of atoms, these transactions were more easily stored and then disseminated when necessary. Beginning with Moses, the Hebrews found that these same atoms could be recombined to represent transactions that existed only in the mind, or pertained to something much greater than anything localizable in any particular part of the world. The alphabet thus proved to be an ideal recipe for the daily re-creation of monotheism in the minds of individuals, and its dissemination to groups and societies and whole cultures over the centuries. Monotheism charged by the alphabet thus triumphed whereas the same idea clothed in the hieroglyph failed.

Of the three major monotheistic religions, Christianity is the most iconic, but even its reliance on literal visual imagery is minor compared to the statuary of its polytheistic predecessors and early contemporaries. And Islam, less under the polytheistic influence of Greece and Rome, emerged as an even more insistently abstract, less iconic religion than Judaism, forbidding pictures not only of God, but of the Prophet. Eventually the Protestant Reformation, which will be one of the main subjects of our next chapter, attempted to return Christianity also to a more abstract basis, with its emphasis on the primacy of the words in the Good Book.

But Greece, though it remained polytheistic in its religion, adopted the phonetic alphabet for its own pursuits in philosophy, science, and politics, from which ensued a whole different set of spectacular, largely unintended consequences. We conclude this chapter with some sketches of those secular aspects of the information revolution in the ancient world.

THE INFORMATION REVOLUTION BECOMES SELF-AWARE

The Greek experience with the alphabet not only differed from the Hebrew in its secular applications: it focused, in the persons of Socrates and Plato, on the very impact of the alphabet itself. Thus the *Phaedrus* contains the Socratic brief for spoken communication and an accompanying critique of writing: reliance on written communication atrophies memory. The written word is unamenable to dialogue, because it can give but one unvarying answer to questions posed to it — namely, the words already written.

Such concerns are clearly reflective of the alphabet, and the relative ease with which it became a central currency of Greek intellectual life. A cumbersome pictographic writing system would have posed no such challenge to orality. Memorization of even epic poems takes far less time than the learning of a hiero-glyphic system with which to record or copy them.

The diminishing degree to which these Socratic concerns were ultimately well taken is something we will consider later in this book, in particular when we look at how electronic text has made the written word indeed immediately amenable to dialogue in our own time. Suffice to say now that, were it not for the alphabet, we would almost certainly know nothing of Socrates' concerns in any case. Fortunately — or unfortunately — for Socrates, Plato troubled to memorialize (to use the legal term for writing, which seems especially apt here) his mentor's critique of writing. Whether the critique came entirely from words spoken by Socrates, or was shared to some extent by Plato, we can be sure that its subtlety and level of abstraction would have made its recording difficult if not impossible in hieroglyphics.

The Greeks, then, were among their many other pioneering pursuits the original media theorists — or, again, the first that we know about in recorded history. In that sense, this very volume is a continuation of a discussion initiated by Socrates. That we at the end of the twentieth century would be so keenly interested in communication environments, along lines similar to the ancient Greeks, is not surprising. As Innis observed (1951), swings in media systems — midpoints in the pendulum when balances between older and newer forms obtain, before the new comes to unduly dominate the older — make for propitious intellectual times. With vantage points between two media, we have unique opportunities to chart the effect of one upon the other, to better trace their underlying structure, to more fully understand their effect upon us. We stand at such a crossroads of digital and analog/print information technology now, much as Socrates and Plato conversed and wrote at a crucial intersection of oral and written modes.

That meta-perspective, one foot in the oral tradition, one in the written, typified the entire Greek engagement with the alphabet and its cultural progeny. Democracy was defined in ancient Athens in terms of the number of people who could hear a speaker's voice, even as the alphabet created an intellectual structure that millennia later would allow democracy on a national scale. Aristotle trusted personal observation and hands-on experience as the bedrocks of the scientific method he developed and wrote about, even as the written mode created a foundation for dissemination of second-hand information and testing and repro- ducibility of results that would stoke the Scientific Revolution — powered by technologically-mediated observation and experimentation — in the Renaissance. This ambivalence toward the very things that writing most made possible, this clinging to the face-to-face encounter that writing — in Freud's words (1930, p. 38), "the voice of an absent person" — in some but not most crucial ways super- seded, runs through all aspects of Greek life of the mind, and in turn Hellenistic and Roman. The vehemence of scholarly attacks on all electronic media, including computers, in our own time is but the same ancient anxiety about the advent of new communications, just inverted to make writing the object of its protection.

Ironically, writing was in far greater need of protection in the ancient world. Indeed, when we consider the insecurity of the written word in an age prior to printing, when each manuscript had to be created by hand, and so was drastically scarcer than anything spoken, the Greeks' reticence to surrender their oral tradition to the written becomes more comprehensible. The destruction of the Library at Alexandria, aptly described by Dampier (1929/1942, p. 51) as "one of the greatest intellectual catastrophes in history," alas shows this distrust of the written was not entirely misplaced. By the time the Library was founded, in the middle of the third century BC, the written word had become far more prevalent and embedded than it had been a hundred years earlier in Plato's Academy. The exponential acceleration of culture from Socrates to Plato to Aristotle to Alexander to Ptolemy, the creator of the Library, gave him and his colleagues hundreds of thousands of manuscripts to collect and store. The Library became the repository of some 400,000 of them — scientific and philosophic treatises, legal codes, political discourses, plays by writers major and minor. Although literacy in Alexandria was never universal by our standards, large segments of its populace learned how to read and write in schools which also taught music, mathematics, and astronomy. This golden age of the intellect was dealt a severe blow when one large section of the Library was destroyed by the Christian bishop Theophilus in 390 AD. The Moslem conquest of the city in 640 AD finished the job, whether by accident or design, whether by conquerors or conquered.

Would more of what the Library contained have survived, had its contents been in the fluid safekeeping of human memory, as Socrates had urged, rather than the stauncher but combustible precincts of papyrus and parchment? The question is unanswerable — it's likely that most of the contents would not have been created, thought, discovered, in the first place in an entirely oral culture, whose capacity for safekeeping is ever leaky. But the destruction of the Library of Alexandria in any case shows the inadequacy of an information culture predicated on a limited number of copies of the information. Dampier (1929/1942, p. 52) calls the Library "one of the wonders" of the Ancient World; unlike the Seven Wonders, it was a wonder of information technology; ironically, the only wonder that survived was the Great Pyramid in Egypt, the product of the very cumbersome hieroglyphic culture that the alphabet and its flowering in Alexandria had replaced.

The aftermath of the Library's destruction, and the dissolution of its political analog in the Roman Empire, was, as we know, the Dark Ages in Europe. The alphabet continued as the written mode, but so difficult was life, so little time did anyone have to learn even its simple set of rules, that literacy plummeted. Once again, a priestly class arose as the sole conduits of knowledge. What the difficulty of pictographs did for the priests in ancient Egypt, the difficulty of life in general did for Christian priests for nearly a thousand years in Europe: it insured their position as guardians of a monopoly of knowledge.

This state continued until the printing press, and its capacity for multiple copies, smashed this monopoly forever.

Like the phoenix which arose resplendent from the ashes, five hundred years after its consumption in flames, the Phoenician invention – the phonetic alphabet, the voices of absent people, the papyrus products of Byblos that we call books – would return in twice that time in a form that defied the local pyre and brought us the modern world.

3

THE PRINTED AUTHORSHIP OF THE MODERN WORLD

Heresy is a most fundamental human trait. It serves as a source of new ideas — as necessary to the survival of our particular species as mutation is to the survival of species in general. Of course, not all mutations are favorable. Indeed, most fail to survive their first expression. The same is true of heresy.

In order for a mutation — or a heresy — to survive, to have impact, it must emerge into a supportive environment. A mutation or heresy has to live long enough in the environment it would re-make in order for the re-making to take place. A land mammal that created an offspring with gills would be giving birth to a dead end — unless the mammal happened to already live near the water, or unless the mammal happened to be human in the later part of the twentieth century, when we might conceivably have the technological wherewithal to produce a suitable environment for such a child. For most mutations and heresies, such favorable circumstances are not at hand.

In a world in which religious authority emanated from interpretations of sacred texts, doubly scarce in terms of the number of extant texts and the number of people who might be able to read and interpret them, few if any circumstances were at hand for heresies to succeed. Rather, their practitioners could be easily marginalized, persecuted, and eradicated — deprived of any supportive environment, about as likely to survive as a mammal with gills out of water. Who knows how many times heretics urged that people should read the Bible for themselves? Such pleas made no practical sense, had no means of implementation, as long as both readers and Bibles to read were in such short supply.

When Martin Luther made this plea in the early years of the sixteenth century, however, the environment had changed. An invention from China had made its way to Europe some fifty years earlier, and would not only make Luther's plea practicable, but would set off a series of related, synergistic events that would at last retrieve the charred hope of Alexandria and revolutionize the world.

In this chapter, we consider how the printing press helped bring the modern age of national states, the Scientific Revolution, public education, democracy, capitalism, and religious diversification into being. We start with Luther and the seed of his ninety-five theses.

THE CHINESE INVENTION OF MODERN EUROPE

The printing press was invented in China as early as 600 AD. Its fate there was in many ways eerily parallel to the destiny of Ikhnaton's monotheism: both inventions were stymied by an ideographic writing system; both went on in a subsequent alphabetic context and support web of related culture to dominate the world. Indeed, in the cases of both ancient Egypt and more modern China, the inventions in the hands of alphabetic cultures went on to undermine the original ideographic civilizations. In the case of ancient Egypt, the eradication was almost total: who writes in hieroglyphics or worships Isis today? In the case of China, it was far from that. But the dénouement in China is perhaps more poignant since it is the undisputed place of invention of the printing press, whereas Ikhnaton's monotheism, though it preceded Moses, apparently came after Abraham.

The incompatibility of ideographic writing with the mass production of text via the press is far more physical and therefore intractable than the problems of literacy that characterized ancient Egypt, although those were part of the Chinese equation as well. In a written language that requires 20,000 unique ideograms for full scholarly literacy, the production of text via a press that uses interchangeable type is simply impossible – the number of possible pieces of type is too large to in any practical sense be interchangeable. Thus, unsurprisingly, the Chinese use of the press was for the most part limited to greetings and announcements comprised of a handful of ideograms. Such full-length texts as did issue from this press were produced with an efficiency scarcely better than creation of hand-written manuscripts. The hobbling of mass production and thus mass printed media continued into our time, with the single-page poster serving as the Chinese newspaper throughout the twentieth century. Computer typesetting is now finally removing that aspect of the ideographic barrier, providing an electronic speed of type selection that renders the realm of thousands of ideographs physically effortless to choose from (see Jones, 1987).

Gutenberg and earlier developers of the press in the West of course had no such ideographic barriers, working with an alphabet whose twenty-six different letters – in contrast to the Chinese 20,000 – were already interchangeable in their representation of a potentially infinite number of words, and thus could not have been better suited to the workings of a press with interchangeable type. The Phoenician invention thus had one last unintended consequence, certainly among its biggest: it made the press possible as a vehicle for mass production of text. The wine press already in use in Europe had interchangeable parts; it was Gutenberg *et al.*'s genius to see how this could apply to letters – to meld the grape press and the Chinese printing press into a press of mass media.

The first wine to come off this early assembly line was the Bible, now known as the Gutenberg or Mazarin Bible (because the first copy to attract widespread attention was located in the library of Cardinal Mazarin), and printed at Mainz, Germany, in Latin, in 1455. As Elizabeth Eisenstein documents (1979), not all church authorities were pleased with this radically new way of disseminating the word of God. Indeed, the printed Bible was criticized in many religious quarters as being a debasement of the manuscript, which when produced by hand was said to be guided by the soul – a criticism reminiscent, in many ways, of the Socratic attack in the *Phaedrus* (secs 275–276) on the soullessness, or unintelligence, of writing *vis-à-vis* speaking. As we will see many more times in our media history, new information technologies are routinely castigated as debauchers of earlier informational styles and values. The attacks on television and computers in the past few decades (e.g., Postman, 1994) – which we will consider and counter in detail in Chapters 6, 10, 11, and elsewhere in this book – are but the current expressions of this perennial hue-and-cry. But whereas the Socratic critique of writing was in large part self-refuting due to our knowing about it only because Plato wrote it down, the concerns that the Church Fathers had about the printing press were not by any means misdirected, especially regarding the impact it would have on the Church and religious life. In its service as the cutting social edge of Luther's heresy and the Protestant Reformation it engendered, the press would permanently slice the hegemony of the Church.

Since Luther of course knew about the printing press, the success of his protest at the edge of its word-sword cannot be considered the purest case of an explosive coincidence (see Haile, 1980, pp. 165–174, for Luther's manipulation of, and by, the new press; by 1523, some 493 German titles were in print, 180 authored by Luther). On the other hand, certainly neither Gutenberg nor the other early printers intended a Protestant Reformation to result from their invention, and nor could anyone have foreseen the remarkable synchrony of Luther's straightforward message – read the Bible for yourself – with the new availability of Bibles, and the multiple consequences that would issue therefrom. Had the press been a catalytic convertor whose product was an ever-growing volley of projectiles aimed at the Church, the consequences would have been no more destructive of tradition.

Indeed, as in all self-escalating catalytic reactions, the fracturing of religious authority as people began reading the Bible for themselves soon got out of hand, even from the Lutheran point of view. Ulrich Zwingli and John Calvin had interpretations that differed a bit from Luther's when they read the Bible for themselves, and soon there were Reform Churches distinct from both the Roman Catholic and the Lutheran. Information can be a powerful acid, an agent of dissolution more than a match for any Church Father, monarch, or other pillar of central authority. This tension between information at large and the sway of central authority, between the puncturing of monopolies of knowledge and attempts to re-seal or re-establish them, would continue unabated down through the present, as governments now frantically try to erect restrictions, clumsy and unenforceable, on the Internet. The most recent example of this Counter-Reformation in the United States is the Communications Decency Act of 1996 (see Chapter 14 in this book, and Levinson, 1997a, for more).

At the dawn of the sixteenth century, the ingredients for the multiply mutually reinforcing catalytic conversion of the medieval into the modern world were all in place. Print, aptly termed a "gunpowder of the mind" by David Riesman (cited in Postman, 1979, p. 65; see Riesman, 1950, for more), not only lit at least half a dozen fuses, but worked as the fuel for many of the explosions, and would continue as the sole proprietor of this role until joined by the telegraph and the photograph and a new progeny of invention in the nineteenth century.

A report from the sixteenth-century scene, assisted with the wisdom of hindsight, might have noticed the following: the fracturing of the Church's power by the Protestant Reformation helped make way for the emergence of other, non-religious, secular forms of power, including the rise of national states and their political power, and the Scientific Revolution and the power of new knowledge it entailed. Further, the press conveyed not only new religious doctrine, but information about a New World, which would stoke the rise of national states, and reports of scientific discoveries, which fed the rise of science. And these developments in turn further weakened the Church, which opened further niches for their development. Soon public education arose, first to satisfy the need of people to meaningfully participate in the print revolution – that is, to learn how to read – and then as a vehicle for dissemination of the new kinds and amounts of information available. The secular alternative to religious education further reduced the Church's influence, with commensurate benefit to the rise of national states and the Scientific Revolution. And in this hot-house of information – some of which was about things people could buy and sell, invest in, trade in, eat, wear – a new form of economics arose, well-suited to the abstraction and speed of this new age: capitalism, and its abstraction of labor and wealth.

Nor was the increasingly literate public in the slightest unaware of what was happening to the Church, and what was most responsible. Haile (1980, p. 174) conveys the contents of a satirical circular from 1546, "News from the Devil," in which the Pope laments the futility of the Church's attempt to eradicate the reissue of an older work by Luther:

I certainly fear we shan't succeed, even though I and all of my cardinals, bishops, abbots, their canons, and all our clerics have had it purchased throughout Germany, and burned, in the hope that not one copy might remain by which printers' type could be set.

In the next sections, we consider the role of the press in each interlocking sector of the spiraling printed hypercycle which so resoundingly slipped the Church's purchase. We turn first to the New World.

"EXTRA! EXTRA! READ ALL ABOUT IT!" THE PRESS DISCOVERS AMERICA

As McLuhan (e.g., 1962) explored in considerable detail, a key characteristic of oral/aural cultures is the magical, mystical, mythical quality of its most important communications. What is spoken and heard, but unseen, acquires larger-than-life qualities in the re-telling. In contrast, writing fixes its information in discrete, reliably accessible – and, with print, reproducible – units. If you were a monarch with some money to spend, which kind of communication about a new world on the other side of a large ocean do you suppose would be more likely to result in your funding a voyage or two there?

We know from Viking artifacts discovered at L'Anse Aux Meadows in Newfoundland that Europeans in fact were in the New World some five hundred years before Columbus. And yet word of this event set off no Age of Discovery. Why not? An Age of Discovery following the Age of Charlemagne and the emergence of the Holy Roman Empire would have made some geo-political sense.

Part of the reason this did not happen was that the environment in Europe was unsupportive on every other score at the time. Socially, technologically, scientifically, the Europe of 1000 AD was in no condition to embark upon an epoch of discovery and settlement across the Atlantic. But part of the reason also lies in the way that word of the Norse discoveries must have reached people back in Europe, if it reached them at all. Couched in oral sagas, whispered in the cold winds, the words had no endurance. Unlike the winds that moved the Norse vessels, the oral sagas had no power to move anyone other than those who had personal reason to trust the speakers. Thus, the Norse expeditions invited only a limited number of other Norse voyages. The Newfoundland foothold was never developed, and in a few hundred years even the Greenland settlements – on the eve, ironically, of Columbus – disappeared. The Viking penetration of the New World was thus the equivalent of Ikhnaton's campaign for monotheism and most heresies before Luther – bold failed forays ahead of their time – or, to be more precise, ahead of their medium.

As we have seen, handwritten manuscripts in the aftermath of Alexandria were so scarce in Europe that even had word of the Norse voyages been written down, it would likely have had little more effect than the oral sagas. Indeed, legends were extant about voyages to a new world by Brendan of Ireland and others, before and after the Norse, and these also had no impact on Europe. A single manuscript or two, moldering away in a monastery, a captain's chest, or whatever, is barely if at all superior to the spoken word as a conveyor of its memes to the larger culture. And whereas the manuscript with alphabetic writing could and did have enormous impact in the smaller political and geographic precincts of the ancient Mediterranean, it was not equal to the Europe of the early fifteenth century, could be no kindler of an Age of Discovery that would change the world as profoundly in a physical sense as the Protestant Reformation and the Scientific Revolution would in the related spiritual and intellectual spheres.

That spark belonged to the printing press, presciently in place, it seems in retrospect, to spread the news of Columbus' voyage to the New World in a mode that influential people could easily access, contemplate, consider, access again, think about some more, discuss with others, access again, and ultimately come to believe as the truth that it was. As Samuel Eliot Morrison notes (1942, p. 379), the first printed report of Columbus' voyage to the New World, a pamphlet of eight pages, became a "best seller" in 1493: three Latin editions were printed in Rome; six different editions in Paris, Basle, and Antwerp in 1493–1494; a Tuscan edition in Rome in 1493; two more editions in Florence that same year; a German translation in 1497; and several Spanish editions during this time.

The printing of this best seller in diverse languages was by no means incidental to the impact of the press and its news of the New World on the rise of national states: not only did the press excite irresistible interest in the New World, interest best fulfilled by ships chartered by monarchies and carrying the flags of nations, it did so in vernaculars which in and of themselves helped crystallize national identities. As Harold Innis (1950, 1951) observed, prior to the press, the only language of writing was Latin – the language of the ecclesiastic manuscript – in contrast to spoken tongues, which had already evolved into an array of Roman and Germanic speech patterns in Western Europe. Gutenberg's first Bibles, as noted above, were printed in Latin. But news of Columbus' voyage was in no sense a rendition of an ancient, sacred work; it was a hot-off-the-press first edition in every sense. That it was rendered not only in the retro-formation of Latin but the new languages of the day made perfect sense.

The press provided descriptions, in black and white, that could be counted on, banked upon. The British believed it, and sent John Cabot to the New World in 1497. The Portuguese, who already had ambitious programs of discovery down the African coast, and whose navigators might have indeed even reached the New World prior to Columbus (but it was unreported in print if it happened), certainly believed reports of Columbus, and sent Vasco da Gama around the Cape of Good Hope of Africa and Pedro Cabral to Brazil. The French believed it too, and soon Jean Cartier was on his way to the northern part of the New World. Each expedition provoked further interest – and what we would today call media coverage – on its return. Each thus fed off its predecessors, and fed its successors, with the result that money and prestige and strategic advantage flowed steadily and increasingly into national capitals.

In an alternate universe, in which the Protestant Reformation was not about to occur, the Age of Discovery in the end might not have set off a permanent rise of national states after all. Had Rome continued as sole religious authority, with all nations as devout in their allegiance to that religion as Spain, then the discovery and settlement of the New World might have been a renewal of and paean to the glory of Roman Catholicism, as Queen Isabella of Spain intended. But the press printed not only reports of voyages to the New World, but lots of Bibles, which provided a ready alternative to the Church's luster.

So the national passions elicited in the race to establish claims in the New World soon proved, if not entirely secular, certainly no tribute to Catholicism, whatever their origins in the mind of Isabella. And this only further attenuated the authority of Rome.

Which made the Scientific Revolution, nurtured by other products of the press, but stimulated by the flood of new data from the New World as well, all the more possible.

THE PRINTED ENGINES OF KNOWLEDGE

Like the myriad, restless reshufflings that comprise the success of DNA on this planet, the essence of the scientific method that eventually arose from the DNA of our brains is testing, re-testing, dissemination, and repeatability. That science was practiced at all in the ancient world was due to the invention and stabilizing impact of writing – it is unknown in pre-literate societies as a rational, testable process, and exists there only as magic. That science is in the pre-eminent position it now enjoys in our world is due to the printing press.

We could capture the crux of science by saying that it demarcates ideas that any human individual may have, however brilliant they may or may not be, from ideas that in some way have survived a test with the external reality beyond any individual. Furthermore, although any individual may test his or her ideas against reality, the rest of us have no way of knowing whether that individual's reports of such test results are accurate and truthful. We have no way of knowing if the individual by accident or design undermined or biased the test. The only remedy, albeit imperfect, we have for these problems is to replicate the tests ourselves, or rely on a number of others to replicate the tests – a number sufficient to warrant our conclusion that the reports on the testing of the ideas, and the ideas them-selves, are not idiosyncratic or at variance with reality.

This occurs, in a sense, on the DNA level itself, where every encounter that an organism has with reality is a test of the efficacy of its living characteristics, and the DNA that gave rise to them. Of course, on the organic level, reports of failure are rather drastic, often arriving in the death of the individual organism whose DNA so failed. Conversely, the mere survival of an organism, or group of organisms, is its own eloquent report that some organic encounter with reality has received at least a minimally passing grade. Humans have the option of improving upon this trial-by-combat, as Karl Popper pointed out (1972, p. 248), by "letting our hypotheses die in our stead." But as Popper and Donald T. Campbell (1974a) also realized – and as discussed briefly in this book's Introduction – the pursuit of ideas wrapped in theories opens up new possibilities for the commission and perpetuation of error.

One source of such error is the ideology – what Richard Dawkins (e.g., 1993) would call a highly persuasive, seductive meme (see also Percival, 1994; Brodie, 1996; Lynch, 1996) – that insists that reality is a certain way regardless of contrary ideas and reports of their testing. The religious view that the Earth is the center of the universe, based initially on the obvious observation that the Sun and the heavenly bodies revolve around Earth, had by the time of the printing press and the Scientific Revolution become a hostage of dogma, as much an article of faith as it was a conclusion based on observation and reason. Galileo's telescopic observation of Jupiter, and its support of Copernican heliocentric theory, was thus treated as heresy by the Church – which attacked not only the theorist and the theory but its enabling technology, citing Aristotle's advice to always trust the evidence of our naked senses (heavenly bodies revolve around the Earth) when in conflict with the testimony of artificial devices (in this case, the telescope).

Aristotle's view that, although natural and artificial processes were both capable of error (*Physica*, II:8), one natural process – direct perception or sensation of qualities such as colors – "admits to the least amount of falsehood" (*De Anima*, III:3), was and still is well-founded. The perceptual devices that survive and flourish in the biological world (such as human vision) have undergone millions of years of testing, and are not usually subject to the degree of radical error which is always possible with a new technology. Indeed, in Aristotle's time, devices for extending the range of vision were no doubt far less reliable for observations of the planets than a pair of good eyes. But what Aristotle of course missed – not surprising, given the static or de-evolutionary worldview of ancient Greece – was the capacity for technologies to evolve under human development to be far more accurate in some areas than naked vision. And what the Church – which kidnapped Aristotle's science and raised it in the house of worship – also missed was that their dispute with Galileo and his theories was taking place in an arena much greater than the Church's chambers. It was an arena, newly constituted by the press, of all readers in Europe.

Thus, though Galileo lost the battle on a personal level, and was eventually obliged to recant under pain of being fully condemned as a heretic, his theory – and the new instrumental mode of science it both rode upon and promoted – triumphed on all accounts. The printing press played a dual crucial role in that victory, first conveying reports of Galileo's and other astronomers' observations to other scientists for their testing, possible refutation, and corroboration, then conveying news of those very corroborations to the growing, much larger, emerging audience of informed public opinion.

Further, as we have seen at other levels of the complex hypercycle of print and the emergence of the modern world, the mass dissemination of scientific information stirred the generation of new ideas that fed the process of science – the raw material that needed to be tested to become science. Upon reading a scientific treatise, a small group of people were motivated to replicate the observations or experiments reported. A much larger group became the *de facto* court of public opinion. Yet a third group, even smaller than the first, were moved to extend, trim, or otherwise revise the theories. And a fourth group, no doubt the smallest of all, went on to generate new theories of their own. Publication of these in turn triggered the testing of the first group, and a new, self-replicating and self-transcending cyclet of knowledge was on its way.

Hundreds, soon thousands, of these cyclets developed, and of course influenced one another. Meanwhile, the forces that opposed this growth of knowledge – mainly, the Church – were already being weakened by the Reformation and the rise of national states. These were natural allies of science – its siblings in the print-fueled hypercycle – and what it could do to improve life on Earth.

Thus did the Socratic qualm about the written word giving but one unvarying answer find at least partial redress in the press, and its capacity to provide great multiples of copies of many unvarying answers. As the numbers of different unvarying answers increased, with each book published about each theory and series of observations or experiments, answers in effect became varying for each reader with more than one book from which to choose. The responsiveness and fluidity of local speech was simulated, to a degree, in the options for knowledge provided by the rapidly globalizing press. A much fuller refutation of Socrates' objections to writing would await the advent of electronic text (see Chapters 11 and after in this volume); but Gutenberg's revolution was a most important start, or resumption of the start extinguished almost a millennium earlier in the burning of the Library at Alexandria.

Of course, for all of this to work – for people to read the Bible for themselves, read about the New World in national vernacular, read about scientific theories and discoveries which survived repeated observation and testing – people had to be able to read. This brings us to the door of the classroom, and the rise of public education.

THE *RAISON D'ÊTRE* OF PUBLIC EDUCATION

The explosion of knowledge – along with the opposition of the Church, the former main conduit of knowledge, to some of the new facts and ideas, and its general weakening as a font of wisdom on most accounts – would have no doubt fomented an increase in public education in any case. New media create new information, which in turn requires new modes of acquisition.

But the rise of public education, especially at the early grade levels, had a far more fundamental connection to the printing press. People had need of intellectual tools, the skill and wherewithal, to receive and process the information that flowed from the press. People required a facility sufficient for the new vessel of this new information, the book, to dock – and for its passengers, the ideas it conveyed, to debark and be fruitfully engaged. People had to learn how to read.

And reading, as we saw in the last chapter, was never a process quickly mastered. The alphabet was radically easier to learn than hieroglyphics, but it was certainly drastically more difficult to learn than speech, the habit of which is acquired simply by living, whatever the ratio of its hardwired (genetic) and mimicked (environmental) and elicited (genetic and environmental) components. Indeed, other than ideographic systems in Asia, alphabetic reading (and writing) remained the most difficult medium to learn well into the twentieth century – looking at a photograph, talking on the phone, listening to a phonograph recording, watching a movie, listening to the radio, watching TV require no learning on the basic perceptual or performance level at all. The personal computer of course changed that, reversing the trajectory of ever easier-to-use media (watching television requires less social skills than going out to a movie) in the knowledge and skill required for use of its software. Accordingly, formal and informal educational efforts to make people of all ages "computer literate," i.e., increase their understanding about how to best employ its programs, have been underway for more than a decade. This has been no easy task for adults, many of whom looked at learning how to drive an automobile as the last significant skill they needed to master for full citizenship in the technological society (see Chapters 11–15 for more on personal computers and their social effects). But even so, traditional reading of text remains far more primary – essential to even the most iconic of computer systems. Small wonder, then, that learning to read and write became the first lesson and continuing mission of public education.

Ironically, although today's point-and-click iconic computer interfaces are perceived as easier to learn and use than older command-level (alphabetic text) systems, the ancient iconic systems of hieroglyphics and ideographic writing were so difficult to master as to defy learning via any system of mass education. Thus, formal collective education as we now know it can be traced back to the increasing implementation of the alphabet in ancient Greece. Socrates' contemporary – and satirist – Aristophanes recalls that the heroes of the Marathon (490 BC) were educated the "old" way, via private tutors, in contrast to the Athenian children of his day (c. 400 BC), who go off in the morning "to their teachers" (*Clouds*, secs 964–965, 986, cited in Marrou, 1956, p. 69). Indeed, Marrou notes (p. 71) that the very word "teacher" is a synecdoche from the Greek "teacher of letters"; the other instructors in the early Greek schools, whose specialties were gymnastics and music, went by names other than "teacher." At the same time, schools of higher learning arose in Plato's Academy (387 BC), Isocrates' school of rhetoric (393 BC), and Aristotle's Lyceum or Peripatetic School (c. 335 BC). Although all three were intended to educate the elite, the Lyceum was the first institution to assemble a publicly accessible collection or library of books. Ptolemy I modeled the Library, Museum, and educational structures in Alexandria (c. 295 BC) – what we could today call a university – on the Lyceum, with one crucial difference. As Peter Green (1990, pp. 89–90) observes, Alexandria and later centers of Hellenistic education were "open to all those who could read" – an entrance requirement democratic in fact as well as principle, since the "Greek alphabet . . . with less than thirty symbols . . . could be learned, and was, by almost everyone" by the time of Alexandria's flowering. The printing press both recaptured and greatly expanded this process – bursting the oligarchic pockets of knowledge that had arisen anew in Europe's Dark Ages – bequeathing to us the educational system in operation around the world today, in which learning how to read is every student's "major" for the first six or more years of schooling.

The growth of literacy under the impact of public education of course had a continuing reciprocal impact on the growth of knowledge, the taste of which had goaded the increase in literacy in the first place. And a series of profound secondary effects ensued. Democracy, defined in terms of speaker-and-audience ranges and numbers in Athens on the eve of its revolution in reading, could in a society of mass literacy now be construed on nationwide levels. The same informed public which played a role in the Scientific Revolution could serve as an informed electorate. But, as we noted earlier (see Ellul, 1962/1965), literacy was not necessarily an absolute ally of the democratic process: to be able to read was also to be amenable to the influence of demagogic texts, and the proclamations of monarchs. Thus, as we shall see in subsequent chapters, literacy became a battleground, first between monarchs and citizens who wanted a free expression of ideas in the press, and in the twentieth century between totalitarian and open societies (although radio broadcasting, not print, became the leading edge of totalitarian government in our century; see Chapter 8). In short, the rise of national states — stimulated in part by the printing press, and secured (at least intellectually) to an increasing degree by literacy — was by no means fully equatable with a rise of democratic states, even though literacy made democracy across large geographic areas practicable.

The rise in literacy via public education also transformed the educational process itself, chiefly (from a structural point of view) by retrieving and enlarging the Hellenistic emphasis on public, state-regulated, universal scribal culture, and making the book, or other source of print, the amanuensis of every classroom. To this very day, books set the outer pace for the conduct of every class, ranging from primary to graduate levels: the speed with which students can read and communicate intelligently about book-constructed venues of knowledge determines the tempo of the class. The liberation of text from its fixed position on printed pages, and the combination of teaching/learning/discussion and reading that constitutes courses taught entirely online via personal computer and modem, is at last offering an alternative to this now five-hundred-year-old system (see Chapter 12; also Levinson, 1995a, 1997a).

The ideal of public education as free and universal, however, continues — at least on the primary and secondary levels — and has indeed been abetted by increased access to information on the Internet, just as the printing press has since its inception facilitated free public education by making relatively low-cost books available to students.

It did this by crystallizing not only notions of national identity, and the government as a provider of education, but a very different, in many ways rival, conception of property, labor, goods, and services as private, commercial enterprises. That system — capitalism — would provide a standard of living sufficient for people to be able to educate their children, rather than have them toil in the fields (or, eventually, the factories it created). Capitalism thus provided a general economic foundation every bit as essential for public education as the books and governments brought forth by the press. But the practice of private enterprise when applied to the press itself would soon come into conflict with some of the prerogatives of nation states, and leave us a world in which the progeny of the press are yet at odds.

THE CAPITALIZATION OF INFORMATION

Knowledge has always been power, as witness the role that monopolies of knowledge among priests and others have played throughout the millennia. But knowledge first became a commodity in mass culture, to be bought, sold, traded, and otherwise exchanged, in the aftermath of the printing press. Today, computers have quickened, expanded, and otherwise amplified this process into the "information society" that we now inhabit.

The Age of Discovery, as we have seen, was first financed by monarchs who believed what they read of Columbus' voyages to the New World – who found it bankable information. The mercantile class soon became a primary financial engine of this age. They too were moved by the new information about overseas resources, markets, and possibilities, and sought to move others by it. The tempo with which this information was conveyed – first via announcements and broadsides, then by newspapers – was set by the press.

Several powerful currents were put in motion. The need that merchants had for dissemination of information about their products and services resulted in the eventual emergence of an advertising industry. The need that merchants also had for accurate reporting of events, and how they related to markets and business, created pressure for a press that was not merely an arm of royal propaganda – and this, in turn, played a decisive role in the struggle between democratic and authoritarian/totalitarian forms of the press. By the time of Jefferson's revolution in the United States, he could reasonably rely on a free press as a check on even a democratically elected government – and seek to secure this freedom in the First Amendment to the US Constitution – because the press was adequately supported via advertising and other modes of free enterprise. (Although broadcast media in the twentieth century were similarly able to function quite well without government stipend in the United States, these fell under some government control nonetheless, as we will see in Chapter 8.)

The capitalization of information, then, in part made possible the third rung in an imperfect evolution of power that went from Church to monarchs to people. On this level, at very least, Marxism was wrong in its claim that capitalism served to enslave. Meanwhile, over the centuries the printing press fueled capitalism in other profound ways – including the paperization of money, the first step in an increasing abstraction of capital in which electronic fund transfer is a high-water mark in our own time. Recalling, again, the clumsiness of hieroglyphics and its consequences, in comparison to the efficiency of the abstract alphabet, we might say that gold and other tangible forms of money functioned as a hieroglyphics of commerce and wealth, in contrast to the "alphabetic" speed and efficiency of ever more abstract paper money, checks, credit cards, and electronic fund transfer.

As we pursue the threads of the press and the multi-dimensional hypercycle of mutually catalytic effects it unleashed – the shattering of the Church's monopolies of faith and knowledge, the rise of national states, the Scientific Revolution, the rise of public education and literacy, the growth of capitalism, democracy, and central national authority – we find a world that increasingly resembles our own in the dynamics and tensions at work. This is because that world, the modern world, is indeed ours – a world of multiple and usually waning religious authorities, of national states and science in place of religion and in the ascendancy, of literacy the most important pedagogic imperative – most reinforcing one another, although with some deep conflicts such as freedom versus central control still very much at issue, in part because both are facilitated by the press. Indeed, the aggregate that is our modern way of life has all in one way or another been a consequence of the press. And since that consequence, our modern world, was surely not intended, certainly not in the specifics and proportions in play today, it and we represent a pre-eminent example of an unintended consequence, the prime product of the information revolution.

But if we live in an informational and thus social and technological world given to us by the press, and still supported by its output, we have also been joined by other important media players. The press and its two branches of children – the book and the periodical – did an enormous amount, separately and between them, in the time of their uncontested media hegemony. But there were miracles of communication, dreamed of by a species that saw the world in images not abstractions, yearned for by humans accustomed to an immediate response to a spoken word, that the printing press for all its extensional power could not deliver. The very humanity of these and other forms of pre-technological communication made their loss in the press, the tradeoff inherent in a global dissemination of abstract, delayed messages, all the more frustrating.

We join the information revolution in our next chapter at a time when some of these natural modes of communication are beginning to be retrieved by technology. More than 350 years have passed since Gutenberg started printing. The results of his work have brought us dozens of heresies that have matured into separate Churches, Isaac Newton's great synthesis of physics on Earth and in the heavens, national states and an age of colonialism stretched so far that the United States of America has already declared its independence from Britain. Immanuel Kant has published his *Critique of Pure Reason*, Jefferson and his colleagues the

Declaration of Independence and the Bill of Rights to the Constitution. The French have overthrown their monarch in an internal democratic revolution, only to have Napoleon seize power and put most of Europe under subjugation. But now he too has gone, leaving an even newer world as his legacy.

All of this and more has been reported in the press. Is there any way to get a reliable picture of it?

4

THE AGE OF PHOTOGRAPHY AND THE AGELESS IMAGE

The nineteenth century is known as the Age of Invention. When we consider its inventions of communication, it could also be known as the Age of the Image and the Echo.

With the notable exception of the telegraph – at once the first electronic medium, the first industrial use of electricity, and the most abstract of any communication mode before or since (Morse Code is an abstraction of writing, itself an abstraction of speech, in turn an abstraction of what it describes) – all the major communication inventions of the last century worked by capturing or reflecting a literal energy configuration from the real world. The still images of the photograph fix the impressions made by light after it bounces off objects. The telephone turns sound waves into analogous, physically similar, electronic patterns. The phonograph recording is literally a record of sound waves woven into the contours of a durable physical medium. Motion pictures are individual photographic images presented to the eye so quickly that they give the illusion of motion – in effect, reconstituting the motion of the real world. And in the twentieth century, first radio and then television carried on in this analog tradition. Only the computer at last changed this course, trafficking in digital expressions of text as abstract as Morse Code – though, unlike Morse Code, invisible to the user. And the computer is now increasingly moving to digital processing and display not only of text but icons, sounds, and images.

The power of the icon – the lure of what is immediately comprehensible to our eyes and ears – is not surprising. Despite the enormous facility and impact of the alphabet, the price we paid and still pay for our immersion in its culture is a distance from the real worlds it conveys. Something in the very bodies and brains our DNA gives rise to, something in our genetic connection to the living, material world around us, makes us respond on the profoundest of levels to music that plays upon our ears, to images that enter our retinas. Without it, we no doubt suffer a form of sensory deprivation. As McLuhan so aptly observed (1962), the alphabet separated the cerebral from the more sensual parts of our nature.

Thus the photograph, appearing after three hundred years of print's increasing domain, was on one level a potent and much needed corrective. In this chapter, we look not only at what it corrected, but at how those corrections transformed the world they were fitted upon – and the lessons this would hold in store for the continuing information revolution in our own century.

THE IMMACULATE CONCEPTION OF PHOTOGRAPHY

The copying of the real visual world of course began eons before the photograph, at very least tens of thousands of years ago in cave drawings found in Chauvet (*c.* 28,000 BC) and elsewhere in Europe. These depictions, ranging from the realistic in Chauvet to the more abstract, and more recent, in Lascaux (*c.* 14,000 BC), obviously predate not only the photograph but the alphabet. Indeed, the accepted (and presumably most likely) path for the evolution of writing has it moving from pictures to pictographs (e.g., stick figures) to hieroglyphics and then alphabet. This withering of reality makes sense as a communication strategy: stick figures can be drawn more quickly, by more people, to represent more things than can full-bodied renderings, just as the alphabet is more efficient than hieroglyphics.

Of course, there are other possible explanations for the prehistoric trajectory. Freud's equation of the creative lives of the artist, child, primitive, and neurotic (1908; 1918) can lead us to wonder if some bare-bones, abstract line drawings are expressions of a less, not more, developed communication technique. And, for all we know, some abstract form of writing, either unrecognizable to us or just not surviving in any durable impression, may have been employed prior to, or in tandem with, the paintings in Chauvet and Lascaux. In a related vein, Alexander Marshack sees evidence of a computational or recording system in a series of V-shaped markings on a piece of ox-rib some 300,000 years old (see Rensberger, 1978), and has argued that the exacting technical requirements of more recent paleolithic cave art points to some system of recording to keep track of such components as pigment ratios (Marshack, 1972). The discovery of some 7,000 nearly identical circular markings in Australia (Wilford, 1996) suggests a system of recording – perhaps even abstract writing – tentatively dated at 75,000 years old.

Nonetheless, we know two things with some certainty about the prehistory and history of realistic representations of the visual world. First, the oldest paintings thus far discovered (30,000 to 15,000 years ago) predate by many millennia the oldest inscriptions that are unambiguously forms of writing (cuneiform and hieroglyphics, as old as 6,000 years, and definitely progressing from more to less realism, or less to more stylization, in both cases). Second, several millennia after the invention of the alphabet – the most stylized, abstract written medium of all until the telegraph in the nineteenth century – and several centuries after the alphabet's exponential augmentation by the press, we find that realistic painting no longer serves a practical, workaday communication function. What had begun, at least insofar as pictographs in hieroglyphics are concerned, as a form of record-keeping, had branched out in the West to abstract writing as the lifeblood of communication on the one hand, and realistic portraiture and landscape painting as art on the other.

This was the environment into which the photograph made its entrance: visual imagery as art, abstract writing as communication. One was more or less unique, idiosyncratically individual, subjective; the other was reliable, repeatable, mass-produced. What made the photograph so revolutionary, then, was not what it did – for artists had been reproducing the images of the world for 30,000 years – but the way it did it. By the nineteenth century, painting had the verisimilitude of Chauvet and far more. Certainly the first photographs – and, indeed, in one respect as long as they were black-and-white – were not the equal of the best paintings in their lifelikeness. But photography produced lifelike images much more efficiently and reliably. And although photography debuted with one-of-a-kind direct "positives" – the daguerreotype – in the late 1830s, it would soon develop images every bit as reproducible as the letters of the alphabet, and publishable in the same press.

This revolution in efficiency would eventually encompass not only the viewer but the taker of the photograph. A half-century after the daguerreotype, the Kodak camera would begin to put a piece of visual reality into every person's potential grasp – just point the camera at a face, an object, a scene, or an event, and take it away – much as the alphabet had done for the act of writing. This alteration in the relationship of humans to their visual environment, which first made access to reproductions of the visual world almost as easy as access to the visual world itself, and soon allowed most people to make the reproductions themselves, served as one of the prototypes for a line of media whose users were producers as well as consumers. Though the alphabet of course operated in this way, the press as a one-way mass medium did not; nor would radio and television; telephone and the personal computer, however, would both be media whose very use created content. We will explore the consequences of the media-empowered producer later in this volume.

But although the photograph's efficiency of image production was a highly influential characteristic, it was by no means its most original, unique, and profound. That distinction lay with the image's reliability – in the very way it was made – which of course was related to ease of production, but had most to do with the nature of the photographic image itself.

A painting, regardless of its verisimilitude, is inevitably the product of an artist's optical system, fed into and through the artist's brain and its genetic construction and lifetime of experience, consciously and unconsciously directing the hand that moves the brush on the canvas. However similar different human brains might be, however "objective" the genetically-derived components of optical, aesthetic-cognitive, and motor operating systems in artists, no one would disagree that a significant part of that process, indeed, the most significant part, is subjective. For what distinguishes the work of one artist from another are not the programs common to all human brains, but each artist's uniquely personal expression.

In contrast, regardless of where the camera is pointed, the photograph at the instant of its conception is product of a standardized, non-living, technological piece of equipment. Given the same lighting conditions, a given camera can be counted upon to take exactly the same picture of the same object over and over again. This is because its optical system, its "brain," its hand upon the canvas (the way the incoming light makes an impression upon the film) is the same every time. Whereas the artist's subjective experience informs every aspect of the painting process, the photographer's subjective input ends with the decision of where to point the camera. Thereafter the image is in the hands of the light and the camera. It was with good reason that Joseph Nicéphore Niépce, who contributed as much to the invention of photography as his partner Louis Jacques Mandé Daguerre (see Gernsheim and Gernsheim, 1968), called his 1820s process "*l'héliographie*" – sun drawing.

No doubt the personal experience, taste, and vision of the inventors play a major role in the construction of any camera – their ideas, inevitably subjective in part, are embodied in the camera, as indeed all technologies are embodiments of human ideas (see Levinson, 1988) – but from the perspective of the photographer, that construction is now objective and not subject to change at the time the photograph is taken. Various built-in options can of course give the photographer more leeway, more room for exercise of personal vision, but even these choices are pre-set, the embodiment of ideas other than those of the proximate photographer.

Thus, the French film critic André Bazin (1967, p. 12) astutely observed that the photograph is free of the "sin" of subjectivity. We might think about, and enjoyably discuss, which aspects of subjectivity are sinful, and why – but if we substitute "unreliability" for "subjectivity," we can easily see one high-profile component of the sin. Surely, a painting of a crime is in no sense as reliable an account or indication or record of a crime as a photograph, and proffering a painting as evidence of what happened would in most cases be laughable.

Interestingly, the digitization of photography via all manner of computers – which can reconstruct an image as fast as a mouse running across a screen – is now undermining that very reliability of the photograph as a mute, unbiased witness of reality. But to understand the import of that, we first need to look at the role that the photograph-as-record has played in the past 175 or more years.

STAINS IN THE MIRROR

On some streets in Manhattan, parking meters require deposit of 25 cents for every ten minutes up to an hour; fines for parking next to an expired meter begin at 40 dollars; one can plead that the meter was broken, not expired, but how does one prove this? The Parking Violations Bureau is always glad to send out an investigator after the fact, but if in the interim an irate citizen with less control but maybe more sense than you slammed the meter and thereby knocked its needle back into operation, your claim that the meter was broken has lost its substantiation. The court will always listen to eyewitness testimony, but members of your family and friends – the people most likely to have been in the car with you – are obviously biased. No, by far the best evidence, lawyers and government factotums agree, is a snapshot of the broken meter – eloquently direct and unimpeachable in its testimony, especially if it is a Polaroid "instant" photograph, unmediated by any laboratory. (This, at least, is what I have been advised the few times that I alas have been obliged to contest parking tickets in the courts of New York City; see also Dornsife, 1978, p. 364. Of course, for this defense, the driver has to have the foresight to keep a camera in the car at all times.)

Most new media are regularly derided as inferior to their predecessors. It wasn't until 1677, more than two hundred years after Gutenberg's rescue of the written word from its slow corruption by hand, that written contracts were held preferable to oral agreements in the British Parliament's "Statute of Frauds." The telegraph was also subject to initial distrust, and television and computers are still cast as despoilers of literacy and morality, if not truth, justice, and the American way. Photography, perhaps because it was without precedence in its clean capture of literal reality, underwent no such period of pillory or even much doubt. As early as 1851, wood engravings from daguerreotypes by Richard Beard were used to document *London Labour and the London Poor*, a massive, pioneering sociological tract by Henry Mayhew and others (see Newhall, 1964, p. 139).

The photographic process formally announced by L.J.M. Daguerre in 1839, and which bore his name, used a direct-to-positive technique that developed the image on a shiny, silvered surface. These first photographs were thus literally as well as figuratively mirrors not only of the world, but of anyone who looked at them, and tilted the photograph at a slight angle. Soon the mirror – whose reflections of the world were not only accurate but endured – was pointed not just at people in poverty but people at war. Roger Fenton and James Robertson took photographs of the Crimean War in the late 1850s with Fox Talbot's improved "negative" process that allowed any number of copies to be made from the original; photography was on its way to becoming a news medium. By the time of the Civil War in America, Matthew Brady and his crew were ready to make the first sustained photographic documentary of a war. His photographs were no longer literal daguerreotypic mirrors, but they were reflections of the deepest levels of human struggle nonetheless – of the complex emotions experienced by humans who think about wars, as much as of the soldiers who fight them. The lessons conveyed in the images were a long time in taking root. "War," Beaumont Newhall aptly observes (1964, p. 67), "has ever been an ungrateful subject for the photographer." It would continue much as it always had been – as a cold instrument of foreign policy wielded by leaders on the one hand, as a glorious swashbuckling adventure by all too many people caught up in its ideal on the other – well into the twentieth century. But by the time the Vietnam War was fought on television in living and dying color, it could no longer be sold as an exhilarating crusade or a rational political equation. In consequence, as Richard Heppner details (1993), the United States military fought the Gulf War in 1991 with one eye on the battlefield and one eye on the camera.

If war and other human outrages were ungrateful subjects of the photograph, the non-human world of nature and the physics within and beyond were uncaring. But, as Einstein observed, the universe is not malicious in the way it seems to withhold its secrets from us, merely difficult, and the photographic record has been able to help coax many a secret from it. Written descriptions of data and discovery may be socially trustworthy, but photography of an object (and, later, with motion photography, of an event) could serve as a reasonable, initial datum substitute for the object itself. Indeed, in rescuing an image, as Bazin put it (1967, p. 14), from its "proper corruption" in time, the photograph can provide an encounter with a scientific object of study superior to that allowed in the actual world with its incessant intrusions and vicissitudes (assuming, of course, that removal of the image from its *in situ* reality does not unduly change it). Further, the attachment of photography to microscopes and telescopes opens entire worlds to such close-to-firsthand inspection, by scientists and the public-at-large who do not have access to such magnifying instruments. Photographs of what might be fossils of Martian micro-organisms found in the remains of a meteorite in Antarctica, and of distant stars which when seen through the Hubble look as if they might have planets, were at the cutting edge of this public inspection of the universe in the mid-1990s.

But here the cutting edge may be blunted a bit by coming up against a fundamental problem inherent in all such advanced photography: the further it reaches for its subject, the more the photograph is not just a simple record of visual reality but itself the result of complex, and ever fallible, technological manipulation. The problem arises even with the straight, non-photographic use of the microscope. We stain a specimen on a slide to see it more clearly; but what might the stain obscure or lead us to see that is not really there? Photography of Martian microbes and distant planets is of course highly enhanced, which puts it in a category shared by the general digitization of photography mentioned above, and indeed by all media in which humans are producers as well as consumers: the greater the opportunity for human refinement of production, the less reliable the medium as an objective legal, social, scientific, or whatever kind of record. This problem is not insurmountable – we can certainly employ checks and balances on any technological adjustment of an image to ascertain its accuracy – but such controls are themselves subject to error, and some increase in the overall noise in the system as we increase technological manipulation is inevitable. We will look at this in more detail in Chapters 11–15, especially at how computers and hypertext have blurred the distinction between reader and author (but for more on the digitization of photography, see Meyer, 1994, and Greenstein, 1996).

For most people, however, microbes and stars, even wars and parking meters, are distinctly secondary as objects of photographic interest. For most of us, perhaps even all of us, the images we most want to see rescued from their proper corruption in time are those of our loved ones, of us, of the parts of the world that we daily walk through or may on occasion actually travel to. At this basic human level, no one questions the authenticity of the photograph. At this level, then, we may find the photograph's most profound contribution to our lives.

IMAGE IMMORTALITY

A sad but instructive fact about the first decade of photography is that its most frequent subjects were deceased children (Reif, 1977). How did such a state of affairs come to be?

The cost of portraiture was very high. Most people could not afford to sit, or have their children sit, for painters. Nor, indeed, was the first thing on most people's minds to run out and have their family photographed. Nature's pencil, after all, was still new and unsharpened.

And yet, as word of its miracles spread, and a child died from tuberculosis or another ravage of an age in which diseases of all sorts ran rampant, the thought might have occurred to a grief-stricken parent: what, other than my memories, have I to keep of my child? Might not a photograph provide such a recollection outside of my head – a recollection that my other children, and their children, and their children in turn might some day be able to regard? Thus was an image, of the most precious kind, truly rescued from its corruption in time.

Of course, as photography became less expensive and more prevalent, more and more families and children posed for photographs. By the 1850s, a daguerreo-typic portrait could be had in the United States for 12½ cents; "picture factories" churned out as many as 1,000 per day (Newhall, 1964, p. 47). Meanwhile, the most popular subject of private photography was the posed female nude. The very impersonality and speed that made photography an ideal medium for scientific and social documentation commended it as a keepsake of more personal things.

From the very beginning, the mechanism of photography was far less expensive than the mechanisms of portraiture and art. A camera is obviously far easier to construct than an artist – once people know how to make them – and a photo-grapher similarly requires far less training. Further, once George Eastman harnessed the principles of mass production to making cameras, and introduced the Kodak box camera in 1889, the image-capturing device became as widespread as any other product of late-nineteenth-century manufacturing.

Thus did the saving of images from their natural disappearance become a mass phenomenon. Indeed, unlike the products of the printing press, which as we saw in the last chapter required years of education to intelligently engage, the products of the camera required no learning at all to profitably perceive. Images born free of the processing of the human nervous system were commensurately easiest for human understanding to embrace. Few, if any, paintings are as self-evident as the photograph, usually comprehensible just by the glancing.

But this says something about photography and subjectivity. The sin that was locked out of the delivery room was by no means banished from the medium, nor the world of other visual renderings photography affected. How could it be otherwise, when a human face was so often the object and always the subject of the photographic gaze?

THE GAZE ACROSS TIME

There is a lesson here for the criticism, often heard, that artificial media tend to dehumanize us, separating us from the real world, our emotions, our deeper selves (see, e.g., Ellul, 1964). The truth is that we invest our deeper selves, as Kant saw, in whatever aspects of external reality we encounter – whether mediated by photochemical plates or travelling more directly to our live optical nerves. The photograph of a pleasing meadow need be no less a recipient of this cognitive and emotional investment than the meadow itself. The meadow in the world no doubt has its advantages, in that it may come with a breeze and the perfume of its clover. But the meadow in our hands, in a photograph, has advantages too – we can see it in the dead of night or winter, or years after the meadow outdoors may have been paved into a parking lot. Nor does the photograph make the paving in any way more likely – if anything, it can arouse even more appreciation of the original meadow.

And what of photographs of people? Surely few of us prefer them to the real thing. And yet most of us see in them elements of humanity which might otherwise not be available. I mean this quite literally. Several years ago, at a flea-market in Stanfordville, New York, I picked up an old photograph, likely from the 1870s. It was of a young woman, I would guess to be in her twenties, looking straight into the camera – and thus straight into my eyes, across more than a hundred years of time. What had she been thinking when that photograph was taken? Had it ever entered even her wildest speculations that more than a century later, when she would be long dead, some student of the media would be holding it, looking at her face, her eyes, on a summer's day on a meadow in upstate New York? Not very likely.

Meanwhile, whatever we might call my contemplation of those possibilities, it was surely a subjective, aesthetic experience of a kind not usually found in daily life on our planet. To be in touch with someone a hundred years in the past, even if that communication was one-way, is something rare. Another genre of that experience could be had by reading any book written in the last century or earlier. But the iconic power of the photograph is, not surprisingly, far more personal — breathtaking in a way no text could be.

Indeed, this personal directness stems from the very impersonality of the photograph's creation. An artist's rendering of a face, however accurate, tells us not only about the face, but about how the artist feels about it. A photograph of a face tells us just about the face — the feelings we see in it are hence just ours, and the person whose face it is. No third party acts as an intermediary. Thus, contrary to photography's critics (such as Sontag, 1977, p. 154), who see in it a usurpation of reality not committed by painting and its "interpretation of the real," the artificial medium of photography eliminates the painting's requirement of a human intermediary between me and my perception of the real world. Which is the more "authentic" human involvement (to use a favorite existentialist adjective, often said to typify modern technology by its absence)? There is of course no clear-cut answer, except that giving Miles Standish the option of receiving information other than through John Alden can scarcely be a dehumanization.

Which, of course, is not to say that art's interpreting, rather than capturing, of reality is in all or even most cases disadvantageous. The import of photography vis-à-vis art — missed by some at its inception, still missed by some now — is rather that they do two different things, both of which were once done only by art.

Having looked at what photography does, we conclude this chapter with a look at what it does not — a look at art in the age of sun drawing.

THE MIGRATION OF SUBJECTIVITY

Upon seeing a daguerreotype for the first time, the French painter Paul Delaroche is said to have exclaimed: "From today on, painting is dead!" Whether Delaroche said this in 1838 or 1839 is in dispute (see Gernsheim and Gernsheim, 1968, p. 95); what's beyond dispute is the fact that painting has obviously amply survived this panicked notice. Indeed, Delaroche himself seems to have quickly seen the light: Josef Maria Eder (1945, p. 348) reports that, within the year, Delaroche was saying of Daguerre's invention that it was "a great advantage for art."

Delaroche's change of heart apparently came with the realization that photography could serve as a trustworthy *de facto* sketchbook for later artistic creations. This was true, but of trivial consequence compared to photography's other contribution to art — a contribution which stemmed from the very threat that Delaroche first perceived.

We can well understand the source of Delaroche's initial concern. The photograph, as we have seen, is both less expensive and more objective and reliable than the painting, by huge orders of magnitude on all accounts. Why would anyone other than a person very wealthy in money and time want to sit for a portrait when a photograph could be taken? The fact is that few people did, and Delaroche's prediction was by and large sustained in the realm of portraiture.

Landscape paintings were more resistant to encroachment, owing to such early photographic deficits as lack of color and limits in size. But here too the efficiency of the photograph ultimately carried the day, with the result that for many years now most scenes of most places are photographically captured.

So how, then, did painting not only survive but thrive?

By focusing on the one thing it could inevitably do better than the photograph — by further developing into an art form its very subjectivity in the conception of the image, the very subjectivity that photography had eliminated.

That there would be a market for paintings that exulted in the point of view, in the subjective aspects of the human eye, should come as no surprise, given the intrinsic human appetite for the subjective, and our projection of it onto all we do. The Impressionists were the first to consciously offer a subjective alternative to the photograph, in a movement which transcended visual art to inspire music and poetry, and became the Hegelian spirit of the end of the nineteenth-century age. Visually, it began as an attempt to in effect best the photograph at its own game: if photography captured the world by registering the light that bounced off it on a photographic plate, why not skip the registration of the world altogether, and just render an impression of the pure light? Of course, although such rendering might seem to be even more objective than the photograph, no one can really see just pure light in this life. So the renderings of the pure light were in fact just the artists' impressions of the light — subjective impressions of the mind rather than objective impressions on plates, interpretations of what the light *should* look like. And in these ethereal interpretations that seemed to float a micron above the canvas, in the works of Manet to Monet and all in between, a new form of art was born, one which was at once beautiful, ideal for social commentary, and utterly beyond the reach of any photograph at the time.

Succeeding generations of artists adopted essentially the same strategy, offering Expressionism, Cubism, and the whole array of twentieth-century art as alternatives to photography, gambits that made photography look clumsy in any attempt to replicate these renderings by human hands. For the subject of modern art, as many have observed, is no longer the natural world, in either its tangible or light forms; it is rather the artistic process itself, with art thus becoming an instant meta-form.

The moral for the evolution of media is very profound: when a new medium triumphs over an older medium in a given function, that does not mean the old medium will shrivel up and die. Rather, the old medium may be pushed into a niche in which it can perform better than the new medium, and where it will therefore survive, albeit as something different from what it was before the new medium arrived. The key, as we will see throughout this book (especially Chapter 9 and its discussion of radio's success in an age of television), is whether the old medium is able to hit upon an already extant human need or perceptual mode.

Thus did Delaroche's fear that the photograph would be loved too much prove unfounded. But he was wrong only that the love of the image rescued so cleanly from time would eclipse the human love of images based on other processes — not that the photograph, and its progeny the motion picture and television, would be loved. For they were, and are — whether because of the sheer ease and sensual satisfaction of the direct image, or because it cuts across time, or both. The photograph in its heart-stopping immediacy of permanent images was every bit as exciting in its day as television is in ours. Indeed, it still is. And one of the questions which we have begun to focus upon here, and will give further attention to later, is why media which evoke such public affection often seem to provoke along with it the consternation of the academic world.

But in our next chapter, we will see that a medium which was a contemporary of the photograph, and its complement in being highly abstract not iconic, and extending across space not time, received a somewhat different initial reception from its public.

5

TELEGRAPHY

The suspect messenger

Harold Innis (1951), whose sage views on communication and culture we have already encountered in our grand tour, observed in a pre-computer age that media tend to extend communication either across space or time, but rarely both in equal balance. Thus, paintings on cave walls and hieroglyphics on tombs convey their messages across millennia, but travel nowhere in space; they are classic time-extending media. In contrast, the alphabet on papyrus or paper, far easier to write on vehicles easily capable of transport, is a space-extending medium *par excellence*; but whether burned in the Library of Alexandria or subject simply to toll of decay, its earliest examples are long since gone. Of course, alphabetic media can be treated as time-extending devices, and accorded special care as they were until the introduction of the printing press. They can be hoarded and treasured and conserved for future generations, rather than disseminated to the world at large; but this was clearly an imposition of a human social order upon the medium, not something intrinsic to the medium itself.

Indeed, the impact of the printing press – midwife to the modern age – can be attributed to its being the first medium in history to extend more or less equally and powerfully across both space and time. Speech, in a much more limited way, also extends in both directions – via the legs of its listeners across space, via their memories across time. But the noise factor in such imperfect extensions is so high that no spoken society that we know of – no human group that communicates solely though speech, with no written back-up – has achieved anything that we might agree constitutes a "civilization." Under the lopsided extensions of hiero-glyphics and then the alphabet, elements of civilization were indeed achieved. But the modern world required the printing press – and, from the perspective of this line of discussion, its twofold impact across space and time. Books were – and are still, in many but not all ways – ideal dual vehicles of dissemination and storage.

From the perspective of our eve-of-the-millennium vantage point in the information revolution, a medium that extends across both space and time seems unsurprising, even *de rigueur*: computers, after all, provide both instant movement of information around the world and massive storage in small sectors of easily accessible space. The storage is perhaps not as far-reaching as the dissemination – computer disks and media may decay more quickly than paper, just as paper fades faster than carvings on cave walls – but the dissemination is so immense that it in itself constitutes a kind of storage, a vastly dispersed proof against decay.

We will return to the computer later, but for now we can observe that Innis' view of the seesaw of space and time extension, with balance-points such as the printing press being rare occurrences, engendering of golden ages, was a view of the ancient world and its media. For rather than being a remarkable exception, the printing press and its balance ushered in a new age of simultaneous space-and-time extension, with the digital culture of computers but the current expression.

In between, we have the nineteenth and first half of the twentieth centuries, whose media transformations began with the photograph and the telegraph. Just as the photograph's radically new contribution was its precise, immaculate extension across time, so was the telegraph's an instant extension across distance. These of course were not the same media, but they constitute a matched pair, invented at the same time. Indeed, courtesy of Samuel Morse, they were to some extent developed by the same inventor. Morse is better known for his work on the telegraph and the code that bears his name, but when visiting Paris in 1838–1839 to promote his new invention, he met Daguerre, saw his photographs, and wrote to his brothers in New York City: "You may recall experiments of mine in New Haven many years ago . . . to ascertain whether it were possible to fix the images of the camera obscura. . . . I . . . gave up the attempt. M. Daguerre has realized in the most exquisite manner this idea" (Eder, 1945, pp. 272–273). Morse and Daguerre became good friends, and Morse went on to do pioneering work in photography in America.

His telegraph – which was based on Ampère's idea and as always on the partial work of others – was subject to a practical limitation in the necessity of wires, and a skill limitation in the need for some people to learn Morse Code. But to the degree that these were satisfied, the telegraph could send a message instantly to anyone, anywhere in the world. Thus, the photograph and the telegraph can be taken as two different faces of a media system which, like the printing press before it and the computer after, extended across both time and space. For people who suddenly found both at hand in the middle decades of the nineteenth century, that was indeed their paired import.

Yet the public's reaction to each new medium was not the same. For while the photograph was immediately and palpably recognizable for what it conveyed and the accuracy of the conveyance, the proximate products of the telegraph were after all dots and dashes usually very far away from their human origins. And dots – not images, not even words directly – can sow distrust, especially when communicated at a speed which previously only sheer human imagination had dared traverse.

DUPLICITOUS MERCURY

That Hermes (Mercury) was a god of speed and deceit, of communication and thievery, should come as no surprise. Anything that can be here one moment and gone the next – now you see it, now you don't – will understandably attract suspicion, however otherwise helpful and reliable it might be. Although our imaginations give us the impression of operating at faster-than-light speeds – we can imagine ourselves to the planet Mercury and back in an instant – in fact they do not. Indeed, although our face-to-face communications provide a similar impression of being immediate – and in effect are – all technologies that extended this communication prior to electronic media operated at very much slower speeds. One of the prices we paid for receiving our news via print rather than word-of-mouth was the inevitable delay of the printed mode. That the delay was eminently worth it, in numerous ways that brought us the modern world, we have already discussed (see also Chapter 9 for more on the evolution of media as tradeoffs with net gain; see also Levinson, 1979). The point here is that, by the time of the telegraph, and in fact through the end of the twentieth century, the delay was expected, with the result that the very instantaneity that was the great suit of the telegraph was also a source of unease.

But Mercury was god of communication as well as speed, and the placement of sleight-of-hand in his bailiwick must after all count somewhat against communication in general, since communication is by no means always swift. Indeed, the now-you-see-it-now-you-don't concern cannot count fully even against speed-of-light communication, since the very nature of information is such that it stays in its place of origin even as it is disseminated instantly and universally. Thus, though Mercurial speed was certainly an aggravating factor, at root the ancient ambivalence towards him and his tasks – and our anxiety as well – likely stems from an ambivalence about the communication process itself, whatever form it might assume.

When we contemplate the ubiquity of noise, how any representation, however accurate, is inevitably a distortion – always less, sometimes more, than the original – we can well understand this distrust. There is no such thing as perfection in representation and communication. A perfect duplicate, were it technically possible, would in its very duplication undermine the original by creating a universe in which the original, owing to its duplication, was no longer one of a kind. Thus, even in this ideal case, which I call the paradox of duplication, the representation is unsettling, and more than just a representation. And, of course, in more common, less extreme cases, we can literally measure the loss in information between representation and original – the inevitable increase in noise in what engineers call "generations." The introduction of remedial media, in this case, can never be entirely effective, since the new medium will inevitably introduce a new noise component of its own.

Meaning, however, can be and usually is fully or mostly recovered. Remedial media can help in a relative sense – Dolby sound systems provide clearer, if less "punchy", sound. But concern over possible loss of meaning in one form or another is what motivated Socrates and his preference for spoken dialogue to writing (one can ask the speaker a question and thereby clarify or reduce noise, whereas the written text provides just one unvarying response), Aristotle and his advice to trust the testimony of the naked senses over technology, the clergy's attack on the press, deconstructionism's self-defeating brief against language (for a fine obituary of which, see Turner, 1996), and indeed the critique that has been in attendance at the opening of just about every new medium, electronic and photochemical, for the past two centuries.

The thrust of this volume is that such critique has been by and large wrong – not unfounded, in the metaphysical sense that noise is indeed ubiquitous, but simply not the case, not warranted, inasmuch as noise does not usually deform media beyond net practical value and benefit to the world. In a phrase: more people have been informed than misinformed by media. But the not unreasonable basis of such concern about misinformation – the presence of accidental noise in every informational transaction, the potential for deliberate noise or deception – means we have to take special care in responding to these critiques of media. It may well be that the current attacks on computers, like prior attacks on TV, motion pictures, et al., are just the flailings-about of informational elites attempting to defend their eroding turfs. But we need to acknowledge that the defense of any older communication system may be grounded in a not necessarily illogical desire to hold on to the noise we have in favor of the noise we may get, lest we be subject to the claim that we are blind to the inevitable margin of error – Hermes' toll – that all communication exacts.

The telegraph, as the first electronic medium, provided an especially vivid occasion of initial concern about this toll. We turn now to Reuter, his use of the telegraph, and its report of Lincoln's assassination.

THE HATCHING OF DISTRUST: THE PIGEON, THE TELEGRAPH, AND BIO-TECH 1850s STYLE

In addition to moving instantly across distances that otherwise took weeks to traverse, trafficking in a code that was itself an abstraction of alphabetic language, and being otherwise heir to the caution accorded any communication that lacked a human face, the earliest messages sent across the Atlantic by cable were beset by a series of technical difficulties that lasted some nine years. The first attempt at laying a cable under the ocean in 1857 ended just 380 miles off the coast of Ireland, when the cable snapped and sank 2,000 fathoms under the sea. A year later, a full 3,000 miles of cable were put into operation; some 700 to 800 messages were sent; but the signals became unclear and died out completely after four weeks. The American Civil War intervened, and it was not until 1865 that a new attempt was made. This time, a brand new cable was laid, stronger and more conducive, but a part of it eventually broke off. It was recovered and spliced to a new piece in 1866, after a second cable had been laid; and continuous, reliable transatlantic service has resulted ever since (see Gibson, n.d., pp. 74–86, and Garratt, 1958, for details).

Meanwhile, Baron Paul Julius von Reuter (1816–1899) had a nose, not just for news, but for the timeliness that was its essence. Notwithstanding all the advantages of the printing press and the massive number of newspapers it produced, the speed with which its news was delivered at the beginning of the nineteenth century was still entirely a function of muscle, as in human and animal locomotion, and sail. The rail would soon add reliability and endurance, but not speed. And rails were not operable across big bodies of water, not even (as yet) the English Channel.

Reuter's news agency gained an early edge in 1849 with its recruitment of pigeons to bridge the gap between the new German and French telegraph lines.

The birds went on to a century of distinguished service to Reuters, including bringing forth news from the beachheads of Normandy in 1944. By 1851, the first underwater cable was in operation – between Calais and Dover – and Reuter set up offices in London. But much to his dismay, the British press refused to publish foreign news borne to it solely by telegraph; Reuter's business was by and large limited to sending and delivering private commercial messages by telegraph and pigeon. Finally, in 1858, *The Times* consented to publish a report of a major speech by Napoleon III, received by Reuters via telegraph from France. The speed for the first publication of a message sent by telegraph across the English Channel can thus be reckoned as follows: a few minutes to transmit and decode, a few hours to be printed in the press, seven years from the time the underwater cable had first been opened. Thus did distrust disable the very advantage of the telegraph, its nearly instantaneous speed. Leavened by the press's social (not technological) resistance, minutes and hours had been transformed into years.

The Atlantic Ocean provided a different kind of test case for the telegraph, but one instructive of the same lesson. With the transatlantic cable still a year away from reliable service, on 26 April 1865 Reuters received news of Abraham Lincoln's assassination eleven days earlier, via a telegram sent to London from a station in Londonderry in northern Ireland. The incredible news had first crossed the Atlantic on the SS Nova Scotian. But so suspect, still, was the telegraph, and so astonishing the news it conveyed across even the relatively small distance from Londonderry to London, that the report was at first denounced as a hoax started by London Stock Exchange speculators. It was of course confirmed by subsequent dispatches beginning two hours later, and Reuter's pre-eminent position as a news agent was established. His office had aptly been named Reuter's Telegram Company Ltd some two months earlier (see Storey, 1951, and Read, 1992).

Myth and motion pictures – like the delightful *A Dispatch from Reuters* (with Edward G. Robinson in the title role, 1940; see Castell, 1995, p. 280) – turned the two-hour limbo that followed receipt of the initial telegram about Lincoln into a more dramatically-gripping several days. But the conviction for even two hours that the initial telegram was a hoax is sufficiently telling. Reporters nowadays are of course expected to confirm their stories and sources, and no one would regard any news agency or network, however sophisticated, as being beyond the manipulation of some organization bent on perpetrating a hoax. But what is suspect now, unlike Reuters' report in April 1865, is the message not the messenger. That is why Walter Cronkite, CBS-TV's news anchor from 1962 through 1981, was deemed "the most trusted man in America" (Head and Sterling, 1982, p. 232).

By the 1970s, television news was likely to be trusted in America, because by then the American public had been receiving its services for more than two decades — as indeed it and the world at large had enjoyed more than a century of news conveyed by electricity and electro-magnetic carrier waves. The primary lesson of Reuters' baptismal experiences with the telegraph is thus that the new kid on the block, especially if electronic, will be doubted and resisted — a phase which generally gives way to public acceptance, if not of its own accord, certainly when a yet newer medium comes along to occupy the niche of initial suspicion. Indeed, the current computer revolution is to some extent unique in that it has both improved the status of its predecessor, television, as well as rapidly moved on its own to partially shed its initial image of a cold, dehumanizing instrument (as evidenced, for example, in widespread use of the Web).

In order to better appreciate the significance of the current digital age and its reception, we need to look more closely at these mechanisms of distrust and rejection of new media. As we have seen, such mechanisms relate both to communication or transfer of representations in general, and to the speed of electronic transfer in particular. To roughly gauge the relative operation and impact of these factors, we can briefly consult the evolution of communications media across history for a pattern — revisiting some of the older media we have already discussed, and encountering some subsequent media for the first time.

A THUMBNAIL HISTORY OF MEDIA CONDEMNATION

When speech was as new as digital communication is today, poised to launch hominids on the path to full *Homo sapiens sapiens*, those who were entrusted or self-appointed guardians of traditional hominid culture would no doubt have assessed the new medium — had they had such power of assessment, absent spoken language — to be undermining and ultimately destructive of their way of life. And they would have been right. If current ape and chimpanzee "culture" is anything like the culture of our pre-linguistic hominid ancestors, certainly our world, animated by the cognitive, communicational, technological progeny of the spoken word, is not much like theirs. Not to mention that our more fully linguistic ancestors likely destroyed our less linguistic cousins, if not by direct extermination, than by competing more successfully for passage of their linguistically valent DNA into subsequent generations.

Indeed, although some formal critiques of new media accurately focus on what aspects of older media are threatened – Socrates' critique of writing as jeopardizing memory and immediate dialogue being an excellent example – and although the communication act itself comes fraught with a concern about the inevitable noise in any information exchange, there is probably a deeper fear afoot in most attacks on new media. It is a fear at once well-founded, unavoidable, and yet superfluous in the sense that by the time it is felt, not much can be done about it. It is a fear that the new mode of communication will undermine an older way of life – a way of life not necessarily best by any means, but certainly more comfortable than what is to come, because the older way is known.

Although we can sympathize with such fears on the human level of appreciating the pain attendant to any kind of cultural loss, our ethics also need to note that for most people the old way of communicating and thereby living is usually inferior to the new. Indeed, new media since the printing press have in every case served to ultimately further the democratization it engendered, with the result that critics of the new media have usually been defenders of the elite, attempting to bar the new onslaught of the masses. Motion pictures at the beginning of the twentieth century – described by a Professor William A. McKeever (1910) as "a school for criminals" – and television for the second half of this century have been special targets of crusaders for the cultural faith. Computers seem to break that mold as they do so many others, attracting some alarm not only as detractors but as vehicles of the informational elite (see, e.g., Ohmann, 1985; Rifkin, 1995; Sale, 1995). But, as we will see in detail later in this journey (see also Levinson, 1989b, 1996), the real victims of digitally created and exchanged information are the elitist aspects that still cling to the book and its "gatekeeping" publishing culture. Thus, the computer also has its share of old-time "McKeeveresque" critics, who see in it a threat to traditional culture (e.g., Heim, 1987; Postman, 1994; Birkerts, 1994).

Such critics of new media, while usually right that something of the old is being undermined, have often been wrong about exactly what that is, and its eventual import. Socrates was right about the atrophy of memory, but he radically underestimated the enormous advantage of writing and its storage of information – time extension – both for the intellectual process in general and the stuff of dialogue in particular. Similarly, as we have seen, Delaroche's death notice for painting in the wake of photography proved justified only for realistic portraits and some landscapes.

Opponents of new media also suffer, more often than not, from having little or no experience with the media under attack. This is a failing far more pertinent than the one invoked by the baseball fan who demands of his buddy, "Who are you to criticize the way Mickey Mantle played center field – have you ever been in the outfield?" In that case, perception of the performance, and the performances of other ball-players, provides experience sufficient to offer a critique of Mantle (however incorrect it might be). But how could Neil Postman offer a rational critique of online education in February 1994, admitting at the same time that he had neither taught nor participated in nor in any way observed a course taught online via personal computer and modem? Had he perhaps observed some deterioration in actual student performance after online education, or discovered that students online learn less effectively than their off-line counterparts? Possibly Socrates' misjudgement of writing was in part based on a similar lack of actual experience with the new medium – writing had been around long enough in Athens for Socrates to have observed its impact, but there is no evidence that he ever actually participated, or attempted to participate, in a written dialogue. Reason alone, as Kant noted, has its limitations. Untempered by actual experience, it can easily become ideology – and, in the case of media critics, an expression of deep-seated fears about any shaking of the *status quo*.

To the extent that critiques of new media are incorrect – whether based on lack of actual experience, or misunderstanding of the experience available – such critiques are a facet of the unintended consequences of invention that are everywhere in its implementation and effect. In the case of faulty critiques, the unintended component comes not so much in the fact that a criticism is mounted – for surely most inventors learn early on about the recalcitrance of the *status quo* – but in the criticism's projection of dire consequences that never come to be.

In the cases of Socrates and Delaroche, the critiques erred in assigning too much negative influence to the new medium. Postman takes a similar tack in his contention that television and computers work to undermine the rational process.

But sometimes a critique of a new medium can err on the other side – in a dismissal that radically underestimates the impact of the new communication device. Reuter's experiences described above are one example.

But by 1881, the telegraph had long since proven itself to everyone. Reuter's news agency and its reliance on the telegraph had made it the premier operation of its kind. In the United States, the telegraph had expanded across the continent along with the rails, and William Orton, President of Western Union Telegraph, was a colleague of the great rail barons. In that year, Orton's friend Chauncey Depew approached him for a little advice. Depew had been offered the opportunity of purchasing one-sixth of all Bell Telephone stock into perpetuity, for the sum of $10,000. In 1881, the telephone was just five years old, and $10,000 was no insignificant amount. So Depew came to Orton, undoubtedly an expert in telecommunications, with a question. Should I make the investment?

No, Orton confidently advised him, the telephone will never be more than a scientific toy (see Hogarth, 1926).

In the next chapter, we will see how this toy changed the world – and is still changing it.

6

TELEPHONE

The toy that roared

The fast dance between photograph and telegraph that balanced extension across time and space in the 1830s created a new imbalance or bias towards the visual, which itself had already been greatly augmented by the printing press and the alphabet before it. Indeed, subsequent to the emergence/invention of speech, every medium through the photograph and telegraph operated in the realm of sight. Photography was revolutionary in being the most literal, and the telegraph was a radical departure in its instantaneity across huge distances and triple level of abstraction away from the given world. But both were more of the same as far as the optical system they played to; and both accordingly set out a call, long overdue, for reciprocity for the acoustic realm.

The call was answered by the telephone in 1876, and its instant transmission not of writing, or code that represented writing, but human speech – plain human talk – across the same effectively universal earthly distances as the telegraph. This daring spatial foray, which reduced the abstraction of the telegraph to the basic human denominator of the spoken word (only hypothetical mental telepathy would be a more basic or direct way of communicating words), was accorded its temporal balance a year later, when the phonograph did for sound what the photograph did for the image. Indeed, Edison's first expectation about the use of the phonograph when he realized what he had invented was that it would be a telephone recording device (Josephson, 1959, pp. 160 ff.; Chew, 1981, pp. 2–3). His expectation was fulfilled nearly a hundred years later, with the telephone answering machine, but the global entertainment impact of the phonograph in the interim provides another outstanding example of unintended consequences. As we will see in the rest of this chapter, the telephone in almost every aspect of its development, including the media it gave rise to, has been a textbook case of unexpected consequences.

Clearly a key factor in generating these unintended results are the seesaws across time and space, the tugs for balance between sight and sound, that seem to channel and even dictate the development and implementation of new media almost regardless of the initial expectations of their inventors. What is the basis of these rhythms that turned the tango of the photograph and telegraph into a four-way square dance of photograph (extension of sight across time), telegraph (extension of sight across space), telephone (extension of sound across space), and phonograph (extension of sound across time) — and indeed would expand the dance into other modalities in the twentieth century, moving faster and faster, in a kind of kinetic Virginia reel?

The basis can only be in us — not only as the proximate creators of new media, but as the selecting force in the choices of our populace as to what media survive. Humans, without the most primitive media of pictographic writing, communicate across space via speech and time via memory. Or, to the extent that we repeat things via speech, we communicate across both time and space in the fundamental, organic cognitive/verbal communication module that every human comes endowed with — or endowed with the capacity to learn, in superficially different ways (so I am here in full agreement with Chomsky, e.g., 1975; see also Levinson, 1979, pp. 245–273, for speculation on the co-evolution of speech and the capacity for abstract thought). So humans, to update Kant, come programmed with a balance of time and space projectors that we shine upon the world. And of course we hear as well as see the results. This in turn suggests that the balance which we orchestrate in our media is but a reflection of our own internal, pre-wired balance. The pace has quickened in our construction and re-creation of this balance as our science and technology have given us the wherewithal to bring this extended balance into existence more quickly. Indeed, when I define technology as an embodiment of human ideas (Levinson, 1988; see also Vincenti, 1990, for an independent, similar view), I mean embodiment not only of ideas on a specific strategic level (the telephone embodies ideas about how to send a voice across a long distance, the phonograph embodies ideas about how to store a voice across time) but on a deeper, Kantian, organizational level (telephone and phonograph together express and implement our cognitive space-and-time projecting structures). And, of course, communication technologies convey ideas on a third, more obvious level — in the ideas spoken in a telephone conversation, in the melodies and ideas brought back to life in a music recording.

Nearly twenty years ago, I termed the powerful tendency to bring media ever more fully into human consonance "anthropotropic" (Levinson, 1979) — the humanly selected evolution of media towards ever more human function.

I suggested a three-part schema, wherein we (a) initially enjoyed a balanced though unextended communication environment (eyesight, earshot, and memory were its limits), (b) developed media to break beyond such limits, but paid a price for these breakthroughs in the balance and other human factors they sacrificed (the total lack of resemblance of the alphabet to the real world is a prime example), so (c) increasingly seek media which preserve and continue the extensional breakthroughs of the past, while retrieving the elements of the naturally human communicative world that were lost. Among the many consequences of this viewpoint is how it refutes the cynical, unexamined but widely accepted assumption of much of the twentieth century that new media and technology serve to dehumanize us (e.g., Ellul, 1964).

In the last quarter of the nineteenth century, however, progress was very much in the driver's seat – certainly more unambiguously so than now, more unanimously so than in the early era of the printing press (when the Church opposed Galileo), more so than when the photograph and telegraph were first implemented – probably more so than at any time before or after in our recorded history, with the possible exception of the heyday of Hellenistic culture. But this did not mean that media in the 1870s and following decades were initially any better understood. Let us revisit, now, the birth and childhood of the misunderstood telephone . . .

EVOLUTION BY MISADVENTURE

Natural selection, as we know, proceeds by the environment's choosing of organisms and organic characteristics which it had no direct role in first instructing into being. In the technological realm, the analog is a machine or a process invented for purpose A being chosen by society for usage B – the ubiquitous unintended consequence, a central theme of naturally selective and humanly directed evolution alike, and no better exemplified than by the story of the telephone and its offspring.

In a nutshell: It begins with Alexander Graham Bell, whose pursuit of a hearing aid (a "harmonic telegraph," to transform speech into electrical signals which could be visually written as in a telegram) resulted in his patent for the telephone in 1876. Elisha Gray, who *was* pursuing the invention of a telephone, lodged his patent a mere few hours after Bell (see Brooks, 1976, for details), therein becoming a footnote to history, and allowing the phone company to say that its system worked as clear as a bell rather than in shades of gray. A year later, Edison stumbled on the phonograph, and, as mentioned earlier, initially thought its main usage would be as a telephone recording device. Interestingly, Bell and his family, for three generations, had been interested in the recording of speech: his grand-father was an elocutionist and expert in the physiology of speech; his father worked on a universal phonetic alphabet, whose letters resembled the shapes of the mouth during speech; and Alexander Graham Bell and his brother Melville attempted as boys to construct a "speaking machine," replete with mechanical tongue, larynx, and vocal chords (see Bell, 1922). But Edison was the one who invented the phonograph, accidentally, and misjudged its main initial impact on the world, and Bell was the one whose fascination with music and the recording of sounds led to the invention of the telephone – both inventors substantiating Arthur Koestler's (1959, p. 15) observation that "the manner in which some of the most important discoveries [in science] were arrived at reminds one more of a sleepwalker's performance than an electronic brain's [i.e., a computer's]."

For his part, Edison was sleepwalking again a decade later, when he envisioned the motion photography process he was just developing as mostly a visual adjunct to the phonograph, whose role as a vehicle of musical entertainment had now been established (Josephson, 1959, p. 388). Meanwhile, William Orton, President of Western Union Telegraph, declined an offer to purchase all of Bell's telephone patents for $100,000; his stated reason: "what can we do with such an electrical toy?" (Josephson, 1959, p. 141). Orton was at least consistent in his myopia, soon advising his friend Chauncey Depew in 1881 to turn down an offer to purchase one-sixth of Bell Telephone stock into perpetuity, on the grounds that "the invention was a toy" (Hogarth, 1926). (Depew, alas, was no more lucky in politics, withdrawing an initially enthusiastically received bid for the Republican candidacy for President in 1888 in favor of Benjamin Harrison, who went on to win in a year of public unhappiness with the Democrats; see Halstead, 1892, p. 422.)

By the turn of the century, the number of telephone calls had exceeded by 50:1 the number of telegrams sent in America (Gibson, n.d., p. 73). Also by then, Marconi had brought to fruition his idea about using electromagnetic carrier waves for a "wireless." Hertz, the discoverer of the waves predicted by Faraday, had flatly predicted that the use of such waves for broadcast would be impossible, requiring "a mirror as large as the Continent" of Europe (Cherry, 1985, p. 23). Fortunately, Marconi had ignored this prediction. But the wireless he had sought to create was a wireless telegraph, or two-way interactive device. This indeed came to be when Marconi sent his first wireless signals, more than a mile, in 1895; by 1901, he had flashed a signal across the Atlantic. But the high expense of transmitting carrier waves, in contrast to the relatively low cost of receiving them, frustrated the use of Marconi's invention as a telephone without wires for the populace, which he also hoped it would be. Instead, David Sarnoff's vision of a "radio music box" transformed the wireless into radio as we now know it – a one-way mass medium that brought into being, as its most important consequence, the instantaneous, the simultaneous mass audience (see Chapter 8; see also Dunlap, 1951, for a fascinating year-by-year account of the work of Marconi, and his contemporaries Reginald Fessenden and Lee de Forest, which shows how their goal of radio telephony was gradually fulfilled with the quite different medium of one-way radio broadcasting; see also Hogan, 1923, pp. 19–21, for more on Fessenden; and Chester *et al.*, 1971, pp. 22–25, for more on de Forest and Fessenden). Marconi even had interactive hopes for television, predicting a "visible telephone" as an outgrowth of his invention in May of 1915 – about three months prior to Sarnoff's proposal of a radio music box (Dunlap, 1951, p. 56).

Of course, a one-way radio box with pictures is what eventually resulted. And most recently, the Internet, the Web, and most telecommunications via personal computers and modems since the 1980s have piggybacked on the voice lines and networks put in place for the telephone: the backbone of the digital revolution in telecommunication was thus a wholly unintended consequence of the telephone (see Levinson, 1995a).

The source of much of this surprise, aside from the unexpected currents that swirl around all invention, no doubt resides in the unique role of speech in the human condition. The telephone traffics in a medium so fundamental to our humanity that it seems odd to call speech a medium at all. All undamaged humans speak. Children need not go to any school to learn the essentials of spoken communication. It costs nothing to speak – talk is cheap indeed – and one can well see, from such a perspective alone, why a businessman like William Orton, accustomed to selling a highly abstract mode of communication requiring trained operators to encode and decode every message, would be prone to dismiss the telecommunication of speech as an "electrical toy." The same universal quality of speech no doubt led Marconi – who prided himself on pragmatic common sense rather than abstract scientific theory (Cherry, 1985, p. 23) – to assume that the wireless would soon engender two-way radio and television telephones. But the Darwinian pull of unprogrammed consequences when embodied in technology was as much a match for common sense as for scientific theory.

Nor were initial expectations for these speech-extending media soon to be realized after the media became well established in other areas, and possibilities for the initial application were open for exploration. The phonograph was in use for more than a century before telephone answering machines became popular. A hundred years after Marconi sent his first radio signals, truly wireless cellular telephones are at last beginning to catch on (cordless phones are not fully wireless, as they require a "home base" attached to a wire, cable, or fiber-optic line system). And audio-visual telephones – prominent in the public's imagination at least since *Tom Swift and his Photo Telephone* (Appleton, 1914), and briefly brought to the fore with Herbert Hoover's picture telephone conversation between Washington and New York City in 1927 (see Phillips *et al.*, 1954, p. 22) – continue to nibble away at the borders of our widespread use, in video conferencing, "C-U See Me" on the Internet, and other specialty areas, but they have yet to provide an alternative to telephone in the way that television has for radio. Writing in 1972 (p. 207), Brenda Maddox noted that "if any single piece of new communication technology has been advertised in advance, it is the picture telephone, yet there is little sign of any demand for it." The same is by and large true today. (See Levinson, 1979, pp. 283–290 – "The aging heir apparent" – for discussion of why; see also Levinson, 1977, for consideration of why some media seem to stall in the "toy" stage of implementation.)

The ubiquity of speech in human life, and our tendency to take for granted and thus misunderstand that which is all around us – "the obvious is usually invisible" (McLuhan, 1967, p. 41) – continues to cloud our perception of the phone and its impact even today. For although we have long since seen the error of Orton's assessment, and know the crucial role the phone plays in all manner of serious business, we often overlook the equally profound impact it has had on our most personal areas of space.

THE PUBLICATION OF PRIVATE PLACES

In an age before the car phone, McLuhan (1976) mused that the only place a person could be alone, or beyond the reach of the public, was in his (or her) car. The cellular telephone has of course changed that, leaving its possessors no place to be alone, but the observation of what the phone did to the home is more on target than ever before. Whereas once upon a time one's home was one's castle – meaning that the act of closing its doors provided some measure of protection, informational as well as physical, from the outside world – the advent of the telephone gave every Tom, Dick, and Harry with a dime direct acoustic access to our inner sanctum.

To make matters worse, the phone's ring is an entreaty that cannot be denied. Every one of us has dreams in progress — yearnings whose fulfillment may lie just in that voice at the other end of the phone's ring. As a writer, I'm keenly aware of the open ends, the potential leads to greater things, that each of my published stories and articles implies. Any phone call could be from some Hollywood producer who has doggedly tracked me down after reading one of my science fiction stories, ready to give me a huge sum of money for film rights in a movie of my story starring the best actors and actresses, directed by last year's Academy Award winner. To be human is to have such fantasies, and the telephone conspires in its every ring to perhaps speak to them.

The phone not only has informational access to our homes, but extraordinary purchase on our attention. No other medium has such power. Not the online world of the Internet and the Web, where one must make the first move to receive as well as send information — that is, where one must first log on to an online system in order to receive any waiting e-mail, in contrast to the phone that rings unbidden. Not television, which is almost always vulnerable to interruption by the telephone, or just good old-fashioned sleep. Indeed, the long-standing joke among media theorists is that twentieth-century lovers sometimes suffer "telephonus interruptus" — the putting on hold of love-making to answer a phone's ring — and the joke is not at all far-fetched.

The telephone answering machine no doubt remedies some of this problem, and serves as a good example of how humans can rationally design technologies to reduce problems of other technologies (hence my term "remedial media"). But so potent is the phone's presentation of possibility that even this fix is incomplete: dare I trust my answering machine to put my initial best voice forward to that potential Hollywood producer at the other end of the line?

Thus the telephone, even when sheathed in the prophylactic of the answering machine, is so potent an inseminator of our dreams that it remains the one medium that can pull us away from our physical beds.

But the telephone is revolutionary not only in what it may promise, but in the most intimate way it makes that offering.

THE EXTERNALIZATION OF INTIMATE SPACE

McLuhan's critique of the alphabet focused on the way that its visual representations of reality provided a more detached, arm's-length relationship than representations offered through spoken words. To appeal to the eye, McLuhan convincingly argued (e.g., 1962), is to present a discrete, fixed stimulus, always somewhere in front of the face; in contrast, the ear can be effectively approached from anywhere in a 360-degree surround. McLuhan saw this difference between acoustic and visual space as among the most fundamental in understanding the impact of media (see Levinson, 1990). And he went on to explain much of the impact of the electronic age, especially television, as emanating from its treating the eye as an ear (to use the apt phrase that he paraphrased often, with attribution, from Tony Schwartz; e.g., McLuhan and McLuhan, 1988, p. 77; see Schwartz, 1973, pp. 14–16).

Much of the impact of cyberspace can be explained by its "acoustic" properties – in the way that its information, to look at but one example, emanates from a continually expanding anywhere-and-everywhere with computer connections, rather than the mass of still-fixed, discrete sources of printed books and news-papers. But text and images online, for all their acoustic features, are still offered to the viewer at a point of perception on a screen that resides in a fixed position, a few or more inches in front of the eyes. This is a close personal distance indeed. But it's an ocean away compared to the intimate acoustic distance of the speaker's mouth and voice from the listener's ear on the telephone.

As Edward T. Hall and other psychologists and ethologists have been exploring for decades (e.g., Hall, 1966; Eibl-Eibesfeldt, 1970), invisible but rigid regulations about appropriate distances between individuals and groups govern the interaction of all organisms, humans included. These rules apply not only between species – where acceptable distances, i.e., those not likely to trigger aggression or defensive behavior, are usually a lot longer than arm's length – but intra-species as well, where distinctions between self and mate, members of the family, and others carry very precise distance concomitants. Humans can of course on occasion override these specifications by dint of necessity and our rationality. We ride in crowded subway cars, packed in all but intimate proximity to total strangers. But such exceptions only briefly suppress our deeply felt sense of the distance rules, which entail a sharply defined (though largely unconscious) hierarchy of expectations about how far we should be standing from total strangers, how far from strangers with whom we are conversing, from colleagues and professional and business discussants (doctors being an exception), from friends, family, and lovers.

The whisper in the ear – lips of the speaker literally at the ear of the listener – is permissible in snippets between friends, but is by and large the domain of lovers and loved ones. And yet this is exactly the acoustic distance obtained in a phone conversation, whether the party at the other end is one's lover, an unknown voice offering a great deal on insurance, or a wrong number. No wonder that the obscene phone call — the lewd proposition from a faceless voice — came into its own on the phone. An obscene telegram would lack equivalent impact.

The telephone is indeed a highly sexually charged instrument (see Lum, 1984), as teenagers well know. By the 1980s and 1990s, some callers knew even better, as "phone sex" became a lucrative business. But the phone's biggest impact on the sexuality it so effortlessly conveys occurred years earlier: if we look for the technological determinants of the sexual revolution in the second half of the twentieth century, we find the telephone right up there with the atom bomb, the automobile, and the birth control pill. The bomb engendered a general psychological environment of live-for-today; the car and the pill provided physical conditions for facilitation of sex; the phone offered occasions for essential informational preludes and aftermaths.

THE GENIE AND ITS CRITICS

The technological genie within the telephone that allowed it to so easily breach the social walls of the home castle was electricity and its capacity for instant communication. The nineteenth century is often considered the dawn of electronic communications, which it indeed is. But it was also, at the time of the telephone and phonograph, equally matched with revolutionary non-electronic media (photochemical for the photograph, completely mechanical for the phonograph). And this form of balance between energy and soma in communication would continue into the twentieth century, when the electro-magnetic radio and the photochemical-mechanical motion picture became the big new players, soon to dominate mass entertainment and other forms of popular culture.

Critics in our century, as we have seen, have been increasingly prone to view both electronic and photochemical media as operating at the expense of older printed media, with electricity especially often cast as the grim reaper of the printed word. McLuhan (e.g., 1962) is in part responsible for this attitude, insofar as he positioned the alphabetic-visual in opposition to the acoustic, and then placed electronic media in the acoustic camp. Postman (e.g., 1979) is far more explicit — and, unlike McLuhan, just plainly incorrect — in his repeated contentions that television, the archetypical electronic medium prior to personal computers, is outrightly destructive of rationality, civility, and a whole passel of cognitive processes and social attitudes we rightly cherish and see connected to literacy. But as I pointed out in my review (Levinson, 1979/1980) of Jerry Mander's *Four Arguments for the Elimination of Television* (1978), I likely have watched at least an hour or two of TV a day since I was a child in the 1950s, and I am, as far as I can tell, still rational, if not always civil, at least in my criticism of some media critics.

Postman's error, and the mistake of most critics of electronic media, is not their connection of rationality and literacy; the error lies rather in their view that electricity and its applications are mortal competitors of books, magazines, and newspapers, and therein of literacy. On the contrary, at the very origin of electronic communication, we have the telegraph, which not only spread the written word faster and farther than any medium before, but was an enormous benefit to newspapers and the reporting of news. And at the current, temporary terminus of electronic communication, we have the liberation of text via personal computer and modem, generating a rising tide lifting all vehicles of literacy.

Thus, the critics are mistaken at both ends of the progression. And, as we will see in the next chapter, they were wrong about the impact of electricity in the middle as well.

7

ELECTRICITY

The book's best friend

Every process in life and technology, communication included, has its pre-conditions. As we discussed in the first chapter, most of these are "soft" rather than "hard," in that they make the process possible, allow it to happen, rather than dictate its existence and result. They thus form a background environment, often so recessed as to be overlooked or taken for granted. Who jumps to the immediate realization when looking at a skyscraper that the elevator was an essential precondition or collateral technology?

The absence of an essential precondition can in retrospect be seen as a reason why a given technology, seemingly workable, fails to develop. The lack of an interchangeable alphabet likely kept printing from becoming a mass medium in China in 800 AD (McLuhan, 1962, p. 185); William McNeill (1982, p. 49) also sees the anti-capitalistic philosophy prevalent in Confucianism as stifling the mass implementation not only of print, but gunpowder, rocketry, and other Chinese inventions that played such major roles in the West. Roger Burlingame (1959) explains Leonardo da Vinci's inability to actualize most of his inventions as due to a lack of "collateral" technology; and, as is well known, Charles Babbage designed a computer a century prior to its enabling technology (see Bolter, 1984, pp. 32-33; Levinson, 1989a). A precondition's absence as a cause of technological non-development is but an extreme case of the usually hidden ways in which the nature of a precondition governs the technology it enables.

Hearing and seeing – biological technologies of perception – are no less subject to such fundamental preconditions. On the surface, they seem rather equivalent: both require sensory/perceptual systems – auditory and optical – to process appropriate energy forms. And both of course require exposure to those energy forms, and the information they convey, if perception is to occur.

But here the similarity ends. For whereas acoustic energy is available in the environment twenty-four hours a day – day and night, in light, darkness, and rain – visual energy or light is far more fickle and selective as to when and how it makes itself available to our viewing in the natural world. It gets dark every night – meaning that unless some artificial form of light is available, media that appeal to the optical nerve are just shooting in the dark, in this case, literally.

In other words: since light is obviously a precondition of vision, and vision just as obviously a precondition of visual media, some form of light is a necessary precondition for the successful operation of all visual media. This conclusion may also be obvious. But, in general, the implications and consequences of all visual media being held hostage to light, and the role of technologies that have come to the rescue, have been seldom explored. McLuhan, characteristically, takes a stab (1964, p. 23) in his observation that "the electric light is pure information," the content of which is everything it illuminates. This may be a way of noting the necessity of light as a precondition of all media that play to the optic nerve. And, aiming close to the origin of life itself, Guenter Waechtershaeuser (1984) argues that photosynthesis can be construed as a process of knowledge perhaps older than the locomotion emphasized by Campbell (1974a).

The singes of flamelight found in Lascaux certainly testify to the antiquity of light as a media requirement. The alphabet and then the printing press may have sprung the word loose from cave and other walls, but the word was no less dependent upon some light via which to read. Kerosene and later gas light provided fairly good reductions of darkness in the nineteenth century, but both also entailed significant safety hazards.

And then came the electric light.

THE DAY-EXTENDING MEDIUM

Electricity extended the abstract written word across space in the early part of the nineteenth century with the telegraph, and the spoken word across space in the later part of the nineteenth century with the telephone. The non-electrical photograph extended the literal visual world across time in the early part of that century, as the non-electrical phonograph would do for sound in the later part.

But the advent of electric lighting at the end of the nineteenth century provided a new kind of across-the-board benefit that facilitated all aspects of human life dependent upon daylight. This of course included the world of images extended by the photograph – which was in its inception quite literally a product of the sun, and continues to be inextricably linked to light. And the incandescent beacon also shone upon letters already extended across space and time by products of the printing press, and across space by the telegraph. Perhaps this universality of extension is responsible for electric lighting being taken for granted or overlooked as an extraordinarily potent communication medium, so palpably augmenting the field of vision and its constituents, including books. Indeed, so significant as a communication medium was the electric lightbulb's turning of night into day, that its inventor Thomas Alva Edison could be justifiably regarded as the most important inventor of media in the past two centuries on the basis of that alone, with his creation of the phonograph and development of a motion picture process left out of the bargain.

The impact of the electric light on literacy was not missed by historian David de Haan (1977, p. 21), who observed that "electricity did more to facilitate the habit of reading books than anything before it." When we consider that Edison filed the crucial patent for his carbon filament lamp in 1879 (see Josephson, 1959, pp. 221 ff., for details), and note the effect on literacy by the following indices between 1870 and 1900 (Emery and Emery, 1992, pp. 155–156), we can agree that de Haan is pretty close to the mark in terms of sheer numbers: the American population doubled in thirty years; the number of daily newspaper names quadrupled and copies sold increased six-fold; the circulation of weeklies tripled; the percentage of children attending public school rose from 57 to 72 per cent; and illiteracy declined from 20 to 10 per cent of the overall population. Furthermore, when we consider that during the day, when artificial lighting is unnecessary, most people are not in circumstances that are the most convenient for reading – being otherwise engaged with making a living, taking care of a family, etc. – we can understand just why the electric light made such a crucial difference: it created a space for reading, after dinner, which was already the best time, socio-economically, for reading to take place. Whereas the unsteady light of flame was the only serious competition to starlight heretofore, the rise of the artificial day of electric light literally and figuratively outshone the stars – though in a way which reflected back upon the stars in the books about the stars and all else in the universe that were now so much easier, and safer, to read.

Thus, rather than being eclipsed and left behind by the harnessing of electricity to communication in the nineteenth century, the book and its siblings the newspaper and the magazine were carried along and even exalted. The role of electricity in reading was, to be sure, indirect – extending the environment in which reading took place – but it was no less profound in its empowerment of the written word than it had been with the telegraph in the past and would be with the online network in the future, where electricity would literally carry encodings of printed words.

Of course, given that there are only twenty-four hours in the day, and some of them must be spent sleeping (and, usually, working), an intense competition among media for people's time and attention always existed. The electric light's extension of useful time could in no way eliminate or even lessen that competition for the highly finite resource of human attention. Further, the bloom of electronic media in the entertainment realms created by motion pictures, radio, and television certainly offered attractive alternatives to the written word, and a source of not entirely unreasonable concern for critics such as Mander (1978) and Postman (e.g., 1979) – who are at least not wrong that someone watching television is usually not reading a book at the same time.

But the critics do miss that someone watching a television program might be moved by that very program to read later – to take up the printed word which the electric light also made a more powerful contender for our notice.

Indeed, thus forearmed and charged, the book has more than held its own in the twentieth century.

THE PAPERBACK REPLY

Convenience is a most relative of human phenomena. Computer speeds that seemed miraculous in word processing, data management, and telecommunications in the early 1980s seem arthritic in comparison to the swift mz's and bps's of the late 1990s. In an earlier age in which the awkward handwritten manuscript was the standard packet of text, the book in any printed form was a liberation. By the 1930s, it had become heavy to carry – economically as well as physically. Radio, after all, exacted just one cost, at the time of initial purchase, and thereafter conveyed its narratives for free.

Indeed, the book, though universally available since the printing press, was rarely an incidental expense. As recently as the year 1800, it cost what amounted to a week's pay for the average worker in America: 1 dollar (Whetmore, 1979, p. 19).

I have in my possession a history book from not much later: *Compend of History, from the Earliest Times; Comprehending a General View of the Present State of the World, with Respect to Civilization, Religion, and Government; and a Brief Dissertation of the*

Importance of Historical Knowledge by Samuel Whelpley, A.M., published by Richardson & Lord, Boston, in 1826. When I purchased it at a book auction in Amherst, Massachusetts several years ago — for 4 dollars — I was struck by the little card I found attached to the front page. It says, in a delicate Victorian scrawl, "This belonged to our Grandfather Isaac Thompson. It must have been bought in the last decade of his life when he was struggling with poverty and his supporting a large family. It shows his taste and worth."

It does indeed. It shows a man who loved wisdom and books so much that he would purchase more than just a Bible for his family — at a time when the cost of that purchase was no doubt a substantial part of his disposable weekly income. High among the many pleasures I have in writing *this* book is forwarding his grand-child's message into the twenty-first century.

By the middle of the nineteenth century, improvements in printing technology reduced the price of books, and led to the mass production of magazines to fill up the idle time that the presses enjoyed between newly efficient print runs. *Harper's New Monthly Magazine*, started by the Harper brothers in 1850 to promote the books they published, is still a major magazine in the 1990s; it had attained a circulation of 200,000 by 1861 (Pember, 1981, p. 40). Books which were inexpensive by any criterion soon poured forth from numerous publishing houses, including "penny dreadfuls" and "dime novels." The latter was seized upon as a standard of trash by Professor McKeever in his 1910 condemnation of "motion pictures . . . more degrading than the dime novel" (p. 184). With literacy undeniably in the ascendancy, educators could still afford to be picky about which texts they deemed fit to read.

As Herbert Gans (1974) convincingly argues, the opprobrium accorded these cheap reads by academics and other agents of the upper classes was motivated as much by their need to keep "literature" a symbol of their conspicuous consumption as by real defects in the fiction. In any case, the unleashing in the 1930s and 40s of the paperback as we know it today — whereby undisputed classics in literature could be purchased for 25 cents — decisively defeated the conservative critique of paperback book culture, at least on logical if not emotional grounds.

The calculus of convenience was just right for the paperback: it was just a little more expensive than a movie theater ticket, and provided entertainment that was permanent. A half century before movies on video tape became readily available for purchase, this gave the paperback a unique time-binding edge over its motion picture and radio rivals: we might say that although the book was bound in cheap paper, it nonetheless effectively bound time. Further, the advent of television in the 1950s did nothing to undo this advantage. And by that time, the price of a first-run movie had crept up to 25 cents, making the paperback price, which had risen to only 35 cents by then, even more attractive in comparison.

The 1970s did see the introduction of the first home video players and recorders – a development which broke print's monopoly on retrievability, though at an initially huge expense. By the 1990s, however, the cost of a video rental ($3.95 per movie in most large chainstores like Blockbuster Video in the US) was less than the cost of a new paperback ($4.95), leaving permanent ownership as distinct from rental the only pragmatic advantage of the paperback (pragmatic in contrast to cognitive – i.e., the paperback is still read rather than viewed). We will explore the video and its impact in more detail in Chapter 10.

But by the 1990s, electronic text – the communication of written words in all its forms and applications online, via personal computer and modem – was providing a mode of discourse which broke the bank on all prior calculi of convenience for writing, publishing, and reading.

THE ELECTRONIC LIBERATION OF TEXT

The personal computer and its word processing, along with the online network and its worldwide, instantaneous, hypertext access, seem likely to be every bit as revolutionary and reconfiguring of culture and human existence as the alphabet and the printing press were in their days, and indeed still are. We will consider these impacts point by point in chapters later in this book. Here I just sketch and situate them for closure of the current chapter's survey of the ways in which text has thrived under the attention of electricity in this and the previous century.

As we have seen, a central and not outlandish concern about new media expressed at least as far back as Socrates is to what extent they enable the generation as well as the receipt of information and knowledge. Neither the alphabet nor the printing press scored their main successes in this generative task: the thrust of their enormous impact was rather in increasing the number of receivers, not creators, of the information conveyed. Of course, the number of authors did sharply increase as the press created mass audiences for new as well as older text – raising issues of intellectual property and copyright for the first time, as we will explore in Chapter 17 – but the ratio of authors to readers still remained almost completely in favor of readers, or just slightly more favorable to authors than it had been before.

The telegraph and telephone, quintessentially interactive media, empowered creators and receivers at the same time. The photograph began as a one-way medium of consumption, but by the end of the nineteenth century the Kodak had made it almost as much a medium of mass, individual production, with everyone taking pictures of their families and vacations. Interestingly, the phonograph began as a two-way medium, sold as a device that could record as well as reproduce sound, but by the twentieth century had taken a turn in the other direction, and would soon become a vehicle for the playing of musical performances produced elsewhere and mass marketed.

The phonograph proved to be a harbinger of mass communication in the twentieth century, dominated by one-way broadcast media of radio and television, as well as one-way motion pictures, and, of course, newspapers, magazines, and books, hardcover and paperback, which were all one-message-to-many in their trajectory.

The photocopying machine, powered by electricity but utilizing a photo-chemical reproductive process, offered the first significant balance to this trend, commencing in the 1940s. As McLuhan noted (1977, p. 178), the Xerox turned the writer into a publisher (see Chapter 12 in this book) – if with neither the cultural clout nor distributive facility of traditional publishers, certainly with the wherewithal to get manuscript copies of an article to an audience far greater than that in reach of the carbon copy (the mimeograph would on this perspective be an early form of photocopying).

The photocopy assisted the author in providing numbers of copies for dissemination, but not speed. Through the early 1980s, the telegraph (and the related telex) remained the only media that brought the immediacy of electronic speed to the communication of text; handwritten manuscripts, published books, photocopied typescripts, and all else in between covers and on pages were until that time equally dependent on speeds of physical transport for dissemination. The fax soon changed that – though word processing, already available for a few years, was by then not only changing speed of transmission but something far more fundamental to the writing process.

Word processing cuts to the very creation of text, remarkably bestowing to the written word, at the very moment of its inception, a revisability, a correctability, almost as easy as that possessed by speech. Indeed, inasmuch as the word, once spoken, cannot be erased, the word once digitally processed – prior to any dissemination – is even more revisable. How far the carving on the cave wall, immutable for millennia, has come!

Negotiations required even by the typewritten page – does this correction merit retyping the entire page? – are thus dispensed with entirely in the word-processed document. Not everyone, certainly not all writers, have seen this as an unmitigated blessing; the notion that a writer must be obligated to spend x amount of time with a text, sweating over its words apparently regardless of the content, seems to have some nostalgic appeal. I argue, to the contrary, that the only speed relevant to the creation of the best possible texts is the time it takes to choose the best possible words for expression of the best (clearest, most accurate, truthful) ideas – and by that measure the benefit of word processing in facilitating revision and correction is absolute (see Chapter 11 for more).

Further, the word-processed text is in a form that can be sent instantly to any place in the world with a personal computer, a modem, and a telephone, and be in principle linked or connected with any and all other documents so transmitted and/or stored electronically. Such instant global dissemination of texts without a traditional publisher has also found its critics, among those who worry that the world will somehow be flooded with unfiltered ideas – or texts that are not subject to the traditional "gatekeeping" editorial functions of the book publisher. Michael Heim (1987) has summarized such criticism, as well as concerns about word processing. I would just note here, with more to follow later, that such massive unfiltered dissemination is just what we would want of a Darwinian evolutionary mechanism for maximizing initial generation. The ideal is to keep this initial pool as open and free as possible from inevitably fallible, artificially imposed rules of control – what Joseph Agassi (1982, p. 239), writing just prior to the online age, called "the inability I suffer to communicate with you prior to the consent of the editor to publish" – so that subsequent selection, made by readers (the "you" Agassi writes to) not editors, is given the widest field of candidates upon which to operate.

The other consequence of networked text – the associative, hypertext link – has thus far escaped much criticism, perhaps because it builds upon long-established modes of linkage in printed texts, ranging from marginal commentary in the Talmud to footnotes in modern scholarly works. The electronic rendering of such connections, making them instant and encyclopedic, was foreseen by Vannevar Bush's "memex" in 1945 (Bush, 1945; see also Bush, 1970) and Theodor Nelson's "Xanadu" of the 1960s (see Nelson, 1990), among others – projected technologies that came to be in the Web in the 1990s (see Chapter 13). The only weakness in such self-generating hypertext connections flows from its very strength: one can make any linkages one wants from one's own document to others – an author needs no more permission to link to another document than to cite it in a reference, as I just did above for Bush's and Nelson's texts. But this means that, from the point of view of a given reader's specific interests, the available links may or may not be the most useful. The reader can of course do searches and in effect establish new links; but these are also dependent upon pre-established search engines and criteria, which may not be sensitive to the specific ideas under pursuit by the reader.

But such limitations are inevitable – as Kant observed, our very ways of knowing have inherent boundaries (e.g., we can only see certain colors; to which I would add that our technologies can and do extend the effective range of human vision, though they are subject to other limitations). In the net scheme of things, the globalization and continuing opportunity for individual input in the Web and its systems represents enormous progress in the development of vehicles for knowledge. Indeed, such decentralization in the generation and organization of knowledge will likely be one of the defining characteristics of the next century.

The twentieth century, however, has been characterized for the most part by centralizing technologies of communication. One of these technologies in particular – radio – assisted the totalitarian regimes that rose and fell in this century, and led critics like Lewis Mumford (e.g., 1967, 1970) to liken the aggregate of twentieth-century technology to ant colonies, or what he imagined ancient Egyptian pyramid-building technology to have been like. As a critic of twentieth-century technology *in toto* he was certainly wrong, if only because of the powerful decentralizing influence of the automobile and localized newspapers in the same period of time. And indeed, although radio and television are undeniably the most centralizing media in history, their effect was far from supportive solely of totalitarian impulses, as the benefit that Churchill and Roosevelt drew from radio, and Kennedy from television, amply attests.

But it is also indeed the case that, at the same time the automobile was giving individuals unprecedented freedom of expression in transportation, radio was unintentionally bringing into being for the first time the national, simultaneous one-way mass audience – the audience of Hitler and Stalin, and the subject of our next chapter.

8

RADIO

All together now

An engraving by Johannes Stradanus (1523–1605) depicts the bustling interior of a sixteenth-century print shop. His caption reads, "Just as one voice can be heard by a multitude of ears, so single writings cover a thousand sheets" (reprinted in Agassi, 1968, p. 26; and on the front cover of Eisenstein, 1979). The analogy is a bit off – "can be seen by a thousand eyes" would be the more appropriate apposition to "can be heard by a multitude of ears" – but it conveys the power of print anyway, by likening it to the inherent one-to-many capacity of speech and hearing. Indeed, long before print and the alphabet, hearing was the archetypal mode for perception by the multitudes. It is also the ideal medium for perception of multiples – more than one message at the same time by one party – or multi-tasking.

One of the early consequences of hearing's appeal to the many is that democracy in ancient Greece was defined by the extent to which an audience could hear a speaker's voice – rendering democracy, in media terms, an acoustocracy. In this chapter, we explore what happened in the twentieth century when this natural mass-mode was literally amplified to national levels. One of the surprising, though in retrospect predictable, consequences of this broadcasting of "acoustocracy" was that it strengthened the operation of all forms of government, totalitarian as well as democratic.

Electricity, though of course a necessary condition for radio and television, was by no means sufficient for the advent of broadcasting. The word had already been electrified on the telephone, which worked like the mute telegraph in most other aspects. Thus, the telephone has been for most of its existence an instrument dependent upon a fixed system of wires, via which messages are sent not one to many, but one to one, and interactively. The telephone did make a remarkable breakthrough in situating the two ends of the conversation in people's homes or places of business, departing from the telegraph's requirement of public sending and receipt of its messages. Perhaps this – in addition to the human pleasure of hearing a voice on the phone and the taste for further reduction of artificiality that begat – whetted the public's appetite for something more.

In any case, it was a quest for a telegraph (not, initially, telephone) without wires – without fixed, pre-set modes of conduit – that inspired Marconi to ignore Heinrich Hertz's pessimism about the inapplicability of the latter's discovery to mass communication, and invent the wireless. And that was by and large the extent to which Marconi's intention was actualized in his invention. The radio which the wireless soon became was an unintended consequence of Fessenden, de Forest, and Marconi's separate aspirations for a wireless or radio telephone (see Chapter 6 in this book for discussion and references; see also Levinson, 1988, p. 159), and a fulfillment of Sarnoff's notion of a "radio music box" – a classic example of the difference between inventor (Marconi) and implementer (Sarnoff) in the ultimate disposition of a new technology. Radio took the form it did because the receipt of electro-magnetic carrier waves with an electronically encoded "passenger" – the voice or sound – proved to be a lot less expensive than the transmission.

The result of sound received from a single source by millions of listeners who could only listen, not reply, was different from the telephone in every respect save the voice conveyed, and different from Marconi's original wireless (1895) in every respect save that radio had no wires. Marconi, like Bell and Edison before him, had thus accidentally midwifed a new age into being.

THE ENDS OF LINEARITY

Hegel's spirit of an age has appeal for anyone seeking to comprehend the patterns of popular culture. There was indeed a confluence of styles in music, visual representation, ways of dress, ways of thinking that typified the psychedelic era of the 1960s, the Impressionistic era at the end of the nineteenth century, and other especially clear highwater marks in social history. A bit more diffuse, but also more encompassing and far-reaching, has been a general dissolving of lines in the past century. Such bygone lines – supplanted not so much in physical reality as in popular vision and culture – range from railroads and telegraph poles to Euclidean geometry. We celebrate in their place the automobile, the airplane, the broadcast. Each makes the pre-set line a little more irrelevant, until, in the case of the broadcast, the shortest distance between sender and receiver is no longer a straight line at all, since all receivers are equidistant from a sender communicating via electro-magnetic carrier waves at the speed of light on planet Earth.

McLuhan wrote in detail (e.g., 1962) about the cause-and-effect of the linear alphabet – rows upon rows of letters – on such modes of thought as classical logic and Euclidean geometry (see also Levinson, 1981, for an assessment). Whether the alphabet made such mental processes possible, or whether all three, as I would contend, sprang from the same Kantian/Chomskyan hard-wired cognitive penchant for linearity, and acted as mutual catalysts, there is no doubt that linearity reigned until the end of the nineteenth century, especially from the Renaissance till then. In the realm of mathematics, linearity was already under attack in the 1820s through 50s by Lobachevsky, Bolyai, and Riemann, and their development of systems that dispensed with Euclid's parallel (fifth) postulate (two parallel lines can never meet). One can play a hand of media determinism here, and wonder if such new forms were inspired by the early impact of electricity (Levinson, 1987) – which, even in its fixed transmission via telegraph wires, obsolesces distance as a factor in communication. By the time Einstein drew on non-Euclidean geometry and published his first paper on relativity in 1905, Marconi had received the first wireless signals. Though Einstein's theory would of course be talked about on the phone, discussed by people transported by trains, described and explained and critiqued in numerous printed documents, it came to typify a new century that would be more profoundly moved by cars and radio, and later by the radio with pictures that is television.

As we have seen, and will again in our grand tour of the evolution of media, no technological breakthrough or invention is so unprecedented as to not be relatable to some earlier, less technological mode of human communication – indeed, to some mode of organization fundamental to all life, or the universe itself. Not only did radio retrieve (McLuhan's excellent term; see his 1977 and 1988 for his "tetrad" of "laws of media," to wit, every technology amplifies some processes, obsolesces others, retrieves still others that might have been earlier obsolesced, and eventually "reverses" or "flips" into something quite different) and immensely extend the natural oral/aural mode of naked speaking and hearing; it also, in its dispersion of one voice or message packet to millions of listeners at the same time, replicated the organic strategy of DNA and its placement of identical source codes in myriad cells throughout the body. Moreover, the instantaneous simultaneous global reach of radio seems in accord with the worldwide situation of closely related DNA patterns within and between similar species, and, on yet a deeper level, with fractal similarities cutting across such diverse forms as leaf patterns, snowflakes, rivers and tributaries, and abstract mathematic progressions (see

Goertzel, 1992, for an overview). It is almost as if, as standard-bearers of the universe, in form if not morality, humans cannot help but replicate and extend its fundamental patterns of doing business in the technologies we bring forth. This may well be the ultimate motivating factor of the "anthropotropic" evolution of media mentioned in Chapter 6 (the evolution of media towards more human function – not to be confused with the anthropic principle, which may also be correct, but which holds that the universe's initial conditions need to be considered from the perspective of leading to the emergence of humans). We will explore other aspects and implications of this phenomenon in the next chapter.

Suffice to say, however, that in actual practice few users of a new medium, and likely not much more often its inventors, take such possible connections into account. The accident of radio thus went on to have extraordinary impact in political and cultural arenas in an age before DNA was identified and fractals appreciated as they are today. Indeed, once radio was understood to be far more than a telegraph or telephone without wires, its political consequences were quickly grasped by governments.

We look first at the government control it excited, and briefly outline the history of censorship in the US to understand how this came about.

THE WIDE BAND OF CENSORSHIP

As we saw in Chapter 2, the shift in the economic reliance of the press from government to the merchant class eventually allowed Jefferson (and Madison) to appoint the press as in effect the fourth and in many ways most important check-and-balance of American government. To perform this independent, critical function, the press – along with speech itself – was guaranteed no interference from any of the three formal branches of the government under the First Amendment to the Constitution, to wit: "Congress shall make no law . . . abridging the freedom of speech, or of the press." The intent of placing such language literally in the Constitution via an amendment was clearly to safeguard it from alteration or removal by any lesser law or finding of a court or action of a Chief Executive; only another amendment to the Constitution should have been able to accomplish that.

But incredibly – and, alas, in retrospect, not surprisingly – the First Amendment was indeed countermanded in less than a decade by President John Adams, who never supported it in the first place, and the Sedition Act of

14 July 1798 that he pushed through Congress. The passage of that Act on Bastille Day, the day of French independence, was no coincidence, as Adams saw the Act as a necessary corrective for democracy and freedom which, if allowed to go too far, could result in the blood and anarchy that was then the sequel to the French Revolution. The Sedition Act read, in part:

That if any person shall write, print, utter, or publish, or shall cause or procure to be written, printed, uttered or published . . . any false, scandalous, and malicious writing or writings against the government of the United States . . . then such person, being therefore convicted . . . shall be punished by a fine not exceeding two thousand dollars, and by imprisonment not exceeding two years.

(see Tedford, 1985)

When we recall that the average price of a book until 1800 was 1 dollar (Whetmore, 1979, p. 19), which was also the average working person's weekly wage, we can see how onerous was even just the financial penalty for criticizing the American government.

Some twenty-four newspaper editors and one congressman – all supporters of Jefferson's then out-of-office, rival political party – were arrested and tried. These included Benjamin Franklin's grandson, who was editor of the Philadelphia *Aurora*, as well as editors of major New York, Boston, Baltimore, and Richmond newspapers. Some were convicted, and then fined or imprisoned. Humor fared no better than political argument – an intoxicated fellow in New Jersey was tried and convicted for publicly offering the opinion that he didn't "care if someone fired a cannon through President Adams' ass." To which the New York *Argus* helpfully advised that this posed no real threat to the President, since no person would ever really think of "firing at such a disgusting target" as the ass of John Adams (Tedford, 1985, p. 47).

The saving grace of this early totalitarian flare was that the Act came packaged with an expiration date – Congress was apparently not then ready to flout the Constitution into perpetuity – on 3 March 1801. This was, ironically and fortunately, the day before Jefferson took office as President. The twenty-four years of Jefferson, Madison, and Monroe in the Presidency, plus the eight years of the even more populist Jackson (1828–1836), were more than enough to raise the nineteenth century to the highest attainment of freedom of expression heretofore – and since – in the United States. Meanwhile, by the 1840s, the price of many books was down to 10 cents (Whetmore, 1979, p. 19). Respect for freedom of expression held even through most of America's Civil War, with Lincoln's toleration for dissent interrupted on rare occasion (Tedford, 1985, p. 49). By

1900, nine out of ten Americans could read (Emery and Emery, 1992, p. 156); and as we saw in the last chapter, electric lighting was making that ever easier. The interlocking and mutually supportive factors of freedom of expression and literacy had conspired to make the nineteenth century a golden age of communication from the political standpoint.

One might well think that radio, as a vehicle of speech supported by more than a hundred years of the Bill of Rights and American tradition, would have been from its outset well beyond any attempt at government control. Unfortunately, by the time the US government began paying serious attention to this new medium in the 1920s, its Supreme Court had already dealt speech itself a staggering blow in *Schenck v. the US*, the first of several espionage cases to be argued before the Court in 1919. Justice Oliver Wendell Holmes, speaking for the unanimous Court, delivered the judgement as follows:

The most stringent protection of free speech would not protect a man in falsely shouting fire in a theater, and causing a panic. . . . The question . . . is whether the words . . . are of such a nature as to create a clear and present danger that they will bring about the substantive evils that Congress has a right to prevent.

(Tedford, 1985, pp. 72–73)

Although such a limitation on speech may seem the soul of reason – certainly in comparison to the crude censorship of the Sedition Act, from which Holmes throughout his career took great pains to distance himself – the "clear and present danger" criterion was (and is) deeply corrosive to freedom of expression for two reasons: (a) it offered an occasion, however seemingly reasonable, in which the government not only had the right but, worse, an obligation to restrict communication, and (b) it rendered these grounds for restriction via the normal workings of government, i.e., a Supreme Court decision, and not the extraordinary route of a Constitutional amendment (requiring passage by two-thirds of both houses of Congress, or recommendation by legislatures of two-thirds of the states, and then ratification by three-quarters of the state legislatures in either case), which is what one would expect, and indeed what the Constitution itself requires, of a change in policy that blatantly abrogated the "no law" portion of the First Amendment. Thus, from 3 March 1919 – the date of the Schenck judgement – and onward, the door was in judicial practice open to any restriction on communication that any branch of the US government saw fit to impose.

The government was quick to take advantage regarding radio. The Federal Radio Act of 1927, designed to bring some order into the crowding of new radio stations onto the then limited bandwidth of available broadcast frequencies

– a purely technical problem which required some limited, purely technical, government regulation – averred that broadcasting was to serve the "public convenience, interest, and necessity" (see Head and Sterling, 1982). The more encompassing Federal Communications Act of 1934, which created the Federal Communications Commission (FCC), retained that language and attitude, and held obscenity as not in the public interest. Thus, although language in the various Acts clearly indicated they were not to be vehicles of censorship, in practice that is just what they were and are, since radio stations applying for license renewals are judged by the FCC as to whether their broadcast content is in the public interest (a part of which is: not obscene). Moreover, as the bandwidth for available radio stations widened, first with the advent of FM in the 1930s through the 1960s, and more recently with technologies that more effectively partition the bandwidths available, the sticky rationale for government regulation shifted right along with it: since the 1970s, the reason cited for government control of what is broadcast has changed from scarcity of a public resource (the airwaves) to penetration of people's homes and private spaces without a point-of-purchase decision on the content. According to this new logic, people know what they are buying when they pay for a pornographic magazine, but may be innocently assaulted with obscenity when they turn on a radio or television. Thus Justice John Paul Stevens, delivering the Supreme Court's 1978 majority decision (five to four) in a case (*FCC v. Pacifica Foundation*) concerning a radio station's broadcast of George Carlin's comedy routine about seven unambiguously "dirty" words (i.e., unlike "ass" or "prick," not amenable to double entendre), held that "broadcast media have established a uniquely pervasive presence. . . . To say that one may avoid further offense by turning off the radio . . . is like saying that the remedy for an assault is to run away after the first blow" (Tedford, 1985, pp. 402–403; see also Levinson, "Naughty words and obscene censorship," in 1992, pp. 148–150). Emboldened by such encouragement, the FCC exacted a $1.7 million settlement from Infinity Broadcasting nearly two decades later for its broadcast of "indecent" material on Howard Stern's syndicated radio talk show (see Shiver, 1995).

However, as far as I know, no scientific studies have ever been conducted on the psychological damage that could occur in the instant of time between experiencing such offensive material and troubling to reach out to change the station. Exposure of children to such materials may create some significant problems – though, not surprisingly, these too have been much overrated, and seized upon as pretexts for censorship, as we will explore in Chapter 13.

Predictably, censorship once unleashed spread to all modes of communication, including the press. The FCC's reasoning that "the First Amendment has simply been rewritten for the twentieth century" (Head and Sterling, 1982, p. 489) had begun as a claim that the unique character of broadcasting made it a special case that Jefferson and Madison could not have foreseen; now the logic was stretched to all media in the twentieth century, including those once held sacrosanct. A high – or low – water mark was reached in the Pentagon Papers Case and the Nixon Administration's unprecedented attempt in 1971 to prevent newspaper publication of information, i.e., restrain communication *prior* to its occurrence. This went even beyond the Sedition Act, which attacked free expression after its communication. In New York, a recently appointed Federal district judge, Murray Gurfein, granted the government's request and issued a temporary restraining order on *The New York Times* and its publication of the Pentagon Papers (*The Washington Post*, also a target of a parallel restraining order, fared better in a district court that rejected the government's request). Gurfein soon after refused to make the restraint permanent – thereby allowing the *Times* to resume publication of the material – and eventually the Supreme Court struck down the restraining order in a six-to-three decision (see Tedford, 1985, pp. 337–338).

But the hounds of government intervention, kept at bay in that crucial instance, were far from retired from the marketplace of freely expressed ideas. The Communications Decency Act, signed into law in 1996 and currently under appeal in the US courts, is the latest censorship gambit, this time aimed at the Internet and its empowerment not only of information consumers but creators. We will return to that arena in later chapters.

Thus has radio the dubious distinction of being the unintended occasion for quite the opposite of a liberation of information. All media that we have thus far discussed in this volume – most especially the alphabet and the press – served by and large to decentralize and democratize the exercise of authority. Not so radio. Indeed, the situation in the rest of the world was far worse in terms of government control provoked by radio than in the United States. Thus, even in the democratic United Kingdom, broadcasting came under the control of the BBC, a government agency far more powerful than the FCC in America, and able to easily control the broadcast of information so as to be favorable to the government in power, as in the case of Margaret Thatcher and the Falklands War (see Levinson, 1989b, n. 7).

The power of radio was thus catnip for government quests to control it. But it was more. Perhaps government attempts to regulate broadcasting were based on knowledge, from the inside out, about just how potent a vehicle for propaganda radio could be.

CHURCHILL AND ROOSEVELT, HITLER AND STALIN: RADIO HEADS

Jacques Ellul (1962/1965) persuasively argues that any mode of human communication can be an effective agent of propaganda, or an appeal to the emotions at the expense of reason. Certainly this is borne out in a myriad of everyday conversations and interactions, as well as centuries of printed documents, that cleverly present one side of arguments. But some media are inherently better at this than others.

As Alexander Marshack (1972) puts it, humans are a story-telling species. We can be defined in contrast to other species by the fact that we weave ourselves in narratives; and we can be distinguished, among ourselves, by the kinds of narratives we weave. We take as our raw materials for these incessant stories however much or little the external environment has to offer, and leaven it with amounts – large amounts if the external stimuli are minimal – of our internal expectations, conceptions accurate or not, sufficient to complete the narrative in our heads. In nighttime skies unlit by electricity, we once found gods as well as stars and planets. In evenings millennia later, in our homes penetrated by radio voices from afar – voices we did not personally know – we brought assumptions to those voices, made them our own, received them as members of our family. For who else would be speaking to us in such private quarters, so late in the day?

Radio does not usually converse at the intimate proximity of the phone; but its personal, familial proximity was more than enough to revolutionize entertainment and political relations. Unlike motion pictures, the other major new medium of entertainment in the 1930s, whose conditions of attendance approximated those of the theatrical performance – i.e., people went out, in the public sphere, to go to the movies, just as they would to a theater or restaurant – listening to the radio was an activity one did in the home. (Radios in automobiles would soon extend this, but the inside of the automobile is effectively as private a place as one's home – even more private, in cases of young lovers who need to be away from their parents.) And unlike telephone, radio's messages are literally narratives, stories created by others beyond our personal acquaintance, whether news or entertainment or political address. Radio's information was thus more publicly originated and structured than what was conveyed by telephone, and of course it reached millions of people at once. In so doing, it created a brand new public/ private ratio that television and later personal computers would both adopt and refine. We'll explore that later. Here we focus on the extraordinary political impact that was unique to radio.

We can begin to grasp its extent by considering the following: can it be a coincidence that the four indisputably most powerful leaders of the twentieth century, in totalitarian and democratic regimes alike, held sway in the age of radio?

As James Curtis (1978) has pointed out, Russia in early Soviet as well as Czarist times was a predominantly acoustic, orally oriented society: it had low literacy rates compared to the West, and exulted in the emotional volatility of the spoken word. Although Stalin reduced illiteracy, and had a dull, plodding speaking style, he was able to use radio to rally the Soviet people and insure his own position when both were in greatest peril. On 3 July 1941, eleven days after the massive German invasion of Kiev, Minsk, Vilna, and the Soviet west, Stalin broadcast an appeal to the entire nation, "Brothers and sisters! I turn to you, my friends. . . . " As Robert Conquest (1991, p. 239) observes, Stalin's non-authoritarian salutation was "very unlike his previous self." Although Deutscher (1949, p. 462) describes much of the speech as "laborious and dry," it nonetheless contained Stalin's "awe-inspiring call on the people to 'scorch the earth.'" And, as we know, it worked. "The speech had a powerful effect," Dmitri Volkogonov, who heard it as a 13-year-old, tells us (1988, p. 414), "giving as it did simple answers to many questions that were tormenting the people." Simple solutions to complex problems – this was the stock-in-trade of both propaganda and a medium that extended across a land mass so big as to defy immediate inspiration by anything other than electro-magnetic carrier waves.

In the United States, Franklin Delano Roosevelt was able to use radio to his advantage in another way. Confined to a wheelchair as a result of polio, he was able nonetheless to project an image of strength and action to the American people by his effective radio addresses (see Meyrowitz, 1985, pp. 284 ff.). His "fireside chats," broadcast into American homes in the evenings, became a staple of his administration (Dunlap, 1951, provides a month-by-month account). Unlike totalitarians, leaders of democratic societies have the problem of standing for re-election, having their policies reviewed by the people, from time to time. Roosevelt, no doubt in part because of his radio rapport, was the only President elected to office four times in America prior to the two-term Constitutional amendment. (As a significant local sidebar, Roosevelt's contemporary Fiorello H. LaGuardia, one of the most popular mayors in the history of New York City, read the "Sunday funnies" – comic strips – to the children of New York via radio every week.)

Hitler's situation was different again, but no less amenable to vital enhancement by radio. Preaching a doctrine of Aryan superiority when he looked nothing like an Aryan himself, he approached the German people in three ways: via rallies in which he could be heard but not really seen, via the masterfully orchestrated filmmaking of Leni Riefenstahl, and via radio – which, as McLuhan observed (1964, pp. 261–262), was uniquely suited to Hitler's explosive polemic. In McLuhan's parlance, Hitler would have been too "hot" for any closeup visual medium – like television.

Hitler himself had a keen if exaggerated sense of the power of speech, contending in *Mein Kampf* (1924/1971, p. 469) that "all great, world-shaking events have been brought about, not by written matter, but by the spoken word." He goes on to explain – via a perspective reminiscent of the Socratic critique of writing in the *Phaedrus* (secs 275–276) – that whereas "the speaker gets a continuous correction of his speech from the crowd he is addressing, since he can always see in the face of his listeners to what extent they can follow his arguments . . . the writer does not know his readers at all."

But neither does the radio speaker. Joachim Fest offers a clue to understanding how Hitler could both prize the faces of his listeners and come to embrace the blind medium of radio. By the time he was in power, Fest reports in his biography of Hitler (1973, p. 522), "no conversation was possible in his presence . . . either Hitler talked, and all others listened, or all the others talked and Hitler sat lost in thought." His mind "had hardened into theses he neither expanded nor modified, but merely gave a sharper cutting edge." One-way mass radio proved to be an ideal vehicle for dissemination of these views that were now well beyond correction. A few words on radio – like the images on film which Hitler also admired because they could bring to viewers "the enlightenment which they obtain from written matter only after arduous reading" (1924/1971, p. 470) – could go a long, long way. They were viscerally appealing, and could bring into being an instant community much like that in a movie theater except bigger, but impossible to attain in the one-on-one relationship of each reader to each book. Joseph Goebbels, Ph.D., University of Heidelberg, 1921, Hitler's Minister of Popular Enlightenment and Propaganda, of course understood this too, and hastily arranged for a radio address from the Führer the very evening after he had been wounded in the bomb plot of July 1944. The sound of Hitler's voice quashed the possibility of widespread insurrection, and extended the war.

Winston Churchill was probably the greatest orator of them all. More than a half century after his addresses delivered in the face of the German high-tide in Europe, we can hear them on crackly recordings and find them every bit as inspiring as the British people – and the free world – did then. My own parents, who lived in New York City at the time, often told me that, much as they loved and had confidence in Roosevelt, it was the sound of Churchill's voice on radio that gave them the deepest assurance that the Allies would prevail.

But unlike Stalin, Roosevelt, and Hitler, the man who the *Encyclopedia Britannica* (1954, p. 687) said "more nearly than any other war leader in British history . . . personified . . . and . . . crystallized the national will" was turned out of office by his own people when the Conservative Party was overwhelmingly defeated in the British election of 1945 (Churchill kept his seat in the House of Commons but was no longer Prime Minister). Churchill had campaigned tirelessly, via tours of the country and radio broadcast. But powerful as radio was, it was not omnipotent – no medium ever is. The important lesson for media determinism, again, is that although information technologies can and do decisively influence events and make them possible, they are not irresistible in their impact, and indeed any medium can be overridden by other media and other factors. We can and do rebel against the fathers in our homes, be they personal and physical or radio-political and informational.

Nonetheless, the impact of radio in this brief period of time was staggering. In all four cases, messages emanating from distant strangers were taken into the hearts of people as if they were the words of a father or uncle. These words gave unprecedented hope, aroused their listeners to new heights of commitment and action, be their causes just or otherwise. Indeed, whether the messages were ethically right or not, on behalf of democracy or totalitarian control, meant to defend against attack or unleashing a monstrous attack upon the innocent, did not really matter. Because the sound and impact of the human voice in such close, personal, radio quarters cut through and around detached rational analysis, exciting emotional levels of bonding, which, like all appeals to our adrenalin, have little to do with reason. In this instance, at least, we can see the wisdom in Lewis Mumford's (1934, p. 241) prophetic warnings about "the dangers of the radio," whose "possibilities . . . for good and evil are immense: the secondary personal contact with voice . . . may increase the amount of mass regimentation." The lifting of the barriers of distance, Mumford observes (1934, p. 240), "has mobilized and hastened mass-reactions, like those which occur on the eve of a war."

Of course, World War I and all manner of world, local, and bloody wars before were amply fought and supported by populaces unmobilized by instantaneous, mass electronic media. Indeed, the Battle of New Orleans, costly in human life, was fought after the peace treaty ending the War of 1812 had been signed in Paris. The ship carrying news of the treaty had not yet arrived. The telegraph, whose deployment was yet a few decades away, would of course have conveyed the news instantly and averted the unnecessary battle. So "restrictions on close human" communication are not, as Mumford (1934, p. 240) implies, always saving.

Nevertheless, where the press had brought into being and nurtured a species of nationality that was critical of doctrine from on high – indeed was democratic in some places – and an Age of Reason and its aftermath predicated on active analysis and discussion of ideas, radio in contrast reached these same nationalities in a way that also evoked the primitive passions of the tribe. The "tribal drum," as McLuhan (1964) dubbed radio, beat forth a message that went out to the districts of print, and transformed its readers into something quite else.

Yet the age of radio, like the initially unrecorded voices it carried and the emotions it excited, was shortlived. Television and its more detached mode of visual engagement was well on the way to replacing radio as the prime vehicle of entertainment and political address in the home by the 1950s. By 1960, a majority of Americans hearing the Kennedy–Nixon debates on radio thought Nixon did better (McLuhan, 1964, p. 261); but a majority of Americans seeing these same debates on television thought the opposite; more people saw the debates on TV than heard them on radio, and, as we know, Kennedy won the election by a narrow margin.

But radio, though dethroned as the central medium, was by no means gone. Always out of sight, never out of mind, it managed to transform itself into a very different kind of medium in terms of the information it delivers – where it continues today as the most profitable medium, dollar spent for dollars earned, in the United States.

Just how radio made that transformation – the principles of media evolution it relied upon and its success highlights – is the subject of our next chapter.

9

SURVIVAL OF THE MEDIA FIT

Radio, motion pictures, and TV in human ecological niches

The 1950s were trying times for radio. Over a period of several decades, it had invented from scratch and refined an economic structure that took full advantage of its capacity to reach a huge, simultaneous mass audience. Now that structure was in grave danger of being undermined by television, which had taken that structure for its own, and, worse, was literally attracting away from radio the main spark which made the structure work: the big-name entertainer.

This is the story of how, when those radio idols of the 1940s literally decamped for TV, the structure did indeed collapse for radio – how, by 1960, network sales accounted for only 6 per cent of all radio income (Head, 1976, p. 153). But this is also the story of how, by the 1960s, radio's revenue came to be higher than ever before. In that two-part story – in the capacity of a medium divested of its way of doing business to recover and find a new way of doing business and thrive – in the explanation not only of how but why that happened – resides one of the crucial keys of media evolution. We begin with what was lost by radio.

THE FICKLE SYMBIOTIC NETWORK

In all advertising relationships, such as those that make possible the publication of newspapers and magazines free of purse strings pulled by the government, the medium charges the advertiser based on the number of people likely to be exposed to the ad – the famous cost-per-thousand principle. Other factors such as the size of the ad – measured by space in publications, time in broadcasts – play a role, but the number of expected recipients is central. Thus, the earliest radio stations in the big cities were able to generate considerable advertising revenue from their large listener markets, which in turn gave them sufficient income to pay for top-notch live entertainment, which in turn kept the listening audience large. But, like all businesses, such big stations were ever eager to increase their audiences – no easy task, since the literal power of broadcast towers, and thus the range of the broadcast, was limited. Meanwhile, radio stations in smaller cities and local areas around the country had plenty of willing listeners on hand – if not in individual smaller areas, certainly in aggregate – but a serious problem with no affordable big-name talent. What good was all of their commercial airtime for sale, with no major entertainment to really attract listeners? The ingenious solution – the network – employed telephone wires to carry big-name programming from big cities to affiliates in the smaller areas around the country (thus constituting yet another fortuitous unintended consequence of the telephone; relay technologies that were more sophisticated, including microwave, were later used). Packaged in this programming were the ads from the original "big city" advertisers, which the network could now rightfully claim were receiving national exposure. But these national ads did not take up all possible airtime for commercials, and the local stations were able to use the open slots for their own local advertisers. True, the national ads left them less time for their own ads, but the national, top-drawer entertainment that came with the national ads more than compensated, by attracting much larger numbers of local listeners than previously. It was a genuine win/win situation, and eventually just about everyone in radio was happy (see Head & Sterling, 1982; see also *The Benny Goodman Story*, 1955, for a somewhat fictional but nonetheless instructive account; see Castell, 1995, p. 90, for details on the movie).

And then came television. Moving pictures in the home, along with sound, were much more appealing than just sound alone. The narrative – whether entertainment or news or politics – was much more palpable with images supplied. Radio's big stars like Jack Benny, radio's popular series like "Gunsmoke," began moving over to television and its rapidly ascending higher profile. And with good reason: the "Hooperatings" (a measure of percentage of estimated listeners of Jack Benny's radio show) had declined from 26 in 1948 to 4.8 in 1951 (Head, 1976, p. 153). Radio's total advertising revenue – the total of network and local – dropped in 1954, for the first time since 1938 (Fornatale and Mills, 1980, p. 11). By 1958, the average radio station was earning only half of what it had been bringing in in 1948; and the income radio was receiving from networks was next to nothing (Sterling and Head, 1982, p. 169).

Yet those last figures show that, in 1958, radio was indeed earning some money – half of its 1948 intake is still considerable – even though its network income was negligible. What was radio's secret?

Part of the answer is that it adopted as content a mode of presentation which had long been scorned by the radio network: the recording.

ROCK 'N' ROLL TO THE RESCUE, *APRÈS* MONTAGE

When last we saw the phonograph, Edison's initial expectation that it would serve primarily as a device for recording telephone conversations was surprised by the phonograph's show-business performance as a photograph of song. But although the public loved the music that could be played again and again on their victrolas, everyone knew that other than this wonderful durability, the recorded performance was in every sense a copy inferior to the original. Benny Goodman's records might sell a million copies – because people indeed prized the record's permanency – but no self-respecting radio station would play it when it could have Benny Goodman performing live over the air. Indeed, radio networks in the first two decades of operation prided themselves on banning "second-hand" recordings from their airwaves (see Head, 1976, pp. 142–143, and Head and Sterling, 1982, p. 167).

This suddenly changed in the 1940s, when technology gained the capacity to not only record musical performances but improve them in the recording. This was one of the two technological springboards (electric instrumentation was the other) that propelled rock 'n' roll onto radio playlists in the 1950s, 60s, and after, and worked along with deeper evolutionary factors to make radio thrive in many ways better than television in the television age. But to fully understand the meaning and impact of that change in recording technology, we have to go back briefly, again, to the end of the nineteenth century, and trace the development of Edison's other great contribution to entertainment media – the motion picture process.

The motion picture from its very inception differed from all other media – including phonograph and still photography – in that its presentation of images in motion is an illusion, created by the offering of these images so quickly to the eye that our cognition, in yet another display of our ubiquitous narrative impulse, weaves the images together into one continuous flow. The constituent photographs of motion photography are of course not sleights-of-hand – they capture images that in fact are literal reflections of scenes in the real world – but the motion is a re-creation, not a reflection, of any motion in the real world. And this opened up a most interesting possibility. For that which was re-created, rather than literally copied, could also be changed, perhaps for the better, in the re-creation.

The French magician Georges Méliès was apparently the first to stumble on this possibility, recognize it, and go on to render from it vibrant art. One fine spring day on the Place de l'Opéra in Paris in 1898, his new-fangled motion picture camera jammed as he was photographing various pedestrians and vehicles. He fixed the camera and resumed shooting, but of course the scene had changed by then, with a whole new sequence of high Victorian, art-nouveau, passers-by now in view. When Méliès came home, developed the film, and projected it, he saw men in the picture, prior to the camera jam, magically changing into women, children into adults, and, most portentously, a bus materializing into a hearse. A balky aperture gate in a camera had led Méliès to the principle of editing. (See Bardeche and Brasillach, 1938, p. 11; Jacobs, 1969, p. 11; and Rhode, 1976, p. 34, for details. Of the three re-tellings of the story, only Rhode prefaces his with the proviso "it is alleged that . . . .")

Stopping and starting the camera – what Méliès called "artificially arranged scenes" – was of course a cumbersome way to edit, although Méliès managed to produce some superb movies with this technique, among them a *A Trip to the Moon*, a hand-colored, 1902 film satirizing Jules Verne's *From the Earth to the Moon* (1865) and *Round the Moon* (1870), which was the first science fiction movie. Fortunately, the new celluloid film stock patented in 1889 by George Eastman for use in his still, "roll" camera proved to be an ideal medium for motion photography, and soon for its mechanical editing, or splicing. Edison's director for motion pictures, William Dickson, sent his first order to Eastman for celluloid film that same year – the event, for Edison, marked the literal detachment of motion pictures from his original intention to have the pictures be part of his phonograph cylinder. (On just who initiated this important development for motion pictures, Mast, 1971, p. 24, says "Dickson convinced the 'Wizard' to give up cylinders for celluloid," whereas Josephson, 1959, p. 387, reports that "on hearing of the new Eastman film, Edison promptly dispatched Dickson to New York to get a sample." For more on the complications of intellectual property, and a proposal for dealing with them, see Chapter 17 of the current volume.)

The technological stage was set for motion photography to be more than a photocopy of life in action: scenes that followed one another in the real world could now be separated on film; scenes that had no connection in the real world could be brought together in the motion picture; and all at the behest of the filmmaker's inner vision, via the expedient of a splice.

It remained for another director of Edison's motion picture operation, Edwin Porter, to accomplish and surpass Méliès' magic by the technique of cutting and rejoining pieces of celluloid film in *The Life of the American Fireman* and *The Great Train Robbery*, both made in 1903. Their viewers had no trouble following sequences that jumped from place to place and back and forth in time, for they made perfect sense in the narratives that Porter was seeking to elicit in the audience's heads. D.W. Griffith played on these and a whole host of similar cinematic tricks he invented a decade or more later; and the subsequent advent of Soviet montage completed the transformation of film from a passive reflector to an active producer of worlds in motion. In a now-famous 1919 experiment, Lev Kuleshov put stock footage of a pre-revolutionary actor's face (Ivan Mozhukin, who had fled to Paris to become a bourgeois movie star) before one of three different images: a bowl of hot soup, a woman lying dead in a coffin, and a little girl playing with a toy bear. Each sequence was shown to a separate audience, and each audience saw a radically different emotion – hunger, horror, parental love – in what was literally the same actor's face with the same expression. As Mast (1971, p. 191) aptly notes, "Editing alone had created the emotion – as well as a brilliant acting performance!" (See also Jacobs, 1969, and Monaco, 1977, for more on Porter and Griffith.) Kuleshov had shown, and Sergei Eisenstein went on to further demonstrate and explicate, that the story of a film comes not in its individual images but their interaction. Film, never quite just a recording of theater to begin with, would go on to become a major player in the supplantation of linearity in the twentieth century: the multi-dimensional, simultaneous visions in the director's mind, and how the viewer's own deep need for narrative could be coaxed into seeing these, would be the operating manual for cinema.

The phonograph, to return to our story of radio, enjoyed no such metamorphosis for the first seventy years of its existence, serving instead as a faithful recorder of sounds in the order and shape in which they arrived. The fate of these sounds was sealed in the recording technology – whether cylinder, wire, or disk, the early forms of recording offered no opportunities for physical reconfiguration comparable to the splicing of celluloid in film (see Levinson, 1977). Indeed, the motion picture itself was only liberated, as we just saw, after Edison literally set it free of his phonograph cylinder.

By the 1940s, however, the confinement of recorded sound had changed. The introduction of audio tape not only allowed for editing via splicing, but opened the doors for overdubbing and multi-tracking that at last lifted recording from copy of reality to art-form. By the 1950s, Les Paul and Mary Ford were singing to their own voices via overdub. By the end of the 1960s, the Beatles had stopped touring, because their live performances simply could not match what they had attained in the studio – using four-track recording primitive by today's standards – in the making of their pathbreaking "Sgt Pepper" album (Levinson, 1977).

Of course, the difference between the Beatles and Les Paul – and even Les Paul and Benny Goodman – was far more than just new recording technology. There was a new, unprecedentedly powerful music at hand (and foot) too, feeding the new recording technology as well as being driven by it. As William Benzon (1993) has detailed, rock 'n' roll was a uniquely American music, soon picked up in England, that was part of an evolution of African-American culture, and its need for identity. That need had yielded jazz before and would yield rap right after rock. In each case, the African-American music, once unique to its culture, had been co-opted by the larger American community, obliging African-Americans to come up with something new.

But rock 'n' roll was something more. Its very name – slang in the African-American community for sexual intercourse – carried a dual taboo charge, racial and sexual, as psychologically irresistible as it was physically catchy. Its emergence and then co-option by the larger American teenage community (see also Curtis, 1987) couldn't have happened at a better time for radio.

What could radio play with its network structure literally being tugged out from under it by television? Easy: records, whose technical quality was now equal and soon superior to live musical performances. Records, which sounded exactly the same whether played in New York or Albuquerque. Records, whose rock 'n' roll energy and implications spoke far better to kids than Jack Benny, "Gunsmoke," and even Lucy and Desi, who slept in separate beds on television anyway.

But impressive as this new array was (see Fornatale and Mills, 1980, for more; see also our next chapter for the FCC's response), it would not have been enough on its own. For radio to survive the advent of television, it would need not only new content, but something deeper in its relationship to people – something in the way it was listened to that would allow it to make full use of its new venue. This hidden advantage had been part of radio's constitution and function all along, but was not especially called upon until now, in its time of urgent competition with television.

THE NATURAL NICHE OF THE EAVESDROPPING MEDIUM

Consider two examples of new media usurping old, and what lessons the radically different subsequent survival histories of the old media have for our understanding of media evolution:

Case 1   In the years immediately following Griffith's transformation of film from a replicative to a creative medium, and the deployment of montage first in the Soviet Union and soon elsewhere, motion pictures became an enormously popular medium. True, they were speechless – not necessarily silent, for music could be played live in the wells of theaters, and sometimes was, and roughly synchronized sound on film was attained as early as 1889 (that pivotal year for motion pictures) by Dickson (see Mast, 1971, pp. 225–230) – but the quick snippet of dialogue printed on the screen nonetheless had its charms. Thus, the first commercial "talkie," Al Jolson's *The Jazz Singer*, was released in 1927 amidst the usual qualms. Would the public accept this strange hybrid of a mostly silent movie, peppered with a few singing performances by Jolson, and, even more astoundingly, with some bits of real, verbal conversation following the songs? The public not only accepted but loved it. And they loved talkies so much that within two years silent movies were about as commercially viable as Egyptian hieroglyphics: "By 1929," Mast reports (p. 230), "the silent film was dead in America."

Case 2   Radio, as we saw in the last chapter, was enormously popular and influential as not only an entertainment but a political medium in the 1930s and 40s. Of course, it was sound only – the converse, in a sense, of sight-only silent movies, and another example, in the balance it gave to silent movies, of the general balancing act of media noted by Harold Innis (1950, 1951). Radio's tenure as a medium that typified and dominated the popular culture lasted more than two decades beyond the heyday of silent movies, but, in the end, radio too was confronted by its talkie, its *Jazz Singer*. And its face was television. Just as sight-only motion pictures had been bettered and buried by sight-and-sound motion pictures, so it seemed to observers in the early 1950s that sound-only radio would be similarly up-staged and retired by sight-and-sound television. Fornatale and Mills (1980, p. 11) cite a cartoon from then of a young boy dusting off a radio in the attic and asking his father, "What's that?" The evidence for radio's demise was certainly there, in the collapse of its networks. The media logic was also there: a uni-sensory medium replaced by a duo-sensory medium that appealed to the same range of human appreciation, in the same conditions of attendance, the home, with the same penetration into familial space, same simultaneity, instantaneity, and national reach. Television seemed to do all the things that radio did, only better, or more. Radio should have fared no better than silent movies.

But it did. And, indeed, it became more profitable than ever.

The coincidental availability of rock 'n' roll (and related genres, like country and western music) on newly superior recordings certainly was a crucial factor. A medium cannot exist, let alone thrive, without content. But was the world of entertainment and art so devoid of potential, distinct content for silent movies when talkies began stealing their thunder? Sergei Eisenstein didn't think so, and worried in 1928 that the rush to sound might "hinder the development and perfection of the cinema as an art" (Eisenstein, 1957, p. 257). There indeed might have been some sequences which would have been better photographed without sound, but the point was already moot. No one wanted to see them.

The all but immediate and total collapse of silent movies once talkies became available suggests that we need to look for something in the media processes themselves to explain why silent movies were killed but radio survived – and thrived in the aftermath of – its encounter with its own multi-sensory nemesis. Seeing without hearing, hearing without seeing: the two processes seem much the same, yet the first shrivels in the face of seeing-and-hearing competition, and the second becomes the locus for one of the most successful popular cultures in our century. The two processes must thus be different in some fundamental way.

Almost two decades ago, in my doctoral dissertation (Levinson, 1979, pp. 227–234), I pointed out that whereas hearing without seeing is a pervasive, natural, "pre-technological" mode of human communication, seeing without hearing is not. The world grows dark every night but never really silent; we can effortlessly shut off sight by closing our eyes, but we have no earlids; we regularly look at one thing and hear something else; modes of eavesdropping on the world, social as well as natural, seem intrinsic to the information gathering that typifies our humanity.

Radio, then, survived and in some ways even trumped its competition because from the very beginning it satisfied, approximated, literally spoke to, a basic pattern of human communication. (As Dizard, 1997, p. 112, points out, a survey by Statistical Research, Inc. in 1995 reported that more than 95 per cent of Americans over the age of 12 listen to radio at least once a week – with no other medium, including television, receiving such frequent attention.) In contrast, the silent movie – literally and figuratively – spoke to no such pre-existing human circuitry. It certainly spoke, and eloquently so, to the human penchant for narrative. But the machinery it used to do so was alien to human sensory ratios. And when a new machinery came along – talkies – that continued the narrative appeal, but in a way that snugly fit the human perceptual array, it utterly replaced its predecessor.

To be sure, these upheavals, their settlings, and their consequences were unintended. Radio as we know it was apparently the third thing on Marconi's mind, after wireless telegraphy and radio telephony; there is no evidence that he gave any thought as to how it might someday survive the advent of sight-and-sound television by claiming its rightful acoustic place in the human ecological niche of hearing-without-seeing. Similarly, motion pictures, though ironically in Edison's case first conceived as a potential accompaniment to music recording, were developed through the montage stage without much thought as to whether the silent medium would survive the advent of talkies. Indeed, Western Electric's "Vitaphone" (a "talkie" process) was turned down by every major motion picture company in 1925; Warner Brothers, a small company, bought it in 1926 because, as Mast (1971, p. 227) observes, they "had nothing to lose"; a year later they released *The Jazz Singer* and were small no more.

Thus, in each case, a primitive medium was developed to perform some extraordinary function – images in motion for motion pictures, wireless communication for radio – with whatever the technology then at hand allowed. The fact that it made possible the initial extraordinary extension is what brought the medium into being as a commercially viable entity in the first place. But the initial technologies also carried limitations – no voices for motion pictures, no pictures for radio – which proved lethal for silent movies, no problem in the long run for radio, not because these media were planned that way, but because radio's limitations from the outset accommodated an already extant and profound human communication mode, hearing-without-seeing, and its social concomitant, multi-tasking.

Thus, radio survived by (a) capitalizing on the consonance of its sightless communication with the human need to sometimes hear and see different things (including not seeing at all), (b) playing rock 'n' roll records as the main new sounds to be so heard, and (c) thereby moving out of the living room, where it had been a medium of central attention, into automobiles, kitchens, bathrooms, and, via transistors (which provided an important collateral technology), days on the beach. And, once radio began to flourish in this new position as an incidental medium, people discovered that they liked listening to news, talk, and other kinds of music that way too (see Whetmore, 1979, p. 101, and Fornatale and Mills, 1980, pp. 17–21, for more on radio, cars, and transistors, including statistics on car radios; see Levinson, 1992, pp. 132–134, for more on multi-tasking).

Recalling that media seem to evolve to modes that increasingly replicate natural patterns of human communication (while continuing to extend across space and time) – my "anthropotropic" theory of media evolution – we should find the survival of radio and the demise of silent movies to be no surprise after all. For, if media evolve to more human function, then surely those media which more closely perform in such patterns will be more resistant to competition by newcomers, or more likely to endure. We might say that such media, like radio, have attained a human ecological niche. (Or, we might call it the media ecological niche – the niche of human congruence that media must attain to survive.)

In the next section, we briefly look at the operation of this niche principle in the evolution of another familiar branch of media.

A FURTHER EXAMPLE OF NICHE FULFILLMENT IN TWO PATHS FROM PHOTOGRAPHY

Photography began as a medium whose characteristics included stillness and black-and-whiteness of image. At first glance, we might think that neither characteristic approximated a pattern of human perception – the world, after all, moves, and comes in colors – and both would thus be vulnerable to replacement by technologies that continued the remarkable preservation of images in photography, while widening its content to retrieve motion and color from the real world.

Indeed, motion, a more crucial component of human traffic with the world than color, was attained in photography by the 1890s. The quest for color was first accommodated by hand-tinting of photographs after the fact (see Newhall, 1976, pp. 96–106, and Dipboye, 1977), but successful attempts to get color to register on the photographic plate along with the image go back to the 1850s (see Eder, 1945, pp. 466 ff., and Newhall, 1964, pp. 191–194), and by the late 1930s the rainbow was becoming increasingly available in popular photography.

And what became of the processes of still and black-and-white photography that these new, more encompassing media had presumably superseded?

Well, black-and-white photography was indeed superseded – it exists now only in the special nether world of nostalgia and deliberate artistic or dramatic statement (see Levinson, 1977, n. 6, and McLuhan, 1964, p. ix) – whereas still photography has not moved, or been replaced, at all. And we can explain this radical difference in disposition, as we did the survival of radio and extinction of silent movies, by appeal to the principle of the media ecological niche.

Although motion is a ubiquitous part of our world, so is stillness. Look at the room you're in: most of what you see there is no doubt still. So are the moon, trees unruffled by a breeze, most flowers in our garden, and the faces of loved ones, not only usually as they sleep, but when they listen to us as we talk. The capturing of stillness in the earliest photographs thus inadvertently assisted a most human function – the perception of stillness – in its intended purpose of just rescuing images (to invoke that marvelous phrase again from Bazin, 1967, p. 14) from their "proper corruption" in time.

But not so the lack of color in daguerreotypes, tintypes, and ensuing photographs printed on paper until the 1930s. Black-and-white, true absence of color, perhaps exists in our world for brief minutes around twilight, or other situations of very low illumination. Thus, having attained no accidental, natural ecological niche in its want of color, the black-and-white photograph went the same way as the silent movie.

Human consumers, including artists, are of course ever clever in making and wringing the most from the media at hand – including turning their limitations into advantages for certain kinds of uses. Thus, the very silence of silent movies has been cited by devotees of film as creating a space for fluid, purely visual explications that are lacking in most talkies (see, again, Eisenstein, 1957, p. 257, also Jacobs, 1969, pp. 158–166, and Mast, 1971, pp. 232–233); the advent of talkies indeed put out of business many actors and actresses whose voices clashed with their images, slowed down movement of people on film until tracking microphones were introduced, and perhaps set back the art of motion pictures until it was recovered and exceeded by Orson Welles' *Citizen Kane* in 1941. And photography (still and motion) without color has been justly celebrated for the forum it provides for such understudied visual components as texture, shading, form, and angle. Mast (1971, p. 307), for example, extols those very black-and-white features of *Citizen Kane*, in "a scene played entirely in shadow, drenched in smoke, backlit by shafts of light." Such creative uses of media shortcomings are undeniable, and play an important role in the technological history and constituents of art. But they detract in no way from the passage of some media such as silent movies and black-and-white photography from mainstream use while others like radio and still photography, equally challenged, continue to thrive, and the reasons explored and set forth above for these profound patterns in media evolution. (We will consider the related issue of nostalgia, and its role in media survival and evolution, in "Paper Futures," Chapter 16 of this book.)

The niche principle also brings to the fore additional questions about media survival. Often a media inadequacy is neither replaced entirely by a new medium nor obliged by media competition to rely upon its inadvertent advantage for human communication; it is rather not replaced, or shifted in its use, at all. Thus, the first photographs were not only black-and-white (replaced by color) and still (continuing to flourish in an age of motion photography), but two-dimensional or flat. And our world is, of course, three-dimensional. Awkward devices like stereo-opticons provided some aspects of depth at the turn of the last century, and holography has been under development and in various stages of use since the late 1940s, but the fact is that almost all of our still and motion photography (including television and video) remains flat. We can think of reasons: two-dimensional photography, like painting itself since the development of perspective in the Renaissance (see McLuhan, 1962, and McLuhan and Parker, 1968, for possible connections between that and the printing press), can provide a pretty good illusion, or rendition, of the third dimension. Or, perhaps depth, crucial in our actual movement through the real world, is not especially important in our re-tellings of visual reality that comprise the various purposes and kinds of photography. Both such reasons amount to suggesting there is not that much evolutionary pressure for a replacement of flat imagery – nothing like the keen need to capture motion in photography, or provide pictures for radio broadcasts. A further factor may be the unavailability of technology necessary for a mass replacement of all two-dimensional image media. Collateral technology sufficient for holography to be a mass medium may not yet be at hand – and the lack of urgent pressure for replication of the third dimension may account for why that is so, and may continue to be so for a while.

All of this suggests not only the difficulty of predicting any outcome in the information revolution, but of injecting human intention, control, into a process governed by our mainly unconscious expectations and requirements of specific human performance in technologies often brought into being for other purposes and reliant on other technologies for their full operation. But difficulty is not the same as impossibility, and does not mean that our conscious capacity to identify media problems and deliberately create new media that do a better job is somehow foreclosed or even incidental to media evolution.

We look next at the shades we have made for our windows, the image-catchers we attach to our TV screens – each a prelude to the wings we have given words on other kinds of screens.

10

REMEDIAL MEDIA

Views via VCR and window

Some of us seem so in awe of our ideas, any ideas, that we place them on a pedestal, where we suppose them to be ever superior to us and our control. Plato went as far as to claim that we are too degraded a vessel of ideas to have been their originator – he contended, instead, that what we think of as our ideas are actually distorted reflections of a perfection that resides elsewhere, out there, somewhere. Hegel's "spirit of an age," in contrast, is clearly a product of human minds, and very useful for explaining confluences in popular culture. But, as Popper (1972, pp. 175–176) points out, the reciprocal impact that culture has on our minds – the way that we not only shape our culture but are in turn shaped by it – "becomes with Hegel omnipotent . . . and degenerates into the doctrine that the great man is something like a medium in which the Spirit of the Epoch expresses itself."

This view of humans as media in the service of ideas, rather than vice versa, has become something of a rallying cry for media theorists in the twentieth century. McLuhan (1964, p. 56) observes that we are, "as it were, the sex organs of the machine world . . . enabling it to fecundate and to evolve to new forms." On one level, this technological rendition of Samuel Butler's sage quip about the chicken being the egg's way of producing more chickens (see Butler, 1910, p. 134) – picked up also by Dawkins (e.g., 1976) in his view of organisms as packages to enable the survival of their selfish genes, and his analogous designation of "memes" as cultural genes – is an apt personalization of the evolution of media under human selection, operating on unintended consequences of the technologies. When we build radios which unintentionally fulfill the human niche of eavesdropping, we are indeed functioning as the "sex organs" of radio.

But serving as the *de facto* means of a technology's reproduction is quite distinct from serving as a vehicle for that technology's bias or agenda – as is claiming that such agendas are destructive of human interests, and beyond human capacity to control. Jacques Ellul (1964, p. 321) has been among the most extreme and comprehensive in such claims, lamenting how "man was made to do his daily work with his muscles; but see him now, like a fly on flypaper, seated for eight hours, motionless at a desk." Karl Jaspers (e.g., 1931/1951), Lewis Mumford (e.g., 1970), Langdon Winner (e.g., 1977), Jerry Mander (e.g., 1978), Neil Postman (e.g., 1985), and Edward Tenner (1996) are among others who, with widely varying degrees of reason and diatribe, have cast humans as at the mercy of exigencies unknowingly and inevitably brought into being by technology. Again, the roots of such a perspective are indisputable: we invent automobiles, to use an exampled offered by Mander (1978, p. 44), to get us from one place to another; these might have relied on electrical power, but either accidentally or because of the collusion of early oil companies came to rely on gasoline as fuel; some seventy years later, wars are fought and economies are shaken due in some part to the world's reliance on oil as car fuel. No one would deny – certainly not I – that technologies, including information technologies, have unforeseen, powerful effects on our lives. What is open to question – and what I specifically dispute – is how damaging such effects might be, especially on our capacity to provide remedies in the form of new technologies.

Karl Popper (1972), to return to his objection to Hegel, argued that although ideas quickly become autonomous of their creators, and therein exert enormous influence, often unexpected, on human affairs, we throughout this also retain the capacity to criticize and revise our ideas, in light of our observation of their performance. Buckminster Fuller (e.g., 1938), Freeman Dyson (e.g., 1971), Samuel Florman (e.g., 1976), and Henry Petroski (e.g., 1985, 1992) are among the sparse but disparate group of theorists who have, in effect, pursued a Popperian approach to technology (in Fuller's case, obviously prior to Popper's work in this area).

In this chapter, we substantiate Popper's proposition in the realm of information technology – where, we will see, unexpected consequences are not always the last word.

THE RECOVERY FROM IMMEDIACY

Instantaneous communication, wondrous as it can be in reach and simultaneity, leaves something to be desired as the only choice on the menu. Indeed, the ephemerality of instantaneous speech was what writing in all of its forms throughout history was designed to anchor. And the design worked: as we have seen, the stability accorded cultures by the advent of ideographics, the alphabet, and the printing press stimulated the successive rise of civilization in general, Greco-Roman civilization in particular, and most recently the Modern Age in which we still, for the most part, reside. Whatever the unintended consequences of these media, they succeeded in their primary, intended purpose of capturing some of the lightning of thought and ideas; indeed, the unintended effects were always secondary, flowing from the kind and intensity of intellectual energy that could be stored in the new bottles, or from properties of the bottle that determined how far it could travel, how long it could be shelved, to whom it could be accessible. And, just as writing and printing helped fix ideas – in both meanings of the verb – so photography came to save the images of the world. All provided remedies, necessarily imperfect, for aspects of thought and existence that ever ail us by their inexorable passage.

The impact of radio on this immediacy/permanency axis, especially when joined by television, was of course to greatly increase the net level of immediacy in the world. Whereas prior to radio, the evanescence of ubiquitous thought and speech was balanced by the adhesive of all other media – writing, printing, telegraphy, photography, sound recording, motion photography – the advent of broadcasting (literally, to sow or cast seeds over a wide area) disseminated the here-and-now to the ends of the Earth. The result was that the easiest media alternative to fleeting personal speech was the equally fleeting mode of radio and television.

Indeed, our increasing immersion in the present, as when we watch television or listen to the radio – in contrast to even skimming a newspaper, and the capacity that gives us to look back at an earlier page – has been a central target of critics of the electronic age. For Mumford (1970, p. 294), the confinement of "man to a present time-cage that cuts him off from both his past and his future" amounts to a state of "mass psychosis"; for Mander (1978, p. 348), the immediacy of television "qualifies as an instrument of brainwashing . . . a form of sensory deprivation, causing disorientation and confusion." So distraught was Mumford about this "instant revolution" that he included the computer among its most blood-thirsty leaders (the blood of books is what Mumford thought they were after), contending that "it reduces all human experience into that of the present generation and the passing moment . . . [and this] instant record is self-effacing." Here Mumford is obviously railing at an imaginary medium. Although we can grant him that the personal computer, word processing, the Internet, and placement of old texts online via scanning were barely foreseen in 1970 (not completely unforeseen, when we consider the work of Vannevar Bush, Douglas Englebart, Theodor Nelson, and others, which we will indeed in Chapters 11–15), Mumford still should have known that computer storage of information goes far deeper than the present, and is in no sense necessarily "self-effacing."

But Mumford's response to the real rise in world immediacy was exaggerated and uninformed by actual media developments even in the case of radio and television. First, to suppose that a media environment can derange us to the point of "psychosis" is to overlook our inherent senses of past and future, retrospection and anticipation, that we bring, Kant-wise, to our every encounter with reality, technologically mediated or otherwise. This is what Marshack (1972) had in mind when he defined us as a narrative species, harking back to a time when the ratio of instant to permanent was far greater in favor of fleeting communication than it is now or was even in the first decades of broadcasting. True, the weight of given information technologies constantly changes the ratio; but never to the point of extinguishing the need and operation of one or the other. We are thus no more bereft of our sense of the past, psychotic, or even confused, when we watch television or listen to the radio, than when we hear and see a bird chirping outside our window. No amount of exposure to the cardinal's bright colors and song "brainwashes" us into a consciousness without past or future. To the contrary, the cardinal may stimulate us to capture its colors in a photograph, its song on an audio tape, or both on video tape – just as the advent of writing, on the other side of the coin, confounded Socrates' prediction and shortly led to a great increase in dialogue.

This irrepressibility of past and future – along with rationality, another purported casualty of electronic media mourned by Mumford, Mander, Postman, et al. – made itself known in media in several ways. Reading and writing, as we saw in Chapter 7, have prospered throughout the twentieth century – including during the heyday of impermanence in media, which I take to be 1930 to 1980, or prior to personal computers and their augmentation of the written word (see Whetmore, 1979, p. 22, for book sales exceeding $3 billion annually in the United States for the first time in the early 1970s; Dizard, 1997, p. 184, for book sales in the US at $23.8 billion in 1994, and Americans spending an average of $80 a year on books, more than for any other medium; Manguel, 1996, p. 135, for 359,347 new books, not including periodicals and pamphlets, acquired by the Library of Congress in 1995; and Maeroff, 1978, for literacy rates holding steady between the 1940s and 1970s, or through the rise of television). And, when people were not reading, when they were listening to the radio or watching television, their need for retrievability was satisfied, just like the viewer of the cardinal, by conscription of available media (or, in the case of television, as we will see below, by development of a new one) for such "remedial" service.

The arrival of rock 'n' roll records on radio in the 1950s, in addition to helping radio compete with television, gave radio a memory. Every recording heard on radio could be heard again and again, whenever one wished, by the simple act of buying that record. Just as radio survived by moving out of the living room, by becoming more portable – literally in automobiles and little transistor models, figuratively in listening habits – so too did the physical nature of the records played. The 45-rpm record was lighter, cheaper, more durable than the 78-rpm it replaced (see Fornatale and Mills, 1980, p. 41), providing more accessible pieces of memory and anticipation, just as the change from 8" floppies that were floppy indeed to 5¼" floppies to 3" disks would do for different kinds of data three decades later. (The rise of paperback books can be considered an incomplete precursor, in that they were lighter and cheaper than hardcover books, but not as durable.) A commercially profound symbiotic relationship between radio and recordings emerged – every bit as powerful as the network, even more so, because it had technological underpinnings more fundamental than the legal agreements that had kept radio's erstwhile networks in business. Record companies supplied their products to radio stations free of charge, hoping to receive airplay, which in turn exposed the records to millions of listeners and potential buyers. Radio, in turn, used this free content to attract listeners, which served as the basis for advertising revenue.

All the players were happy with this win/win relationship – recording companies, radio stations, even, in retrospect, the writer of this book (I was also happy enough at the time as a listener and record buyer) – except, unsurprisingly, the US government, which in the late 1950s launched the "payola" investigations. The government's announced target, this time, were disk jockeys who were taking money from record companies to play certain records, rather than playing the records because they liked them. But the real grievance was rock 'n' roll, whose combination of sexual energy and African-American origins was anathema to many conservative Americans, well represented in the Eisenhower government in the 1950s (see Fornatale and Mills, 1980, pp. 45–54). And who was the victim of this purported crime of payola? Not the listening audience, whom the government as always was claiming to protect; any listener hearing an unenjoyable song on the radio could simply switch to another station. Perhaps the radio station that was induced by the bribe to play poor-quality music, and therein lost listeners and advertisers, was a victim; but no radio station complained to the FCC, and indeed the broadcasting industry opposed the investigation. The same was true of the recording industry. (As Fornatale and Mills, 1980, explain, ASCAP – the American Society of Composers, Authors, and Publishers – at the time representative of writers and publishers of older big-band music, triggered the payola investigation with a call for a Congressional committee to take a wider look at "corruption in broadcasting"; the corruption they had been investigating at the time was the so-called quiz-show scandal, in which contestants on TV game-shows were given the answers beforehand – the movie *Quiz Show*, 1994, offers a dramatization; see Castell, 1995, p. 942.)

In any event, so mutually beneficial was the relationship between radio and recordings that it handily survived the government's attempt to improve it – and several later attempts at government regulation, like the FCC's attempt to ban the broadcast of songs with drug lyrics in the 1970s (see Head, 1976, p. 389, and Fornatale and Mills, pp. 145–147), which served mostly to eliminate songs that spoke eloquently about the dangers of drugs. Several individual disk jockeys, however, including Alan Freed, the "father of rock 'n' roll," saw their careers ruined as a result of the payola investigations. As has been the case since Ikhnaton and his failed championship of monotheism in ancient Egypt, the right medium for a new religion proved more durable than its prophet.

Meanwhile, audio-tape technology, which in the 1940s had made the revolution in recording possible in the first place, became available to the public at large in the 1950s, giving radio listeners another mode of bottling some of its lightning. A similar fix for television was not long in arriving. Indeed, its rudiments were already in place as Mumford launched his most vitriolic attacks on television in the late 1960s. Here we see a common mistake of media criticism – what I call the "Ellulian error" (Levinson, 1979) because it permeated so much of Ellul's work – of critiquing the caterpillar of the technology, in childhood or adolescent form, before the butterfly has emerged (see also Levinson, 1977, pp. 85–86). Apparently, the view that media dominate us – disrupting our rationality, as per Mumford and Postman, or poisoning our lives, as per Ellul, with their seductive cloak of artificiality – blinds its proponents not only to the evolution of media from technological species to species, but to ongoing stages in the development of individual media. These critics miss, in other words, not only the phylogeny but the ontogeny of media. Their attacks work best on targets that function as negative eternal Platonic forms – i.e., on targets that exist nowhere in the real world of media evolution.

Certainly Mumford, as he spoke of the peril of television to college audiences in the early 1970s, gave no notice to the early "portapak" video cameras that were recording his talks from the back of the room. (I used such portable video cameras myself as a student at New York University in 1973–1974, although I never had occasion to tape Mumford.) Or, if he noticed them, he did not foresee the import of what they were doing. Or that, within a few years – by 1975 – the first Betamax home video recording systems would be marketed by SONY. This at once gave viewers the power to record and retrieve anything broadcast on TV, and the capacity to even plan ahead and record a program a few days into the future, at a time when the viewer might be otherwise occupied. By the mid-1990s, more than 80 per cent of American households with television had VCRs (Dizard, 1997, p. 147). The VCR thus gave viewers of television a mechanism for both retrieval and anticipation of programming. In so doing, it endowed television with much of the navigational qualities long cherished in the book, and recently available in radio by virtue of its symbiosis with recorded music. Indeed, inasmuch as the cost of capturing and retrieving a TV program is nil after the initial purchase of VCR equipment and blank tape, the VCR provides an occasion for exercise of our senses of past and future in some ways more economically attractive than that provided by the book and the record, which must be purchased anew for each new "program." We will return to the enormous benefit of software detachable from hardware – or "refreshability" of the media platter – in our discussions of electronic text and computer screens in subsequent chapters. (See also Dizard, 1997, pp. 143–145, for the growth of video rentals, in which the video functions as a book in a paying library.)

Typically, however, the remedial medium of the VCR, like any player in evolution, brought disadvantages to some, even as it balanced the heretofore unbridled technological immediacy of TV. Advertisers who were paying money to television networks and stations for potential viewers of their ads had no way of knowing if a human being or a video recorder was at the receiving end, and if a video recorder, if the people who later watched it did not "fast forward" right past all the commercials. (The advertisers responded with viewer surveys that took account of whether a person or a VCR was watching television.) And the motion picture industry – the one that had arisen with the public theater as its condition of attendance, already shaken and reformed to some extent by the advent of rival audio-visual programming in the home via television – took another hit when its movies could now be seen in the home rather than theaters. More than 80 per cent of the film industry's revenues came from theater ticket sales as recently as 1980; less than 20 per cent did in 1995 (Dizard, 1997, p. 145; see also Head, 1976, p. 483, for the impact of television on movie theaters in the 1950s).

Remedial media thus provide no more "noiseless" solutions to problems than the original media themselves. Instead, they play a crucial role in offering more than they take away – by providing a net rather than an absolute improvement, as we have discussed throughout this volume. The result when remedial media work is thus usually both net progress as well as new challenges about how to remediate new problems that the remediation may bring into being. New remedial media applied to these second-order problems will of course create third-order problems and so forth – another expression of the ubiquity of noise in the universe and all its facets – but if some net benefit ensues then progress will have been made in its uneven, fallible way.

Our recognition of this process gives us an important tool for understanding the impact and evolution of the personal computer, as we move in the next chapter to the edge of its age. For example, as saw earlier, we might look at electronic text as a remedial medium that addressed the non-interactive shortcomings of writing decried by Socrates, which in turn was a remedial medium relative to the ephemerality of the spoken word.

But first, we consider in a little more detail the remediation of remediation, via consultation of the full story of the window shade, before and after its implementation. Sometimes the level of noise in the final iteration can be so low that the case for further remediation is effectively closed.

WINDOWS ON WINDOWS, BEFORE COMPUTERS

The window shade is a classic example of a remedial medium. Indeed, it also is the culmination of a long and fascinating evolution of a certain kind of medium that goes back to the very origins of the human species, likely in the open savannahs of Africa.

Ideal as that real-life Garden of Eden might have been in many ways – providing essential elements of cradling in the nursery of our evolution – it also (or perhaps as part of the reason it was ideal) provided goads to harnessing of technology that would increasingly come to typify our existence as a species. Stones, at first used opportunistically as implements in shapes in which they were found, soon began to be chiseled for better effect. The harshness of the environment in rainy seasons, or, farther north, in colder times, bade our ancestors seek out natural shelters. And, later, they began to erect dwellings made of walls.

The wall, primitive as it is, displays all the tradeoff dynamics of our most advanced technologies. In response to a problem, the rawness of the external world, our forebears devised a technology of protection. And the wall did a fine job as guardian against the elements. But, in so doing, it also cut our ancestors off from the beautiful, nurturing, non-invasive forces of the outside world. In keeping out the howling winds and freezing rains, walls also excluded sunshine and moonlight and fresh air.

In response to this unwanted consequence of the first medium in this series – the wall – our ancestors must have soon come up with the first remedial medium: a piece of stone left out of the side, a crack in the armor, a hole in the wall. This was a pretty good accommodation. Most of the elements were kept out. But a little light from sun and moon and stars crept in, along with a little fresh air. Of course, under the pressure of very rainy or cold days, this balance collapsed in favor of the inconvenience of being a little wet or cold. The alternative was to close up the hole, just for a little while, or maybe just a little bit, or perhaps both, but this was no pleasure either, for darkness in the day was perhaps too high a price to pay for dryness and warmth.

This is where the window came in, as a marvelous medium that did everything for a room with a view that the hole did, but without the problems of what to do in bad weather (see Wachtel, 1977/1978, for discussion of the window's other archetypal media properties). And yet this extraordinary convenience of the window, in the very vistas to the outside it afforded from the warmth and dryness and safety of the inside, also engendered a whole new class of problems. For, as we saw: that which could easily be looked out of could almost as easily be looked into. Thus the window, a remarkable remedial medium in its own right, one of the most effective in all of human history, turned out to be in need of remediation itself.

Here, at last, the window shade seems to have literally and figuratively closed the curtain on this most instructive performance of remedial media evolution. For the window shade, when combined with the window, finally allows all denizens to eat their cake of visual access to the outside, and have it without the bite of the Peeping Tom. One could envision some superior technology in which walls themselves could be made transparent with the press of a button, and then back again, or set to varying modes of transparency and translucence in between. But these would be just icing on the cake as far as the window shade is concerned. For the window shade more or less performs all of those functions already, certainly the basic one of easily keeping outside eyes from looking in whenever such protection is desired.

Thus the evolution from the savannah to the wall to the hole in the wall to the window to the window covering provides a textbook case of media evolution in response to human need and design, with a beginning, a middle, and even a happy ending. The completeness of this sequence is no doubt due, in large part, to the relative simplicity and straightforwardness of the needs addressed: shelter with access, access with privacy. The situation with regard to more sophisticated information technologies and the multiplicity of needs they address is, unsurprisingly, far more complex. Of the many media we have discussed thus far in this book – alphabet, printing, photography, telegraphy, the telephone, radio, and television – only the alphabet and now likely radio have achieved long-range stability, in both cases because the needs they did not address were satisfied by remedial media that ultimately accompanied, rather than co-opted, the original media. The window shade, then, can be seen as an ideal end of the remediation of remediation. It demonstrates the power of human rationality to direct the course of media evolution in a sea of unintended consequences – in which most other media have yet to come to shore.

Television, the apex of popular media evolution by the late 1950s, was in need of remediation in many ways. It delivered motion pictures to the instantaneous, simultaneous mass audience carved out by radio, and was thus was an improvement of both prior media. However, it cried out for further improvement in its black-and-whiteness, two-dimensionality, ephemerality, and non-interactivity.

Color television came the quickest, within a decade of television's advent, by the 1960s. Holography, as was discussed briefly in the last chapter, was actually developed at the same time as television's commercial launch in the late 1940s, but as of the mid-1990s it was still not available to people in their homes. Ephemerality was effectively reduced by the home video recorder, as we have seen above. And interactivity?

Well, that has been under intensive remediation for more than a decade now too: via a machine that uses a screen, and now shows pictures and produces sounds, but first – and still foremost – lit upon and therein reinvigorated and catapulted to new prominence the written word, the stuff of the alphabet and the printing press which had received its last, and only, electronic boosts from the telegraph and the electric light back in the nineteenth century.

How that machine has transformed the writing process and everything writing in turn conveys and affects, how the global linkage of tens of millions of those machines (Kantor and Neubarth, 1996), as personal in their penetration of the home as the phone, is re-making world culture and the agendas of most prior media, is the terrain of the second half of our tour: the digital age.

We turn, in the next and succeeding chapters, from consideration of where we and our information technologies have come from to where we are now and where we are going. We enter the epoch in the natural history of information technology – our epoch, our epic – epitomized and energized by the personal computer and its adjuncts.

11

WORD PROCESSING AND ITS MASTERS

Prior to word processing, the act of writing required one of a succession of media that each made correction of errors, and therefore revision, more difficult. This was the price paid for equivalent increases in permanency in each stage. Pencil on paper, the medium most used now by children in school and adults for casual encounters with text, is the easiest to change, and the most perishable. Pens make scribbles and signatures that last far longer than those of pencil; but they are all but impossible to neatly erase, and, dependent as they are on the same physical skill of the handwriter, they are no more reliably legible than pencil marks. Typewriters create text that is much more legible, and more durable. But up until the introduction of self-correcting typewriters, at the very vestibule of the computer age, their impact on the page was flatly impossible to neatly correct. And the various modes of typewritten self-correction, prior to computers, could be defeated if an error was noticed after a page had been removed from the machine, or spotted after the typist had proceeded too far down on the page, or simply if more than one correction was needed in the same place. The target of all of these corrections – the bearer, after all, not only of their result but of the very physical changes entailed – was just a piece of paper.

And, should a writer have been fortunate enough to proceed from pencil to pen to typewriter to the further point of seeing the manuscript set in print by a publisher and issued from the press as a newspaper article or a book, the text in that then ultimate form was durable indeed – and utterly, implacably unalterable. Once so published, the text had to await another edition – of the newspaper, magazine, or book – to be corrected, amended, revised in any way.

We can grasp immediately the enormity of the revolution of word processing when we consider that it produces text much more correctable than a pencil on paper, as durable when printed out as any typewritten page, and, when connected to the telecommunication network of computers — now the Internet and its tributaries — more quickly and universally dispersed and stored than any book consisting of bound printed pages, yet still more neatly amendable than the output of any pencil on paper, as long as it is kept in electronic form.

We explore below the impact of this invention on the writing process — and, since writing is a currency of communication second only to speech itself, on some of the sundry wellsprings of the human condition that writing influences.

THE REVOLUTION IN MEDIA PRODUCTION

All human technologies, as discussed briefly in Chapter 6, and as I argue and explain at length in *Mind at Large: Knowing in the Technological Age* (1988), are embodiments of human ideas. A car is a compendium of ideas about how to be seated comfortably, how to see where you have just been, how sand can be processed into glass — as well, of course, as a cluster of crucial ideas about how a vehicle can be made to travel without being pulled by an animal. A toothpick is a much more limited example, but even it embodies ideas about the processing of wood, and how the results can be used to clean teeth or serve as a social ornament of the teeth, lips, and mouth.

One class of technology — communication media — are actually doubly ideational, since they are both embodiments of strategies or ideas about how to communicate, as well as conveyors of the ideas they carry. A book, this book, any book, is thus the implementation of a strategy and decision about how to communicate — to place ideas in a series of bound pages, instead of, in addition to, but fundamentally distinct from saying them in a lecture, or making a motion picture about them. And these strategic, embodied ideas about how to convey ideas are not the same as the ideas conveyed, except in the unusual case of authors like McLuhan, and, on this occasion, me, who choose to write about the very idea of how books are ideas about how to communicate.

Writing a book about books may be a rarity among authors, but not as much a rarity as published authors are as a group in contrast to the rest of the human species. Indeed, implementation of one's ideas into technologies on both the general level (car/toothpick) and meta-ideational level (communication media) has been an extraordinarily lopsided affair, with a relative handful of inventors and authors bringing forth creations in material and text that service everyone else.

The history of communication offers an interesting story about fitful, mainly unsuccessful, attempts to redress this discrepancy between producer and consumer. At the beginning, speech was, and is, of course totally fluid in both directions: all consumers of speech are producers (this pertains to the realm of the deaf as well, where consumers of signing are also producers). The advent of non-alphabetic ideographic writing, as we saw in Chapter 2, exacted a drastic toll not on the balance between consumption and production, but on the percentage of the population able to partake of this communication at either the receiving or the sending end. The result were minuscule cadres capable of so communicating, keepers of the faith and protectors of the monopolies of knowledge so engendered. The alphabet shattered those monopolies, but at the cost of throwing the balance between consumer and producer far out of kilter – as literacy increased, so did the preponderance of those who read the writing of others, without contributing to the dialogue in text. The printing press completed and increased by huge orders of magnitude this process on all levels, as we saw in Chapter 3, bringing into being a world approaching universal literacy in some areas, fed by a tiny brook of authors.

Indeed, prior to personal computers and word processing, only the telephone and its frank traffic in human conversation – voices one-to-one, telecommunicated – recovered in technology the ancient and ongoing ubiquity and balance of speech. The telegraph had the balance but not the ubiquity. Photography, as discussed in Chapter 4, made a significant contribution to the production side with the Kodak camera by the end of the nineteenth century – but even so, when photographs in newspapers that are viewed by millions of readers are taken into account, we have a situation in which far more people view than capture images rescued, à la Bazin, from their proper temporal corruption. The phonograph was first construed by Edison, as we noted in Chapter 6, as a recording as well as play-back device; but it quickly developed into a universally popular medium for listening to the music and voices of others. Motion pictures from their inception were a one-way medium of reception, with home movies meriting just the slightest of qualifying asterisks. And radio and television, as we have seen, both intended by various inventors and implementers at various times to be extensions of the interactive, producer/consumer balanced telephone, instead developed into media even more universal and penetrating than the press – with far fewer "authors" of program-ming in contrast to the numbers of authors in print, with far more recipients of the effortlessly accessible broadcast, and thus a far more lopsided ratio of producer to consumer.

A main cause of radio's divergence from the interactive expectations of

Marconi, Fessenden, and de Forest was, as we saw, the high cost of production and transmission in comparison to reception. People could easily afford to have radio receivers in their homes, but not radio transmitters. The same was of course true of television. And one would have thought the same would be true of computers.

And indeed it was, as long as computers remained mainframes (with capacity less than today's personal computers), requiring feet of vacuum tubes to operate. The shrinkage first to transistors and then to microchips radically changed that – vividly fulfilling Fuller's (1938) "dymaxion" principle of more technological power from smaller, lighter, more flexible units – and brought into being for the first time since the telephone a cutting-edge technology that could as inexpensively produce as receive data. The long-standing hegemony of high communication technology being out of people's hands as producers, available only as receivers – a way of technology that easily spanned the arc from printing press to broadcast media, relieved only by the ephemeral conversation of the telephone, and the personal snapshot of the Kodak – lay decisively, permanently, massively toppled.

But what was it in these new machines that made writing technically as easy as reading? And is that an unmitigated good? I'll give myself away by offering that it is. In the next two sections, we'll explore why.

THE SAVING QUASI-PLATONIC DELAY

Word processing makes writing – and correcting – easier, by speeding the process of externalization of text, that is, by shortening the resistance that inevitably intrudes in the conversion of what is inside of our heads to what we want to be outside. Spoken conversation is the benchmark for immediate efficiency in this conversion – the coincidence of terminology, of conversation and conversion, is meaningful – and the crucial component of this efficiency is speed. Indeed, the very word "immediate" – unmediated – and our expectations of immediacy in the production of speech, points to the way that all other media, especially pre-electronic writing, add some measure of delay to the communication. Only mental telepathy, at this point still in the realm of science fiction, would be more immediate, less subject to mediation or delay, than speech.

But word processing makes writing more efficient not just by reducing that delay, but by putting it to very constructive use. We might say that word processing facilitates writing via the heretofore unique way it delays. Words entered into a computer not only instantly appear on a screen, from which they can be read by the author, printed, or, much faster, telecommunicated to another device, but they exist in the computer in a form that comes into being a split second after the keys are touched and a split second before the text appears on the screen. Further, this intermediate stage – this binary electronic encoding of the text data – endures after the words appear on the screen, and for as long as the text file is saved on the computer. It can be operated upon any time the words are on the screen; in some ways (such as spell-checking), when the words are not on the screen; and can in any case be brought back into sight anytime a stored file is called forth to the screen. It is this virtual, invisible, quasi-Platonic realm (Platonic because it exists a split second prior to the expression, quasi because we ourselves create it, contrary to Plato's pre-human realm) that endows word processing with all of its power.

We see here another example of the non-analogic, "digital" mode of communication we encountered with DNA and the alphabet – except this time the processing is literally as well as figuratively digital. One might well think that the most efficient mode of communicating – of sending forth a representation of an original, to be received and understood as the original – would be to send forth information that literally looked, or sounded, like the original. The alphabet showed this was not so: writing letters that looked liked nothing in the real world was a far easier way of communicating about the real world than writing symbols that attempted to look like the real world; people could, and did, get by in the non-analogic, first instance with just a tiny fraction of the symbols required in the analogic second. Some three millennia later, word processing demonstrated the similar lesson that writing letters which at first looked nothing like letters – looked, in fact, like nothing – was a far easier way of recording, not to mention transmitting, those letters than writing them directly down in physical steps on a piece of paper, or pounding a key that produced an unmediated direct impact on a page. Of course, the operation of DNA has embodied this lesson for presumably billions of years, brokering a myriad of biological structures and systems via a nucleic acid encoding that looks nothing like the organisms it both receives its instructions, in sealed form, from, and instructs into being in the future. Through this, the language of life, we have beings not images truly rescued from their proper corruptions in time. For unlike the analogic camera, DNA is indeed not only a digital but an interactive – in today's high-tech parlance, intelligent – extender across time, thus far the most powerful extender on Earth, and perhaps beyond.

And among the teeming variety of structures it gives rise to, DNA when generating human brains brought forth a system not only able to think and speak about itself, but in the past few years write about itself with almost the same fluidity of thought and speech, plus powers of dissemination that are beginning to rival DNA's. Once entered into a word-processing program on a computer, a text – if the computer has a modem and a phone line – can be telecommunicated to a practically unlimited number of places anywhere in the world, at more or less the same time, and linked to a similarly unlimited number of other texts for reference, comparison, and further contemplation. We will explore some of these literally extended applications of electronic text in the next few chapters.

Meanwhile, for those who value the life of the mind, even word processing unvarnished and unconnected is surely as profound an invention as the alphabet and the printing press.

Yet as we saw with those two pivotal media, not everyone was pleased with their inception, and they did entail some tradeoffs – such as the loss of interaction in writing lamented by Socrates – however limited the drawbacks were in comparison to the new benefits. What disadvantages, if any, can we find in word processing?

REVISION UNBOUND, AND ITS CONSEQUENCES

Revision is often said to be the essence of writing. On the other hand, Isaac Asimov, who wrote or edited some 470 books before his death in 1992 at the age of 72, said he exulted in the first draft, with just a once-over dusting for spelling errors, missing words, and a deletion or addition here and there to completion (see, e.g., Asimov, 1995, pp. 379–386). I'm closer to Asimov than the writing-as-revision school – I usually go for a substantial second draft, but not much more than that – but I can certainly see, and testify to, the enormous assistance of word processing in facilitating any revisions. Indeed, Asimov did also, writing delightfully (1984, pp. 205–208) – first draft, no doubt – of how, after a battle royal with his first computer and its alien programs, typical of most of us, he discovered the joy of word processing and never looked back.

The battle is typical because no adult likes to be reduced, however temporarily, to the status of a child and become obliged to learn such a new and unintuitive skill. Just as the letters of the alphabet are intrinsically devoid of meaning, so are word-processing commands mostly arbitrary; pointing and clicking, which we will consider in our discussion of hypertext in Chapter 13, may be more intuitive, but equally extraneous to those who learned writing as pressing on a key that delivers a word on a page, or applying pencil or pen directly to paper. No such new skills, after all, are required to talk on the phone, listen to the radio, or watch a movie or a TV program – one of the reasons those media became so popular so quickly. Driving a car is usually the last technical skill society expects one to master on the way to full adulthood. Fortunately, children who learn to word-process as they learn to write have no such initial problem.

And the problem is in any case quickly overcome by adults, as it was for Asimov, and was for me. My own first encounter with a personal computer entailed not only word processing but its telecommunication, and therein promised satisfactions not only in writing but in its dissemination. But easing the hardship of revision at the composition stage was an immediate and continuing inducement. Can there be any penalty in rendering revisions easier?

I suppose one could conjure a concern that, if the first words written are so golden, any technology which makes them easier to alter is opening the gates to a potential disservice. But here another incident conveyed by Asimov (1995, pp. 383–384), this one about Oscar Wilde, may be usefully consulted. Wilde is said to have come down to lunch, joining his guests after a whole morning of editing. "Did you do much work," one asked? "Yes," Wilde replied – "I inserted a comma." After lunch, he excused himself, and resumed his writing for the rest of the afternoon. The scene repeated itself at dinner, when Wilde re-appeared, and received a similar query about whether he had had a productive afternoon. "Yes," Wilde answered again – "I removed the comma."

Asimov cited this as testament to the folly of revision, but the point of this comical comma episode for our purposes is that what can be revised can always – prior to publication – be re-revised back to its original form. Thus, a process which greatly facilitates revision poses little danger of ushering in a raft of gems cut to their detriment since, in the realm of easily revised text, the revisions can themselves be just as easily revised and removed if desired. Criticism, as Karl Popper aptly argued (e.g., 1972), is indeed the cutting edge of rationality and the growth of knowledge – a criticism can only do harm when it is for some reason placed above and beyond any subsequent criticism, for then it is shielded from any further identification of error. (Popper's student Bartley, however, erred in arguing that the critical process itself could, and should, always be held open to criticism – for to criticize the critical process successfully, to the point of invalidating it *in toto* as a process, is to refute the very process used to make the refutation. See Bartley, 1982b, and Levinson, 1988, Chapter 2.)

Thus, the concern that, under word processing, good work will be easily revised away is self-eliminating. But – surprisingly in view of the ease of revision that is word processing's most prominent feature – critics of computers have contended that the new facility for creating and revising text will result in a glut of hastily prepared puddings in the food-for-thought market.

The argument, presented by Gore Vidal ("the word processor is erasing literature"), Michael Heim, and others (see Heim, 1987, p. 1, for the Vidal quote and more; see also Birkerts, 1994, who offers even stronger despairing concern about readers of electronic text), can be summarized in one sentence: there is something conducive to good writing in sweating over each piece of paper, agonizing over a change, thinking, and thinking again, and again, before committing word to page. That last part is crucial to the argument – the proposition that (a) contemplation beforehand is essential to good writing, and (b) the speed and comfort of word processing works as an inducement to bypass some or all of such contemplation.

I agree, at least insofar as my own way of writing is concerned, with the importance of the first. I cannot imagine sitting down to write without having given extensive thought to what I want to write first. But I also recognize that such a procedure is what works for me, and I see no need or value in generalizing it to all or most writers. However, for the sake of this discussion, let us assume that extensive prior contemplation is essential for creation of good text. How would the facility of word processing in any way diminish that prelude?

I cannot see any way that it could. One can think about a text as long as one wants before sitting down to write it in whatever way – on a pad of paper, typewriter, or computer. Moreover, the speed with which words appear on the screen is only slightly, if at all, faster than the speed with which words appear on a written or typewritten page; the word processor's keen edge in speed is rather felt in the revision and organization of the externalized text, not its initial creation. Thus, the ratio of thinking to writing during the actual process of writing is the same across all three media.

The only significant difference that could have an adverse, premature-delivery effect is that word-processed text can look so good, in an aesthetic, layout sense, in first draft, as to make an author disinclined to do any further revision, even if warranted. In contrast, a handwritten text is *ipso facto* and unalterably a first draft, unfit for any publication or dissemination save the sending of a letter to a friend, or a draft of a manuscript to an extremely tolerant and/or devoted friend. However, on a continuum that begins with the scribbled page at one end and the word-processed text printed to perfection at the other, the typewritten manuscript comes out much closer to the product of word processing in initial presentable appearance. And more than a century of typewriting has produced no rush of underdone texts that anyone has complained of.

Indeed, the main significant difference between the typewritten manuscript and one printed out after being word-processed is not that the first looks less publicly presentable than the second. The *raison d'être* of typewriters, in their time, was to present reliably professional-looking work – regardless of the very variable hand-writing dexterity of the fingers that jabbed its keys. The main difference, rather, is that typewritten words have to be right – better, more precisely chosen – the first time out. That is probably why Isaac Asimov so loved his typewriters. Prior to his conversion to computers, he had typewriters lining the walls of his office, each with a different manuscript in a different stage of completion, so he could easily jump from work on one text to another. But not every writer is an Asimov. And even Asimov was quick to see and implement the advantages of word processing: in addition to being so easily corrected, files on a computer disk can be far more easily reconnoitered and engaged – fruitfully jumped between – than pieces of paper sticking out of typewriters around a room.

The fact remains that, for all writers, there is a huge discrepancy between the words inside one's head and what can be and is externalized on the page or screen. For many would-be writers, the bottleneck is so great, the imbalance in favor of the words inside so overwhelming, that the process of writing may be blocked. For people who do write, the imbalance may in some sense be an inspiration, but it is also a constant discomfort. And this traffic jam at the edge of the exit ramps of our minds exists and persists, to be sure, quite independently of how fast our ideas may fly after they have made their first landing in the external world. I suspect it is, for better or worse, a condition of cognition quite transcending of any external technology – immune to technological amelioration or impairment of any kind, unless such technology permitted mental telepathy. Word processing, then, in easing the jam at the other side of this exit, likely has no effect on these deeper factors. Certainly its reduction of the physical jam, beyond the cognitive jam, seems unlikely to reduce the positive tension of the writing, which whatever and however inspiring it is, clearly resides well inside the great divide. I find it only a benefit, more, a blessing, and I cannot imagine that any writer – other than a critic of computers – would find it otherwise.

On the other hand, that sentiment is likely a failing of my imagination, for I also know that writing is a highly personal, idiosyncratic endeavor, subject in terms of "what works" to a wide variety of tastes and styles. Indeed, less than a month after I wrote the above, I found myself talking about it to Paul Edwin

Zimmer, a science fiction writer, at a convention in Albany, New York. He assured me that he hates word processing precisely because the opportunity it affords for revision keeps him too focused on the first paragraph he writes – so tempted is he to revise it on the word processor, that he has considerable trouble getting beyond it and on with the rest of the text (Zimmer, 1996). I suppose this constitutes a rare, almost reverse Orwellian case of freedom becoming slavery – freedom from the bottleneck of editing resulting in a greater jam. (See also Dubie, 1994, for more testimony by writers on the impact of word processing on their work: journalists and business writers uniformly love it; poets and writers of fiction tend to be more attached to tools they have previously used.)

But the initial creation of text is not the only external bottleneck that word processing helps dissolve. There is a second external barrier, a discrepancy, far more formidable than the pain of entering and revising text on paper, that we discussed at the beginning of this chapter. It is, simply, the extraordinarily enormous difficulty of getting one's work published and disseminated in a world of print in newspapers, magazines, and books. Word processing, by virtue of the penultimate digital state of its text, and its fundamental connectivity to vehicles of telecommunication, stands poised to lower that barrier too. And, not unexpectedly, critics have hurled even more furious rounds of attack at that eventuality – actually, already under way – too.

In the next chapter we consider the prospects of a world in which all writers are publishers with global lines of distribution.

12

THE ONLINE AUTHOR AS PUBLISHER AND BOOKSTORE

McLuhan (1977, p. 178) captured something of the import of photocopying when he observed, as we saw in Chapter 7, that the Xerox turned the author into a publisher. But the metaphor – like all metaphors – is incomplete. First, although photocopying makes distribution of a manuscript far easier than in the carbon-copy days, the form it adheres to – the bulky manuscript, regardless of its reduction in layout – is a kind of publication only in the limited, literal sense of being made available to a public. In practice, this public usually amounts to a few friends or at most a list of colleagues in a scholarly circle, and the photocopied manuscript in no sense resembles a book or a newspaper. Second, even were an author, utilizing some combination of photocopying, multiple printing, desktop publishing, and binding technologies, able to produce books that looked and felt like books, how would the author get those books into stores, or to the attention of their potential readers? Indeed, as every author who has been published in a small press knows (including the present author for some prior texts), such publications rarely find their way into reviews in the major organs, or onto the shelves of big bookstores. The business of publishing does not work that way.

The Xerox, then, is and always has been more of a possibility than a fulfillment of the author as publisher. The reasons, as usual, are not only economic and social, but technological, in the sense that the underlying technology of paper works to keep the author/publisher distinction strong and pertinent. Words published on paper require a separate set of sheets for each copy of the publication; paper itself costs money; and, since paper in amounts used for books, and even newspapers and magazines, has weight, shipment of paper publications whether by direct mail to subscribers or to bookstores for retail purchase incurs additional costs. Thus, in order for authors to be publishers in paper media, they must have sufficient finances and a whole bundle of skills, talent, and knowledge that have nothing to do with the authored content of the publication, unless it happens to be about book, newspaper, and/or magazine publishing. Inexpensive photocopying only accounts for part of the cost and part of the talent, the part entailed in typesetting and printing. Desktop publishing can give the author the technical wherewithal to do page layout and design, assuming the author has the knowledge and talent. Still unaddressed are the high expenses and considerable knowledge needed for book binding and other aspects of production, and the entire subsequent operation of marketing.

Word-processed text, once deposited on paper, does nothing to change those palpable realities. The text is at that point, regardless of its digital origin, after all just another constituent of the paper medium – just as subject, from the moment of its appearance on paper, to all the characteristics, limitations and advantages, that pertain to any paper. We might say that, from the perspective of communication and dissemination, the chain here is only as fluid as its driest link.

But must the word-processed text always find its final resting place on a piece of paper? Having entered the penultimate intelligent digital state, where any number of corrections are possible, must it in the end surrender to a frozen, "dumb" existence?

As again McLuhan (1964, p. 158; and McLuhan and Fiore, 1967, pp. 74–75) so aptly noted, we tend to look at our new technologies through a "rear-view mirror" – construing all that they are and can be, ironically, through the lenses of the very media they were designed to replace (see also Levinson, 1989a). Yet new media often go on to perform in radically new, unintended ways. Thus, radio was called the wireless – true, but incorrect in its underlying assumption that radio would in any sense replace or even compete with the wired media of its day, telegraph and telephone. It instead went on, as we saw, to carve out a whole new niche of the simultaneous, instantaneous, national, eavesdropping mass audience. And the automobile was called the horseless carriage. Again, this definition of the automobile in terms of what it was not is certainly true, but it missed the many other things that the automobile also was and would be: a consumer of oil, a stimulus for highway development, and so forth. In both cases, focus on the media of the past – on wires and horses – at first blinded some people to the new possibilities and environments that the new media were inventing.

When word processing was first introduced, people quite understandably looked in the rear-view mirror and saw it as a wonderful way of producing texts with less difficulty on paper. Desktop publishing and fax, each in its own way, were similarly launched with a paper trail in mind, although the digital media that make these devices work, like word processing, already had the wherewithal to leave the paper trail behind — to make paper an historical route to, not an outcome of, these new media. For the text digitally encoded can be as easily sent through the telephone wires to another computer, as it can be sent through one's cable to a printer.

We explore three consequences of such text at large — for publishing, hypertext linking, and its combination of publishing and linking in "webbing" — in this and the next two chapters. We first look here briefly at the technology that makes this possible.

THE COMPUTER AS AN ENGINE OF COMMUNICATION

The principle that communication originating inside the home or place of business could be carried by wires anywhere in the world was established for speech with the telephone, which built upon the more formal, publicly accessible but privately inaccessible older wired system of the telegraph. But stepping back for a bit more perspective, we find that the telegraphing of an electrically encoded Morse Code across the world was more revolutionary in terms of radically breaking with the past than anything since accomplished. Telephone, radio, television, and now personal computers communicating via modem and phone lines, are latecomers to this party of eradicating distance, any distance on Earth, via the instantaneous transport of information at the speed of light. "Is it a fact — or have I dreamed it — that, by means of electricity, the world of matter has become a great nerve, vibrating thousands of miles in a breathless point of time?" Nathaniel Hawthorne has his character Clifford wonder about the telegraph in *The House of the Seven Gables* (1851/1962, p. 239). It was a fact.

But the telephone also was remarkable — and influential in more personal arenas of life than was the telegraph — because its electrically encoded signal, its instant coffee transmitted through the wire to be decoded at the other end, was none other than the human voice itself, spoken in the most comfortable and private of places. Compared to the telephone and the still most direct and effortless of communication it engenders, the telecommunication of text into and out of our places of residence and business is also not as pathbreaking as first it may seem to our late-twentieth-century selves, which quite understandably take the phone and the telegraph and their miracles for granted now.

But text communicated via wires from homes is unique in that the telegraph transmits text via wires originating and ending outside of the home, and the phone transmits speech not writing. The telecommunication of text via computers is thus a revolution in writing or authorship, furthered by the fact that the initial instrument of authorship, the personal computer as word processor, is the same computer used for telecommunication.

The digital buffer in which word-processed text resides, ever ready to be altered, turned out to be admirably suited to telecommunication because its digital binary encodings were easily translatable via modem (modulator/demodulator, initially a small device shaped like a cigar box and attached externally to the computer, soon available also as an internal card) into the analogic form necessary for telephonic conveyance in most places in the 1980s. Moreover, the amount of computer processing power and storage capacity needed to digitize text was, and is, far less than that required for sounds and images, with the consequence that far less is needed in telecommunication speed and efficiency to send digital text rendered in analogic signals through the phone. The upshot was that, in the early days of personal computing, means were at hand in 300-bps and even slower modems to effectively transmit electronic texts from personal computers in any home connected to a phone line to computers similarly connected any place in the world. By the time more powerful personal computers with modems operating at nearly a hundred times 300-bps speeds became commonplace in the mid-1990s, able to transmit full motion pictures with sounds almost as easily as a few lines of letters, digital text had already enjoyed a crucial decade of marriage to telecommunication (see Townsend, 1984, and Levinson, 1985a, for details on the early days). Its place in the future – already emerging with ISDN digital phone lines replacing the older analogic lines and modems altogether – was assured.

The early network structures that personal computers and telecommunication gave rise to supported the computer author as publisher/distributor in another important, unintended way. Modems allowed one personal computer of limited capacity to communicate to another personal computer of similar capacity; but modems also allowed these same personal computers to communicate with mini- and mainframe computers of much greater processing and storage capacity, and in effect borrow that greater capacity for the personal computer user's benefit. In the early and mid-1980s, those central advantages included storage space for programs and text for personal computers with little or no hard disk capacity. But from the point of view of the writer, the biggest resource that the central system provided turned out to be readers: other writers, or users of that central system, people who connected to it via their modems and phone lines for whatever reason, who could read one's postings. The first online communities, in which all writers were readers and all readers could be writers, were coming into being.

The significance of the online community becomes clear when we recall that radio and television, the two dominant electronic media prior to computers, are both one-way mass media — attempts to improve the telephone, if we consider the aspirations of some of its inventors, that did not quite work out that way (see Chapter 8). But the urge for genuine, two-way, interactive communication and community beyond the telephone remained strong. Indeed, McLuhan's famous observation that "the new electronic interdependence recreates the world in the image of a global village" (1962, p. 43) speaks to that need, even though that global village of radio listeners and television viewers was and still is more metaphoric than real, consisting as it does almost entirely of voyeurs, not creators, of information. In contrast, the real village consists of denizens who are senders as well as receivers, who participate in its communication and community on many levels. By that criterion, the online community is the first true global village.

An author, whether online or off-line, whether today or at any time in history, petitions for citizenship in a village via the very act of writing. Yes, I suppose there have been and are hypothetical authors in the past and now who have created work truly and purely for the pleasure of storing it in a closet or desk drawer, never to be read by anyone. (I do not include diarists — such as Samuel Pepys — among them, because I suppose that even the diarist on some level wants to be read, if only by the diarist's later self.) I would argue that, for almost all authors, to write is to want that writing read by some community, some village of readers, however small and specialized — even if the great majority of that village, as for the reclusive Emily Dickinson, congregates after the death of the writer. The act of authoring, in other words, seems to intrinsically call for a communication to a public, a publication. To speak, after all, is automatically to "publish," albeit by the fleeting medium of voice. It is only the peculiarity of paper — and parchment, papyrus, and harder media before it — which, for all the benefits conveyed, made the acts of writing and dissemination seem so separate and distinct in the first place.

Words on computer screens are a new kind of medium. Like the addition of blue dye to water, which results not in blue dye plus water, but a new kind of blue water, words on a screen are not just screen plus words but new kinds of words — or a new kind of screen. The words look like the words in books, but they can go places, drastically faster and easier than words wedded to pages. The screen looks like a television, and partakes of its infinite refreshability, but it usually displays words not images, and, more importantly, words that can be created by its viewers.

How far those words can go, who its viewers – and respondents – may be, is determined by the technological and social nature of the online community.

THE ONLINE COMMUNITY AS MARKETPLACE OF IDEAS

One of the ironies of the disproportion between writers and readers, creators and audience, engendered by the mass media of print, radio, and television is that the huge audiences enjoyed by a tiny number of authors left all other authors, actual and would-be, in desperate need of readers. This is why the online community, and the informal, *de facto* circles of interchangeable authors and readers it sprouted, was revolutionary even prior to its maturation into more formal modes of publishing in the mid-1990s (see Rheingold, 1993, for a history of online communities through the early 1990s; see also Levinson, 1985b). Estimates of numbers of current Internet users vary greatly – from 9 to 42 million in mid-1996 (see Kantor and Neubarth, 1996) – but all agree that the number of users is large, and the users are interactive.

Several unexpected characteristics of online communication made the "virtual" community vibrant from the very beginning. Any model of personal computer could connect and take part in it. As long as text was prepared and digitized in a "non-document" mode – i.e., one not designed to look good on paper printouts – neither the modem nor transmitting phone lines nor the central computer could tell if the text had originated in an early DOS, Mac, or one of the dozens of CP/M machines still at hand in the mid-1980s. It was all the same on the central system, which served, in effect, as a translator of the numerous personal computer text formats then in use. So the online community was from the outset, in this important technical sense, universal. Further, although facilities were available for live, real-time, synchronous online "chats," and these were extensively used, the bulk of the interactions took place asynchronously – meaning that people any place in the world could log on any time, at their convenience, and either read or write a note (see Levinson, 1992, pp. 159–160, for more on the advantages of "interactive asynchronicity"). This opportunity to "log on" and read any text when one wanted would have distinguished online communities of even just readers from the early audiences of television – which, prior to the VCR, were offered programming at fixed times, on a take-it-or-leave-it basis.

Here is how a typical asynchronous online discussion proceeds. Johnny, in

Cleveland, logs on to a commercial public online network like CompuServe – having received a free month's time online with the computer system he purchased – and seeks out its science fiction forum. He's a quick learner – the system is easy to learn anyway – and he posts a note about Isaac Asimov, saying how much he loves his robot stories, and what a genius Asimov was for coming up with the word "robot." The note is posted at 8.00 pm Eastern Standard Time. Janet, a night owl, logs on an hour later from London – it is well into the wee hours of the morning there. She reads Johnny's note, and replies. She actually always loved Asimov's "Foundation" series more, and she doesn't think he came up with the name "robot." Maybe "robotics" – she thinks she read that he did come up with that – but not "robot." But she's not sure who did . . . . Several hours pass. It is now 2.00 am Eastern time; 11.00 pm California time; just the time that Deborah logs on from San Francisco. She reads the two posts in the thread. Ah, Karel Čapek coined the word "robot," she writes – in his play, *RUR*. And she goes on to say how much she too loves the "Foundation" series – especially the part at the end of the second novel in the trilogy where a woman – highly unusual for the 1940s when that tale was written – saves the day. Five or six more people will log on from all points before the night is over; two will add their comments to the mix. By the time Johnny logs on the next morning, he finds a feast far more tasty than the morning news for his intellect. . . .

The above, if an exaggeration in any way, errs on the side of underrating the intensity and perspicuity of even the most casual online dialogue – often, nearly always, among a group comprised of at least some people who have never met in person. Leaders emerge, decline, new leaders emerge, information is shared, people teach one other, friendships are formed, fights break out, sometimes people fall in love, sometimes strong dislikes are taken, people make love – all through words, usually entered asynchronously (except for the last activity, which is usually conducted synchronously, one-to-one, in private "chat rooms"), all online, through personal computers and modems. As Andrew Feenberg (1984) observed early on, the leader in most of these discussions is "like a publisher working together with peers and colleagues to produce a sort of magazine in which all readers can become writers."

At the formal end of this "publication" spectrum, Connected Education – the organization I founded with my wife, Tina Vozick – has since 1985 been offering academic courses online for graduate-level credit and degrees in cooperation with distinguished universities and colleges. More than 2,000 people from forty-five states in the US and twenty nations around the world have taken our online courses – all without leaving their homes or places of business, because they take the courses through their computers and modems (Levinson, 1997b). When I travel to New Orleans, or Toronto, or England, I still have the pleasure of meeting in person for the first time a student I have come to know very well online.

Most people would agree that a system that gave students more opportunity to actively participate in learning via writing was a good thing – although even online education has its critics, usually among social "observers" who have never actually participated in an online course (e.g., Postman, 1994). Far more common among critics, however, is an attack on the online empowerment of people to write who are not students in an online course. The gist of this critique is: perhaps it was good that so many people were shut out of the writing/publishing process, perhaps the traditional publisher as gatekeeper played an essential role in filtering out drivel – in contrast to the word-processed online network, where anything goes, and, as Michael Heim (1987, p. 212) puts it, a "glut of possibilities" is unleashed. Let's look at this line of criticism more closely.

THE BELEAGUERED, COUNTER-DARWINIAN GATEKEEPER

Most textbooks of mass media, unwittingly making a virtue out of a vice, tell us that among the most important functions of newspapers, magazines, books, motion pictures, radio, and television – all media that send few messages to many people – is "gatekeeping," or selection of the few messages to be sent from a pool of candidates that is infinite in possibility, and legion in actuality (see, e.g., Hiebert et al., 1982, pp. 119–132). The New York Times publishes not all the news, but "All the News That's Fit to Print" – i.e., that its editors, serving as gatekeepers, judge fit. Walter Cronkite, news-anchor on CBS-TV's evening news from 1962 through 1981, and once rated the most trusted man in America (see Chapter 5), ended each nightly newscast with the words, "And that's the way it is." But, of course, it wasn't. A more accurate, if less elegant, tagline might have been: "And that's the way we gatekeepers at CBS thought you should think it is."

In defense of The New York Times and CBS, we need to recognize that only a limited number of pages can comprise a newspaper, and a limited number of minutes – usually, thirty, in America – a national newscast. So these media have no choice but to be selective. The situation is less intrinsically restrictive in the realm of books – the numbers of volumes in large bookstores are easily ten times the number of newspaper pages and broadcast minutes combined — but literally hard, physical limitations assert themselves eventually here as well. A bookstore, a publisher's warehouse, a library, after all, can only hold a given number of tomes, in areas usually measured in feet not miles.

Online storage is of course not infinite either; digital encodings take up "space" on computer systems, and require computer power to process and transmit. But the capacity in the mid-1990s to transmit the entire text of *War and Peace* anywhere in the world in a few minutes, and store it and the complete works of Shakespeare and more on a CD-ROM, highlights the radically different, liberated nature of limitations when we deal with digitally encoded text and online media. What constructive role, in these new lightened, enlightened circumstances, would a gatekeeper play?

Online communities arose independently of established mass media, and have had little or no effective gatekeeping for much of their continuing tenure. A "sysop" — systems operator — might delete an abusive post, but in my experience this happens perhaps once in 10,000 posts, if even that often. Some online discussion groups — certain Usenet "lists" on the Internet, and all forums on central systems like CompuServe — have moderators whose job, in part, is to decide if a post is relevant, and even move it someplace else if deemed not. Indeed, online academic courses are in effect highly moderated discussion groups, though in an online course a professor usually would discuss why a given note might not be relevant, rather than move it. But, in any case, for every moderated discussion on the Internet there are dozens that are not — because, again, the calculus of digital space allows for virtually unlimited discussion, in both senses of the word "virtually." The gatekeeper, intrinsic to the performance of mass media, is relegated to a special option in the online world.

And yet, just as the FCC, first legislated into being in the 1930s in response to too many stations wanting to broadcast on too few bandwidths, was given new justification by the Supreme Court as a regulator of programming broadcast unexpectedly into people's homes when bandwidths became much less scarce in recent decades (see Chapter 8), so too the gatekeeper, mandated by physical and economic realities of mass media, is now called upon as a purifying filter for online media in which the constraints of mass media no longer apply. Indeed, the absence of gatekeeping, or its perceived ineffective operation, is at the very crux of scholarly, literary complaints about online communication — which, according to its critics (e.g., Heim, 1987, and others cited in his discussion), is as apt to publish garbage as gems of purest ray serene. I agree entirely with this description, but see it as a cause for celebration not concern.

The problem with the gatekeeper — whether unavoidable in the case of mass media or optional in the case of online publication — is that it cuts off the flow of ideas before the intended recipients, the readers, have a chance to select them. The equivalent in biological evolution would be if every new organism, every new mutation, unfavorable or otherwise, had to pass some board of review before entering the world at large. Such a board might well have pre-sorted the human species, the first mammal, life itself, out of existence by whatever criteria it deemed reasonable. In our actual political history, the failure of socialist systems highlights another disadvantage of deciding policy prior to the market. Some initial structure is inevitable and beneficial — were human DNA capable of generating butterflies, that no doubt would have put a crimp in our evolution. But, in general, whether we're dealing with biology, economics, politics, or publishing, the best strategy seems, wherever possible, to let the environment, market, people, readers decide.

One might even look at the FCC, in its best light, as an attempt to limit the power of radio's internal gatekeepers on behalf of the people. But, as we saw extensively in previous chapters, the FCC in practice has just functioned as an additional gatekeeper — one, moreover, with the power to put a radio station entirely out of business. If we value a media environment with fewer gatekeepers, the best course is not to try to check the power of existing gatekeepers with new ones, but to lend support to those kinds of systems that have little or no gatekeeping to begin with.

Online networks, to be sure — including the Web — are full of drivel, just as the critics say. But who is hurt by this? Where is the harm when a reader can dispense with the drivel, and move on to something else, with the click of a trackball — much as the radio listener in the late 1950s, hearing some putatively awful recording that was played only because the disk jockey was bribed, had the remedy of just switching to another station? (See the discussion of payola in Chapter 10.)

Nor are the gate-kept media free of dross either. Janus at the gates of even the best publisher or bookstore is no Socrates or Plato, and plenty of tripe sits right there on the shelves along with the classics, new and old. This was never the end of the world, as long as some good texts made it through, as they did. But people interested in the growth of knowledge should welcome the flood of new candidates that digital text, taking up a fraction of the space of paper, provides.

Of course, the very word "flood" raises another oft-heard objection to the new electronic flow of information, somewhat distinct from the issue of high quality: does not the very quantity of new information parcels, even if it contains parcels of merit, overwhelm our ability to make constructive sense of it? The answer to this concern about overload, I would say, is no. We frequently walk into bookstores and libraries, and encounter many more choices than we can possibly process, but feel overwhelmed if at all only for a moment or two, after which we gain our bearings and make selections. Why? Because we have, since childhood, been exposed to navigational strategies for bookstores and libraries, and have long internalized them by the time we are adults. Overload, in other words, is really a condition of underload – of not enough navigational structures at hand. And these structures do indeed exist online, in numerous programs, some visible, some under the surface, for searching, sorting, linking, storing, retrieving, quoting, building upon online text (see Levinson, 1996, for more on overload as underload).

The structures that make online texts navigable work like both the tables of contents and indices within books, and the classifying systems in libraries and bookstores that make connections among books. The text published online, then, is not only a book but a bookstore. To move through its links is not only to turn from the middle to the beginning or end of a book, but walk from one aisle of a bookstore to another – more, to fly from a bookstore in New York City to consult a text in a library in Tokyo.

The "intelligence" in these online texts vibrates in marked contrast to the "dumbness" of tomes that sit side by side in bookstores without any exchange of information. Such programming of texts has gone far beyond the limited links of postings in the earlier, plainer online communities described above. They have changed the nature of publication, not only in terms of what online books look like, and who has access to them, but what they do.

We enter this realm in more detail in the next two chapters.

HYPERTEXT AND AUTHOR/READER INVERSIONS

The online network stands ready to empower the author as never before, giving creators of text almost the same immediate, unimpeded access to a potentially interactive audience as a speaker – except the author's audience in the online case is global. Just as the word processor frees the writer from excruciating negotiations with pieces of paper, so the online network can free the writer from equally frustrating negotiations with editors and publishers, and writers-as-publishers from the equivalent with distributors and bookstores. All of these dividends in creation and penetration of text accrue to the writer, who, courtesy of the digital genie, has a magic carpet ride from the moment his or her energized fingers stroke the keys – to the moment, which could literally be not much longer, that the results of those strokes reach the eyes of readers. The ride is smooth, digitally coated all the way, the most likely bumps being malfunctions of technology.

And the ride is smooth for the reader, who, courtesy of the same digital programming, if it includes hypertext linking of one line of text to another, or to another on another page, or book, or encyclopedia online, is able to easily locate not only the author's text, but many others.

But might a readership so empowered by hypertext at some point become more than a fulfillment of what authors most want – indeed becoming more widely read, with more involvement – but in a way that diffuses or loses important aspects of authorship, so that, in the end, authors are read more and better but less as authors than they were before?

All genies, including the digital, have their price; all evolutionary advances are tradeoffs.

PATHS: TO AND FROM HYPERTEXT

Whether spoken or alphabetically written, words, as we know, have no intrinsic meaning. Rather, they mean what our culture tells us they mean, plus what our numerous varying, yet overlapping, personal experiences teach us they mean. Words, then, have primary cultural and many secondary personal meanings. The significance of the latter is one of the reasons that each reader derives his or her slightly different meaning from the same text, which at the same time must differ somewhat from the author's personal secondary meanings as well. Deconstructionists perversely exaggerate this diversity with proclamations that all communication, all words, are noise or – worse – lies (see Turner, 1996, for an apt critique). A more reasonable attitude, one consonant with evolution and the growth of real knowledge and the assumptions underlying this volume, is that noise indeed inhabits the multiplicity of word links, but *in toto* they manage to imperfectly describe objective external reality anyway – i.e., go beyond personal distinctions to point at underlying meanings, generally shared. Such an approach to language is consistent with Popper's view that we can improve our knowledge via criticism. Words are a primary tool in this endeavor, and work because we speak and write words far more than they speak and write us.

Hypertext can be considered an active programmed implementation of words, phrases, and their links, crystal clear or slightly implied, to other words and phrases: a map, constantly under revision (as we'll discuss in more detail below), of their meanings and associations. For example, I could undertake a simple hypertext thread in this document – if it were in a digital form amenable to hypertext (and, for all I know, at the time you are reading this, it may be) – and connect every citation of McLuhan to an appropriate fuller reference. Thus, the reader who encounters the sentence, "McLuhan (1964) wrote that 'the medium is the message'," could click on "McLuhan (1964)" and be brought to a complete capsule description of *Understanding Media*, including title, city of publication, and publisher, as is now found in the Bibliography of the book edition (hardcover or paperback) of *The Soft Edge*. I could also try a slightly more sophisticated kind of hypertext, in which a click on the name "McLuhan" anywhere in this volume would bring the reader the complete bibliographic listings of all McLuhan works cited in this volume. Notice that, in either case, hypertext does not actually increase the amount of information available to the reader of the printed volume. It rather increases the ease with which the reader can obtain information already in the text – saving the reader the tiny effort of turning to the Bibliography in the back of the text.

But let's say I wanted to be more adventurous in my hypertext authoring. If I had an appropriate programming language at hand (hypertext markup language or HTML is the standard in late 1996) and access to an online system that connected to other compatibly programmed hypertext documents (the Web is just such a system), I could design my document so that any time the reader clicked on "McLuhan," not only was a complete bibliographic reference brought forth, but, as a further option, the complete text of that reference, assuming that it too was on the Web. Thus, clicking on "McLuhan (1964)" could bring the reader the full text of *Understanding Media* (if it was also online); or, clicking on "the medium is the message" would bring the reader exactly to that part of *Understanding Media* in which the phrase appeared, thereby revolutionizing the nature of footnotes.

But this more ambitious form of hypertext is revolutionary in ways far more profound. In the simple form, in which links are all internal to my document, I remain author of all information. I perhaps surrender something of the order in which passages are read, or jumps are made from one part of the book to another, but readers of course are also likely to jump around in a book comprised of printed pages in bound sequence; hypertext just makes that easier. In contrast, the more complex form, in which words are linked to external documents, brings the reader into a document of someone else's authorship every time a "hot," externally-linked word is clicked upon. A reader who starts here in *The Soft Edge*, and clicks upon "McLuhan (1964)," may soon be reading *Understanding Media*, of which McLuhan, not I, was the author; moreover, if *Understanding Media* is online in hypertext language, then it may also carry links to texts written by third, fourth, fifth, and other authors, *ad infinitum* in principle. Who is the author of that "volume" that started with *The Soft Edge* and went to *Understanding Media*, and who knows where afterward, and could go a different sequence of places every single time it is read? Perhaps, as we'll explore below, we're dealing not with a book or a volume here at all, but a bookstore or a library, in which the traditional notion of author pertains only as a contributor of a component of the overall aggregate of texts.

As radical a departure from text on paper as the above may seem, it only scratches the surface of hypertext. Any given hot word or phrase can carry dozens, hundreds, of possible secondary connections. Should I link "the medium is the message" not only to its place in *Understanding Media*, but to a menu of further linked texts that include *The Medium is the Massage* (McLuhan and Fiore, 1967), and the numerous other ways and texts in which McLuhan played with this phrase (the medium is the mess age, the medium is the mass age, the tedium is . . . etc.)? Or perhaps I, as author of the "flat" text of *The Soft Edge*, am not the best or only person to work out all of its hypertext extensions. Other hypertext engineers or editors, well versed in McLuhan, would no doubt come up with overlapping but distinct lists of McLuhan links for this book, giving the reader multiple hypertext editions of *The Soft Edge* from which to choose as a point of entry. And, of course, "McLuhan" is but one of hundreds, maybe thousands, of words and phrases in this or any book that could be linked, each replete with all the possibilities just described above for "McLuhan." The sheer quantity of such links quickly becomes nearly or effectively infinite; the options for meaning and knowledge that ensue from such myriad collisions, montage-like, are even greater.

In this enormity of reach, hypertext has roots in the simultaneous mass audiences of radio and television. One voice or image in millions of ears and/or eyes around a nation becomes one word linked in hypertext to tens of others to tens of others to who knows how many others at exponential remove around the world; and there are a thousand such individual words to begin with in any document. But hypertext also exploits a power of words that radio and television do not. Words in all cases can be both descriptions of situations and calls or pre-scriptions for actions. "The water feels beautiful" both describes a state and invites an action – jump in and join me for a swim. But unlike all words, which implicitly entail choices of one kind or another, hypertext explicitly maps out and presents a series of choices beforehand, which can be implemented with a click upon the screen. In that sense, hypertext word-links are almost like strands of DNA – each one not only a nucleic acid compound in itself (its description), but a formula, a command system, for the organization of proteins into pre-set patterns in appro-priate circumstances (its prescription) (see Löfgren, 1979, 1981a, 1981b, for exploration of the similar descriptive/prescriptive functions of words, genes, and computer programs). Hypertext, in other words, not only describes or refers to other text, but actually moves the reader to it, thereby reconfiguring the reader's world, pulling the reader into different bodies of water.

The reader of hypertext thus has an array of associative options literally at hand, programmed and actually waiting to be implemented, which for the reader of traditional, flat text on inert paper are usually purely ideational or confined to the mind. This is one reason why large personal libraries are crucial to the traditional, off-line scholar – they afford the only means of immediately jumping from one book to another, of quickly actualizing a cross-volume ideational link.

In some cases, the traditional author wants the reader to jump, to realize those possibilities, much as the montage film director intends the viewer to draw certain inferences from the juxtaposition of images, as in a man's face followed by a bowl of soup means hunger. In other cases, traditional readers and viewers of course make jumps and inferences not intended by the author. Hypertext has both, but it differs from text on paper in that the first kind of leap, the intended ones, are not only deliberate but are "hot," actionable, instantly ready to go, and their implementation may unleash a whole new series of unintended connections, both pre-programmed (by other hypertext authors) and arising wholly within the reader.

I.A. Richards (1929) recognized the importance of unintended interpretations, mutations in meaning, when he warned of the "intentional fallacy" – and stressed that the meaning of a work flows not from what its author intends but what its readers derive (assuming such derivations are not too idiosyncratic, as in, "I like a story because the name of its lead character is the name of someone I personally like"). In Richards' schema, we thus have even the traditional reader beginning to emerge as author, by supplying the relevant interpretations of a text. In one sense, the literal provision of links by the hypertext author may preempt or reduce the choices of the traditional reader, who may be more tempted to follow the author's literally highlighted connections than the reader's own internal associations. In that sense, hypertext strengthens the authorial role. On the other hand, once the hypertext reader follows a link outside of the initial document, the author's intentions quickly become irrelevant, and far more so than in Richards' analysis, since the hypertext reader is now responding to a document which the initial hypertext author had no part in creating at all. And this other hand, this transformation of the very notion of author, seems likely to be the far stronger.

PREMONITIONS OF AUTHOR DIMINUTION

As is now well known, Vannevar Bush foresaw the revolutionary advantage of a device that left the traditional vertical links of library catalogs and indices – in alphabetic order, each listing under or after another – and instead externalized the associative processes of the human mind, via which any given idea was in the right circumstances equidistant, in effect equi-linkable, to any and all other ideas. Bush named this hypothetical device the "memex"; the time was 1945; John von Neumann and Alan Turing were already creating different but overlapping aspects of the groundwork that would actualize Charles Babbage's plans for an "analytic engine" – a computer – devised a century before (see Bush, 1945 and 1970).

By the mid-1960s, when Theodor Nelson first began talking and writing about his "Xanadu" hypertext project, which presaged just about every aspect of today's hypertext environment and more – including coining of the words "hypertext" and "hypermedia" – the mainframe computers that had ascended from von Neumann and Turing's thought and work had already implemented some of Babbage's vision, but none of Bush's (see Nelson, 1990, for details). But like the diverse, independent flares of ideas that hypertext would one day link, its constituents were already in the air. J.C.R. Licklider had urged as early as 1960 that computers should be construed as tools to enhance and extend the operation of the human intellect – "augment" it – rather than in any sense compete with it as per the autonomous artificial intelligence scenarios of science fiction. In 1962, Douglas C. Englebart began planning just how this might be done – in word processing, windowing, pointing-and-clicking, and text-linking (see Skagestad, 1993 and 1996). ARPANET, a US military communication network that was also the world's first online network and would someday expand beyond most expectations and be known as the Internet, had emerged by the end of the decade. Karl Pribram's *Languages of the Brain* (1971) convincingly argued that much of the brain operated on the "holographic" principle of information redundantly dispersed in numerous sites. As the 1970s concluded, researchers in Xerox's "PARC" facility in Palo Alto, California, were developing not only the first personal computers but the first pcs connected to larger central computers and networks. These prototypes would soon be successfully commercialized by Apple, IBM, and others, and connected into a growing number of online networks including the Electronic Information Exchange System (EIES) under the leadership of Murray Turoff and Roxanne Hiltz and the New Jersey Institute of Technology (upon which Connected Education first began offering online graduate-level courses in 1985), and commercial services like The Source and the still-vibrant CompuServe (see Quarterman, 1990). By the mid-1990s, to link back to the sentence that opened this paragraph, much of Nelson's hypertext vision had been realized in multi-millions of personal computers connecting to Web pages either directly on the Internet or via gateways from central, commercial services like America OnLine and CompuServe (Kantor and Neubarth, 1996, cite a survey report of 12.8 million Internet hosts in mid-1996; America OnLine is the biggest, claiming nearly 7 million users in October 1996; see Zuckerman, 1996).

Throughout this time, including as I write these very words, the older mechanisms of publishing, based on the principle of a separate, new piece of paper for every page, a separate book for each copy of a book-length text, has continued operating in scholarly and commercial high gear. I may write here of the single screen whose effectively infinite "refreshability" can display an infinite number of words over time – indeed, I am writing this *on* one of those screens right now

— but the occasion for my writing these words is their forthcoming publication in traditional book form by Routledge. And, though I've no doubt already committed hundreds of thousands of words to screen — certainly thousands of comments in courses I have taught online, and dozens of papers posted online as well — I am very pleased and proud to be writing these words for traditional book publication, especially by a publisher as distinguished as Routledge. But perhaps that feeling is nothing more significant than my being as subject as any other human to the spell of McLuhan's rear-view mirror, and its peculiar aesthetic effect of often casting older media as more legitimate than the new — much as some people still hold the theater to be more "legitimate" than cinema.

So, the printed book, and the author it holds high, reign much as they ever have. Yet on closer inspection, we can see even in this non-digital realm some blurrings of the author/reader distinction — some premonitions of hypertext, stirrings of authorial prerogatives by readers beyond those that Richards sees as intrinsic to every reading. Consider, again, the case of Isaac Asimov, whose masterworks in science fiction appeared in two eventually intertwining series of novels — his "Foundation" and robot books — that were published as follows: *Foundation* (1951), *Foundation and Empire* (1952), *Second Foundation* (1953), *The Caves of Steel* (1953), *The Naked Sun* (1956), *Foundation's Edge* (1982), *The Robots of Dawn* (1983), *Robots and Empire* (1985), *Foundation and Earth* (1986), *Prelude to Foundation* (1988), and *Forward the Foundation* (1993; a year after his death). (The situation is actually even more complex. The texts of his first three novels were first published as a series of shorter stories in the 1940s and 1950. Asimov wrote at least one other novel that qualifies, in my view, as a masterwork — *The End of Eternity* in 1957 — but that has little connection to the intertwining two series. And Asimov wrote three other novels in the 1950s — his Empire novels — which are directly connected to the series, but are in my and everyone else's opinion I've encountered not in the same league as the eleven novels listed above.)

In what sequence is the reader to approach these? If he or she were old enough, the novels could simply have been read in the order in which they were published. But what's the best order now, with the books all available? (A condition which not only is the case now, but will be the case from now on.) A reader today could elect to pick up the books in the original order in which they were published, as listed above. Or, the reader could elect to follow the story not via publication order, but narrative order — for the two are very different. In narrative order, i.e., the books listed in order of the events they describe, we have the following: *The Caves of Steel*, *The Naked Sun*, *The Robots of Dawn*, *Robots and Empire* (these comprise the robot series); *Prelude to Foundation* and *Forward the Foundation* (a bridge between robots and *Foundation*); *Foundation*, *Foundation and Empire*, *Second Foundation*, *Foundation's Edge* (the "Foundation" series — the first three known as the trilogy); *Foundation and Earth* (further mixture of robots and Foundation). Now, were the reader to choose the novels in that order, the author of both the individual books and even that sequence still would clearly be Asimov and only Asimov — he, after all, not the reader, wrote the event sequence that way. But a reader might also choose to jump right from *Forward the Foundation* to *Foundation and Earth*, for the sake of following the robot theme without interruption (actually, *Foundation's Edge* has a hint of robots too). Who would be the author, completely, of *that* sequence? Probably still Asimov, for he is responsible for even that thematic grouping, but somehow his authorship of the entire series when read in the robot-grouping way seems a bit more attenuated than in the other modes. And if the reader, implementing links of his or her own, for whatever reasons, reads the books in yet a different order?

Like the individual texts that comprise the global hypertext "document," there is no doubt at all about the author of the pockets or points — the author of each of the individual novels listed above is Asimov, regardless of the order in which they are read. The complication comes in the compilation. But compilations are probably as old as books themselves — as witness the Old and New Testaments. Today, anthology and magazine editors, and online services, claim "compilation" copyright to the articles or stories or online postings taken as a whole — a copyright which in no way infringes on the copyright of the individual pieces held by the authors. Even more ambiguous situations abound in other media. Who is the author of a film — the scriptwriter or the director (known in France as the *auteur*)?

Our society has found ways to deal with these complications, and will no doubt find ways to deal with authorial complexities of hypertext. (I argue in Chapter 17 that one of these ways is *not* to do away with copyright, as has been urged by some champions of the digital age; I instead propose a way of enlisting a special kind of digital support for copyright.) But preconfigurations in print and other media notwithstanding, hypertext does present some genuinely new challenges, not only in the numbers of readers it instantly and globally brings to the rearrangement festival, but in the radically diminished size of the text units it allows to be rearranged.

In the case of the Asimov series and its reading order, we have novels as the unit of possible re-ordering. In the case of online hypertexts, we have links that jump from the middle of one line to the middle of another, a continent and an author away. Is there some minimal irreducible unit — an author's meme — that we can claim for the author to hang on to in this sea of links?

HYPERTEXT: FICTION AND NON

The content of the text – what it is about and how it is constructed – is not irrelevant to this issue. In the case of this very book – a work of non-fiction, one hopes – I have arranged themes in chapters and subchapters, and placed these in order to be printed and, I assume, read. But I would not be heartbroken, nor, I would think, would any damage at all be done to the flow of ideas presented herein, were readers to encounter the text in a different order. That is, after all, what tables of contents, indices, and references to discussions in other chapters are designed to do – allow readers to carve their own paths through a text. If you're reading this in hypertext right now, the only difference is that the paths have already been set out for you, at least internal to this text and insofar as this text may be linked to other documents (from where, as discussed above, the rest is up to you – or certainly no longer up to me).

But the situation seems very different for fiction. In the above pre-hypertext example of Asimov's novels, they tell a significantly different story when read in narrative versus publication order. In the case of fiction deliberately written for hypertext today – called "hyperfiction" – the initial author is actually telling as many different stories as the pre-programmed links within the story allow. Depending on one's perspective, one could say that the hypertext author is doing either more or less than the traditional author. And, of course, if one hypertext story has links to another hypertext story by a different author, then we instantly have an example of dual authorship comparable to any situation of co-authorship, whether of books, or in the more complex case of scriptwriter and director mentioned above. And when we have dozens, hundreds, thousands of independently authored linked texts?

As some critics of hypertext contend, readers may want to be entertained when delving into fiction to the point that they want to follow, fathom, ponder, deliciously reflect upon stories told to them, rather than stories that they have to click into being for themselves from hypertext. "A tight, satisfying story with plot twists, revelations, and a strong ending doesn't allow much room for the user to interfere," Charles Platt observes (1995, p. 195; see Nayman, 1996, for a summary and discussion of like criticism; and McDaid, 1994, for arguments on behalf of interactive fiction). Of course, to read is indeed to create a story for oneself – perhaps different from the one intended by the author – but what readers most want might be to do this internally, not externally through programmed links. They may crave the feel of a cloth already whole, and find an option to assemble it from pieces to be incompatible with Coleridge's willing suspension of disbelief. Montage, after all, runs on the filmmaker's coaxing the viewer to get a certain meaning out of a juxtaposition of images already brought together by the film-maker. Were the viewer to become the filmmaker, and physically put together the individual images, would the magic of meaning from montage – of a new meaning different from that of each of the constituent images – long survive?

Motion pictures whose endings were selected by preview audiences may be the beginning of a further inversion of authors and audience (*Fatal Attraction*, 1987, is a famous example; see Fleming, 1992, for details; see also Carr, 1995, for the "Interfilm" process, in which each audience decides plot paths and rates the action by pressing buttons attached to their seats); they in effect are transplantations to the big screen of computer games like "Where in the World is Carmen Sandiego?" in which players for more than a decade have been choosing pre-set story paths (see Platt, 1995). But audience-chosen endings or forks earlier in a movie are showcases of linear simplicity in comparison to hypertext online, where millions of readers make millions of jumps across thousands of documents daily. In the truly global, multiplex-of-multiplex movie theater that is the World Wide Web, not only is an endless series or simultaneity of productions showing – depending on whether we look at the links as sequences chosen by individuals, or as a collective of ever-changing links flashing in and out of being at any one time – but the productions vary radically in the texture, degree of original author expression, and internal-link possibilities within the constituent parts. To return to the montage analogy, we might say that in hypertext mounted on the Web there is no individual image, anywhere. Rather, we are dealing with images – texts – which at their smallest linked component, by very virtue of that link, are themselves an image connected to another, a process already in motion.

This view of the Web as implicate aggregate – to borrow David Bohm's (1980) use of "implicate" order, another accurate take on the holographic nature of reality, or its provision of complete recipes for the pie in each of its slices, regard-less of how thin they are cut – further complicates the issue of enjoyment of text. To the question of whether I prefer being told or telling myself a story – and, if both are possible, in what ratio – we have the additional challenge of, if I choose to tell the story myself and go the link route, at what juncture will these linkages, the story itself under my construction, end? If as reader I become my own author, then that entails not only getting from point A to B to C, perhaps back to B, then on to D, E, F, perhaps back to rendezvous with A, then B again, though this time on to G, etc. . . . but also deciding what and when is Z. As hypertext reader become author, I get to provide the closure, to select an ending not only from a multiplicity of possible endings, but in light of the possibility of no ending at all in the never-ending story on the Web.

And this Web viewed on the macro-level, as a Gaia-like organism or universe, poses yet a third, provocative dimension to our consideration of authorship in this new world of digital text (and, increasingly, digital audio-visual media, which we will consider in more detail in Chapter 15) – perhaps the most provocative of all. We started, in Chapters 11 and 12, with the traditional author, and how access to interactive readers online, and freedom from the wooden constraints of text pasted on sliced trees, greatly enhances this author's voice and range. We have seen in the present chapter, however, how this very empowerment of the author through the empowerment of readers works to turn readers into authors via the very act of reading/linking in the hypertext environment. So each reader in effect becomes author, in part, of the text that comes into being as the text is hyper-textually read across documents. But, at any given time, a myriad of readers may be so performing as authors, each wholly unaware of the links being made by the others – some of which may not even yet exist at the time a reader begins a session. So who, then, is the author of the aggregate, book of books under constant revision that is the Web?

To say that its author is the sum total of authors at any one time who have contributed in both text and linkages is technically true, but not really responsive, because the invocation of that aggregate as an author – an aggregate usually consisting of no one who knows what anyone else in the authorship aggregate is doing at the time – is like no other known or comprehensible use of the term "author," and not much like other human forms of collective either. It is certainly not like any other co-authorship in traditional text, in which even posthumous collaboration entails one of the partners, the living one, knowing about the other's work. Nor is it like any anthology in which the authors are unaware of each other's work – for in that case, the editor has knowledge of all the work. The Web, in contrast, has no such editor, no head of its publishing house, no head of the studio, no music director to keep track of all the disparate records played on a radio station, no librarian or even group of librarians who presumably have some idea, at least, of what if not where all the books are.

No, the Web as a whole is, rather, like the book of nature itself, a book without apparent author. Indeed, unlike the natural world – the world of energy, subatomic particles, atoms, complex matter, life, and intelligent life – whose ultimate origins are to some degree unknown, we know full well just where the online, digital world came from. And having thus witnessed its emergence, we say with more assurance than we can about the natural world that this Web has no author.

In the next chapter, we explore more of the consequences of this different world – this hyper-Darwinian digital world that is something very new under the sun, yet apparently no less subject to the jealousy of ancient central authority.

14

THE OPEN WEB AND ITS ENEMIES

Serendipity is, serendipitously, everywhere – including in off-line, pre-digital text environments. Many is the time I have bumped into a wonderful reference because it was mis-shelved in a bookstore, or I happened to take a wrong turn in a library, or a right turn, but took in more than I had intended in my glance at the stacks. We might say that in the pre-programmed links on the Web – the ready nervous system it provides – serendipity has been elevated to both a way of life and an art form.

Some of us are less than comfortable with that way of life – even if it is lived by others. One manifestation of this discontent is the increasing movement of governments around the world to put this self-augmenting super-organism under control, the latest expression of the perennial battle for freedom of expression that we visited at some length in Chapter 8. We will look in on it again later in this chapter, in particular at the US government's attempt to legislate pornography off the Internet in the Communications Decency Act of 1996.

Most of us say we admire something in the wild unpredictability of nature, yet choose to interact with it via safari in capsules that have all the comforts of home. Indeed, this mixture of the informationally unpredictable and the physically safe and convenient is as precise an ergonomic description as any of life online: head in the infinite, rear end in the chair, fingers just a tad closer to accessing the cosmos through keyboard or mouse than the refrigerator for a snack. And we demand a high underlying degree of consistency even in the informational: we expect our computer to work when we turn it on, to connect to where we want when it dials a number, to link just as advertised when we click – just as previous generations expected and we still expect newspapers in the morning, bookstores open at their posted hours, televisions to be broadcasting according to schedule on a given channel at 10.00 pm. The serendipity of joyfully connecting to sites and texts we did not expect has a short leash, and works only when everything else around it is rock steady. We would not long put up with an old-fashioned library in which most things were out of place.

The question then inevitably arises as to how far we should fool with the tuning of unpredictability on the Web. Government intrusion aside, do we want more cataloging and less unbridled linking, if we had the power to shift in that direction? Or should we do what we can to maximize and increase the uninstructed, Darwinian generation of connections on the Web, as the only balance to the older array of print and broadcast media, in which every word and picture – the exception being the guest's patter on a talk show – is 100 per cent programmed?

Outside of my window, I see bright yellow flowers in my springtime garden. Actually, only one, the daffodil, is a flower. The other, whose color looks equally beautiful to me, is a bloom of the dandelion, and is called something else – a weed. Most people, even if they acknowledged the equivalence in color, would hold that the first should be nurtured and the second pulled up and out of the garden wherever it may arise.

I see things differently. In the next section, I'll tell you why – and we'll explore the lesson of the weed for the Internet and its unpredictability.

DANDELION POWER

When I was about 5 years old, I witnessed a terrible thing. A new group of apartment houses were being built near where I lived, and one day the construction crew pulled up a big bunch of buttercups and dandelions that had been growing on the site. I was furious and started crying. I ran home and told my father. It's OK, he tried to console me, they'll plant other flowers there, better ones than the ones they pulled out, you'll see. And they did indeed plant other flowers there – but they weren't as nice as the buttercups and dandelions, and I never did see.

There must be something about kids of all ages and weeds, because a year or so ago, my own son, 11 years old then, walked over to me as I was looking at our garden. The dandelions are nice, he said. Yes, they are, I replied. (He's a voracious reader, and had been studying some botany in school.) They're stronger than flowers, he then said – they survive more easily on their own – and that's why people don't like them. In addition to being delighted with his insight, I agreed that we would never pull out a dandelion.

Flowers are no doubt more reliable than weeds such as dandelions – in part because we have to plant them – and this combination of reliability and dependence on us makes them more appealing. Weeds thrive without us, and on much thinner soil than required by most flowers. Dandelions can pop up almost anywhere their gossamer seeds borne by wind may land, just as texts and links pop up everywhere their digital seeds, electrons encoded with meaning, land on the Internet. In contrast, flowers require our careful planting, digging a place in the soil, application of fertilizers, much as a text intended for traditional book publication requires preparation with the publisher and all manner of vetting. Of course, even weeds, like links on the Internet, require some prior structure and energy to thrive – soil and water, the natural equivalent in this case of programming and electricity.

The advantages of beauty emerging from lack of planning in gardens – and wisdom from lack of planning, or to be more precise, programming intended to facilitate serendipity, on the Web – are pragmatic and profound. Practically, something true, beautiful, or right emerging from less human ministration is preferable to the same emerging from more ministration, on account of the first leaving humans more time to enjoy it, and/or go on to create other things. Further, we can be more relaxed in our enjoyment of and interaction with things of intrinsic strength, that come to us for free – our daughter can pick dandelions, buttercups, daisies and other wildflowers for her bouquets without worrying about stepping on any gardener's toes (as we'll see in Chapter 17, however, the effacement of authorship on the Web can engender serious problems for intellectual property). And on a level deeper than convenience and property, what emerges in a less directed way is commensurately less subject to human error. We might plant seeds in our garden inappropriate to our climate. Any dandelions that grow there are obviously appropriate for that garden's ecology. (See Levinson, 1995c, for 200 words that amount to a prose poem on the lesson of the weed for the Web.)

But the wisdom of nature is not always good for us, insofar as it accommodates hurricanes, drought, famine, earthquakes, and all manner of destructive occurrences. Our garden and we could be taken over as easily by ugly ragweed and the hayfever it aggravates, as by colorfully cheerful and non-allergenic dandelions. To give the government and critics of media their due, it is the ragweed on the Web that they are seeking to control.

The question, as always, is not whether the ragweed is ragweed – even Jefferson acknowledged that some editors "fill their newspapers with falsehoods, calumnies, and audacities" (1802 letter to the Comte de Volney, quoted in Emery and Emery, 1992, p. 75) – but whether ragweed can be controlled without suppressing the beauty and value that emerges right next to it, untended. I carefully administered a pesticide designed to destroy (and advertised as so doing) only poison ivy in my garden this spring, and it killed at least three or four other plants, including two deliberately planted, whose presence our family very much liked. Jefferson probably had the lessons of this in mind for media when he further vowed to the Comte de Volney (1802 letter) to "protect them [newspapers] in the right of lying and calumniating" – following through on his famous letter to Edward Carrington in 1787, in which he offered that "were it left to me to decide whether we should have a government without newspapers, or newspapers without government, I should not hesitate a moment to prefer the latter" (quoted in Emery and Emery, 1992, p. 74).

Is weed control advisable and possible on the Internet, and the more sophisticated kinds of television receivers now becoming available? The US government, following a twentieth-century tradition that still seems to dominate so much thinking at the end of this century, certainly believes so.

CDA, V-CHIPS, AND OTHER BRANDS OF THE LAW

The logic of government regulation of media in potential and real contravention of the First Amendment in the United States has called upon such political considerations as protection of people from communication that poses "a clear and present danger" to life and other things we hold dear, and such technological factors as scarcity of broadcast bands as a public resource (the initial justification for the FCC), penetration of broadcast programs into unsuspecting homes and cars (the later justification for FCC regulation, when broadcast bands were no longer so scarce), and the direct appeal that images and sounds in contrast to printed words make to our emotions (the Mumfordian argument – e.g., Mumford, 1934 and 1970).

Interestingly, text and hypertext on the Web partake of little or none of the above three technological stigmata. First, the Web is all but the antithesis of a scarce resource. Millions of people not only read it but actively contribute new content and links to it daily. True, computer equipment is required, but second-hand equipment now costing only a few hundred dollars – say, a 386-level computer with a 2400 bps modem – can browse and contribute to the Web just fine, especially via "shell" text-only ascii accounts offered by many Internet providers and central online systems like Genie (see Roberson, 1988, for an early recognition of computer affordability via highly functional second-hand systems; Kantor and Neubarth, 1996, report 1–2 per cent of all Web users employing text-only Lynx browsers; depending on estimates of total numbers of Web users, this could indicate as many as a million text-only users, most likely working on inexpensive, older equipment). Thus, the Web is accessible – not only readable but programmable – for the cost of a TV set in the United States today. Second, although an unwanted text or graphic could be lurking behind an innocent-looking link, the online participant is making a far more conscious and directed decision when logging on to the Web than is the radio listener who turns on the radio and accidentally hears obscene words – the listener whom the FCC strives so mightily to protect. And, in practice, something of the content of at least the next link in a chain is usually fairly evident to the hypertext reader. Third, although the Web has an increasing amount of images and sounds – a development whose import we will examine in the next chapter – its fundamental currency remains the written word. Thus, on this score, one can respond to the claim that electricity repealed the Bill of Rights – dubious even when applied to the one-way broadcast of spoken words on radio and spoken words and images on television – by celebrating its return to complete pertinence regarding the reading and writing of electronic text online. (See Head and Sterling, 1987, Chapter 18, and Tedford, 1985, 1997, for discussion of the many occasions for contravention of the First Amendment in the twentieth century, in print as well as broadcast media; see also Chapter 8 in this book.)

Are there any other occasions that have reasonably called for government regulation of communications prior to the Internet? Certainly the First Amendment was never intended as protection against prosecution for libel committed in the press – meaning that although the government could not directly prevent or punish such libel, it could certainly make civil (not criminal) courts available for trials of people alleged to have committed libel, and machinery to ensure collection of any monies awarded the plaintiffs – and surely the same should apply to the Web. But such government enforcement of civil court decisions about libel is government "involvement" in communication only in the most indirect of senses.

At another end of the spectrum of government intervention, we have courts insisting that journalists disclose their sources in murder trials, on pain of fine or imprisonment; some states, in response, have passed journalistic "shield" laws, which explicitly protect the journalist against such judicial pressure. The situation is a nightmare for champions of the Bill of Rights (obviously, I count myself among them), because it pits one important amendment to the Constitution (the right to have a fair trial) against another (no law restricting freedom of press). A defendant's right to have a fair trial can be affected if, as happened in an actual case in New Jersey, the prosecution is based on evidence investigated, brought to light, or provided, by a journalist. If the defendant seeks to have this journalist take the stand and be publicly cross-examined before the jury as a significant witness, and the journalist refuses, citing First Amendment rights (as happened in the New Jersey case), the defendant's right to a fair trial clearly has been breached. (See Tedford, 1985, p. 353, and Whetmore, 1989, p. 61, for details on *Myron Farber and The New York Times v. New Jersey* in 1978, and other journalistic "shield law" issues and cases: Farber served forty days in jail for contempt, and *The New York Times* was heavily fined; but the defendant was not convicted, so Farber was released without complying with the court order; he and *The New York Times* were pardoned by Governor Brendan Byrne four years later.) Journalists and newspaper editors argue that if reporters can be compelled by courts to publicly divulge their sources, then who in any sensitive matter would ever talk to them?

My own inclination on this, my absolute support for the First Amendment notwithstanding, is to err on the side of a fair trial, especially one in which the defendant's life may be at stake (I also oppose capital punishment; but the above applies even were the defendant facing life in prison). The court, after all, is in such cases neither directly restraining publication nor seeking to punish it after the fact, nor even threatening not to renew a broadcaster's license. Thus, though its compelling of journalists to testify indeed has a chilling effect on investigative reporting, the effect is psychological not legal – i.e., the government is not compelling potential sources not to talk to reporters – and thus, unlike the "clear and present danger" decision and its many progeny, not an abrogation of the First Amendment.

Indeed, this position is not inconsistent with Jefferson's view of the government as the main threat to human freedom, on behalf of which the press is needed as a constant ally and check on the government. Were we, as per Jefferson's quote above and as per impossible, to live in a world with newspapers but no governments, then the problem of shield laws would never arise. But given that we do have governments, with powers to arrest, try, and even execute individuals convicted of certain crimes, then I see the government's threat to human freedom in that area – in the spectre of, say, convicting an innocent person – to be so real and grave that we should do everything we can to strengthen an individual in such a position, even if that entails an indirect hobbling of a particular facet of journalism.

In any case, no such complexity or subtlety exists in the Communications Decency Act of 1996 — actually part of an extensive revision of the Communications Act of 1934 — which now makes "transmission of any comment, request, suggestion, proposal, image, or other communication which is obscene, lewd, lascivious, filthy, or indecent, with intent to annoy, abuse, threaten, or harass another person" (Title V, Subtitle A, Sec. 502, sec. 223, a1Aii) illegal and punishable by fines of up to $100,000 and prison terms as long as two years. As an indication of just how broad the government's interpretation of "annoy" can be under this Act, extending to prohibition and punishment of essentially political not personal communication, the Clinton Administration was quick to prosecute Joe Shea, editor of the online *American Reporter*, when he set about to test the Act by publishing on the Internet an open letter to the government describing its passage of the Act in the saltiest of terms (i.e., some of those instanced by George Carlin in his "seven dirty words" routine; see Chapter 8). A Manhattan district court on 29 July 1996 agreed with Shea that aspects of the CDA were unconstitutional; the US Department of Justice filed an appeal, intended to go to the Supreme Court, two weeks later (see McCullagh, 1996 for more on the government's maneuverings in the Shea case, and a parallel challenge of the CDA by an American Civil Liberties Union coalition; see Greenhouse, 1996, and Tedford, 1997, pp. 367–369, for the Supreme Court's decision to consider the ACLU case; see Levinson, 1997a, for general background). Not since the Sedition Act of 1798 has the government been so bold in its enactment and implementation of legislation designed to flout the First Amendment it is sworn to uphold along with rest of the Constitution.

Much of the public fervor in favor of the CDA is born of concern about the availability of pornography to children on the Web. The Act is even more sweeping in that respect, providing the same punishments to whoever

knowingly . . . uses an interactive computer service to display in a manner available to a person under 18 years of age, any comment, request, suggestion, proposal, image, or other communication that, in context, depicts or describes, in terms patently offensive as measured by contemporary community standards, sexual or excretory activities or organs.

(Title V, Subtitle A, Sec. 502, sec. 223, a2dB)

As we saw with the "seven dirty words" case, exposure of children to "offensive" content on broadcast media has long been of great concern to some parents, and an occasion for FCC regulation (see also Meyrowitz, 1985, for discussion of the general blurring of differences between children and adults due to exposure to the same television). But the enormous growth of cable television in the past two decades — subscribed to by nearly two-thirds of American homes in 1995, and mainly responsible for reducing viewing of broadcast network TV to an all-time low of 57 per cent of homes with TV (Dizard, 1997, pp. 121, 90) – has given children access to levels of nudity, love-making, and violence (although network TV always had a good dose of the latter) not previously available.

In response, the Clinton Administration has championed and signed into law in the new Telecommunications Act not only the CDA and its above language, which provides for outright government censorship, but the requirement of a "V" chip, to give parents "the technological tools that allow them easily to block violent, sexual, or other programming that they believe harmful to their children" (Title V, Subtitle B, Sec. 551, a9). This, at least, is no blatant violation of the First Amendment, though it raises questions as to what right parents have to control the viewing habits of, say, their 16-year-old children.

The invocation of children as beneficiaries of the government's protection in both the CDA and the V-chip components of the new law raises a different series of questions about the First Amendment and its guarantee of freedom of expression. Guarantee for whom? The twentieth century, as we have seen, has often made a mockery of that guarantee for adults, and on that basis we can say, certainly of the part of the CDA under which Joe Shea has been prosecuted, that it is *ipso facto* unconstitutional. But what about children? Are they guaranteed freedom of expression – and exposure to information– under the First Amendment, and should adults have equivalent freedom in their communication with children?

On the one hand, children who could read their parents' newspapers were certainly on hand when the Bill of Rights was written and adopted as part of the Constitution, so the lack of any restrictions on the press at that time certainly suggests that children were not then considered a group whose interests exceeded the First Amendment. On the other hand, the Internet gives access to far more vivid and provocative material than any newspaper – and, in its instant connection to anywhere via Web links, is radically less foreseeable in terms of what its content might be than any newspaper or broadcast or even cable medium. Indeed, one of the great strengths of any voyage of discovery on the hyper-Darwinian Web is the qualified unpredictability of its outcome. But is this a strength for children, and parents concerned about their well-being?

The issue is further complicated by the fact that the category "children," under the law, pertains to a range of human beings from under 1 to 18 years of age, at opposite ends of Piaget's cognitive stages of development.

CHILDREN ONLINE

Children have been on line – and not just at school cafeterias – for well over a decade. A story that has been circulating for nearly as long – and I honestly do not know whether it is apocryphal, but that doesn't matter, because it certainly could have been true – tells of a man who fell in love with an online correspondent living on the other side of the country. He was married; she was not. He begged her to let him come to her; he'd divorce his wife. She demurred. But the man was deeply in love now, and wouldn't take no for an answer. So he told her he'd be flying across the country to be with her. Shortly before he left, he received a call from a mutual online friend, someone who lived near the woman, and apparently knew about the romantic relationship. (In the version of this story I heard, the relationship was a flirtatious romance rather than an explicit online "affair" – although as indicated in Chapter 12, quite explicit sexual details are sometimes communicated via text online; see also Levinson, 1985b.) The caller pleaded with the gentleman not to leave his wife. The gentleman scoffed. The caller explained: the "woman" you are preparing to leave your wife for is an 11-year-old girl. The gentleman told the caller: you're crazy, I can tell the difference between a woman and an 11-year-old! And he hung up, and caught the next plane. And, of course, the caller had been telling the truth.

There are many lessons about online communication one could draw from this – the most obvious, and entirely true, being the ease with which certain kinds of deception can flourish in a faceless, voiceless medium. Of course, in a casual conversation at a party or a bar, one might be able to be deceptive about different aspects of personality difficult to conceal in sustained online conversation. The Irish slang word "fawney" became "phoney" in twentieth-century America, in recognition of the degree to which "one's feelings or even identity could be readily falsified on the telephone" (Chapman, 1987, p. 327; see also McLuhan and McLuhan, 1988, p. 153). Every environment caters to certain modes of deceit; Jacques Ellul's (1962/1965) observation that every device of communication, print as well electronic, triumphs in one kind of propaganda or another, bears emblazoning on the face of every medium – it cannot be repeated too often. But the most important lesson of this particular media deception involving a married gentleman and his 11-year-old online true love, for the present purposes, has to do with government illusion or self-deception: for the Communications Decency Act would have had no effect on such a disadvantageous online alliance.

Beyond the always obvious case that laws are notoriously poor in preventing two consenting people from doing anything, even (and, in many instances, especially) if one or both are under age, the crux of this online romance was that it was based on deception. The gentleman had no way of knowing he was communicating with a minor, and hence would not have been in violation of any CDA provision had the law been in effect. The CDA says nothing, after all, about lying online; nor does it prohibit unknowing communication with a minor, and wisely so, as such a provision would not only be utterly unfair but even more difficult to enforce. Perhaps our deceived romantic violated the general prohibition of "obscene, lewd, lascivious," etc. communication (a1Aii), which applies to any "person," not just minors. Perhaps. Yet, as the story has been recounted, its essence was romance not sexuality, which gives us no reason to suppose that the language employed was anything less than decorous.

Thus, the CDA stands virtually powerless to do anything about such an event. Like all legislation intended to censor, it works best against easy political prey, like Joe Shea's deliberate letter attacking the CDA itself. Like all antibiotic censorship, it inevitably does less and more than it is supposed to.

Yet the episode is disturbing indeed. Has society no way of preventing this or making it less likely to occur?

Of course we do. As is always the case with children, we can expect a little better parental supervision of the 11-year-old. Nor is this the simplistic kind of supervision that says an 11-year-old should not have access to a computer and modem, or should not without a parental chaperone. That, again, like government censorship, would be both too little and too much: too little because the child could log on via a computer in someone else's house; too much because to deprive any child of a computer, or of a computer without a parent standing by, is to deprive the child of much more than an online romance. No, the supervision needed here is a gestalt, in-depth awareness of who the child is, how she is behaving in the numerous encounters that comprise her life. The online romance in this instance apparently had been going on for several months. Surely in that period of time, even moderately attentive parents would have sensed something unusual in their daughter (or, if this was a repeat performance, something unusual the first time it happened).

The same full-court parental involvement renders the V-chip unnecessary. As a simple technological fix, it cannot be completely effective anyway unless all parents set their chips to block the same stations. As Harlan Cleveland (1985, p. 32) aptly notes, information is inherently "leaky"; in this context, the result is that parental attempts to control the TV viewing of their children via V-chips can be defeated by just one parent who elects not to use the chip, and whose children are friends or in school together with the other children. Unlike the remedial medium of the VCR discussed in Chapter 10, which successfully projects the inherent human senses of past and future, retrospection and anticipation, upon ephemeral television, the V-chip goes against both human nature (curiosity) and the properties of information (namely, its diffusiveness) in its attempt to control the across-the-board exposure of any given child to objectionable information. It fails as a remedial medium — which must work in consonance with human psychology to succeed — and even more so as a substitute for parental attention and discussion, which are far more effective methods for helping our children better understand and deal with all kinds of information they will sooner or later come into contact with, V-chips or not. About the only good thing that can be said about this facet of the new Telecommunications Act is that, as indicated above, it is not government censorship.

Fair enough, even a proponent of the CDA might agree. Pornography on television is not as technologically participational as pornography on the Internet — never potentially interactive with real human beings, including children — which is the main abuse that the CDA is designed to prevent or reduce. Does failure of this legislation to prevent one kind of abuse such as the deceptive online romance warrant its not being allowed to stop another, such as exposure of children to pedophiles on the Internet?

The first response that comes to mind is why, if pedophilic propositioning and pornographic abuse of children is the government's main concern (as indeed it should be), does not the CDA simply come out and state clear-cut prohibitions against that? Why couch such a prohibition in language so vague that it hauls Joe Shea into court for publishing a letter that lambastes, in strong language, the Congress? Assuming that the members of Congress are indeed not children, one can only conclude that we have another case here of censorship, as per usual, being as leaky as the information it attempts to contain. Not only does it not contain what it is supposed to, it leaks out like a caustic acid and damages other activities and lives.

But even a more focused form of censorship would have a seriously disabling effect on the whole enterprise of the undirected, interconnected Web.

To return to our story of serendipity and the garden: the effort to control poison ivy in our garden by the application of a government defoliant runs a high risk of killing dandelions — and daffodils too — and would not extirpate the poison ivy not in our garden but still at large in society (i.e., pedophilic pornography not online). Lengthy chains of online links that led to fascinating places might well be broken in the middle, leaving readers hanging, if they perchance happened to connect somewhere in that middle to a line in *Lady Chatterley's Lover*. Holding authors of pages responsible for what their links led to would deprive the Web of the very quality — lack of overall planning, and the evolutionary dividends that ensue — that makes it the most truly original medium in history.

But is not a garden without dandelions worth reducing the risk, by even a modest margin, of a 2-year-old toddling into it and suffering the incomprehensible itch of poison ivy — a 2-year-old, moreover, with no special brief for dandelions and what they represent over daffodils, only an evolutionarily conditioned tendency to trust its parents and their environments? Arguments for protective censorship certainly increase in persuasiveness as the age of the would-be protected falls.

Fortunately, however, for the many other aspects of society and human freedom that would nonetheless be damaged by even the most justified censorship, the problem of the youngest, most vulnerable children is self-correcting on at least two accounts. The first, more general, corrective is that the younger the child, the more likely he or she is to have some direct parental supervision — thus reducing the need, proportionately as the children are younger, for the government to in effect mandate their separation from dangerous gardens. The second countervailing factor arises from the properties of a personal computer connected to the Web. Unlike a garden, no one — young child, adolescent, or adult — can just wander into it. Rather, even though serendipity can play a major role once the online encounter has commenced, a certain amount of deliberative skill is always necessary to initiate it — to invoke the Web browser, log on to a particular page, etc. — and very young children of course do not have this skill. One simply cannot toddle into an online environment.

This, then, places literal gardens, TV, and radio pretty much on one side of a divide, and personal computers and the hypertext Web on the other. Of course, a young child could walk into a room and see something disturbing on a Web page already on the screen, left there by someone older; but in such an instance, the computer screen would be functioning more like a TV, un-Web-like, in its conveyance of information to a passive viewer. Which is not to say that radio and TV *ipso facto* warrant more censorship than online communication. The very passivity of one-way broadcast media, as mentioned above, makes its forms of pornography non-participational, and thus less intrusive. And there are other good reasons, such as the pre-eminent role of one-way, mass, simultaneous broadcast media in politics, that radio and TV ought not be censored. But on the special, vexing question of pornography adversely affecting children, the Web's worst danger of actively involving children as pornographic participants is self-limiting in that children below a certain age lack the capacity to participate. (One might also argue that the younger the child, the less he or she is likely to at all comprehend and thus be affected by even audio-visual pornography, so that its broadcast on unsupervised television poses diminishing threats as well. I would agree – and this is another good argument against the need of the V-chip – but the inherent technological safety advantage of online communication, in being more difficult to use by young children than broadcast media, still holds.)

Of course, like most distinctions involving human beings, this one no doubt admits to exceptions. Not every child is a toddler or a teenager, the first unable to understand pornography, the second an adult both biologically and cognitively, according to Piaget. In between, there may indeed be children old enough to read and at least partially comprehend pornography, but not old enough to deal with it. But even this assumes a discrepancy between intellectual and emotional comprehension, or between comprehension and vulnerability, that may not be the case for most children, whatever their age. Rather, if the capacity of pornography to do harm is predicated on its comprehension, and that comprehension, at whatever level, also entails the wherewithal to place the pornography in larger perspective – to view a mixture of, say, violence and sexuality as not the way people are, but the crazy or whatever way people are portrayed just in the text or movie – then the problem of the child's perception of pornography is still intrinsically self-limiting.

An important component of this issue is the prevalence of text on the Web, and the degree of literacy therefore required both to read and navigate it. Presumably, some children would have the capacity to turn on a computer and point-and-click long before they were able to read much of what was on the screen. To visit the garden metaphor again, these kids might be able to get, physically, into a dangerous vicinity, but would be immune, by virtue of their low literacy, to any text that might cause rashes.

But this level of immunity may be declining, even as I write this, as graphics ranging from still photos to full audio-visual productions gain increasing prominence (though not prevalence by any means) on the Web. Keith Ferrell (1996), until 1996 editor of *Omni*, a major magazine (with circulation of almost a million) which in 1995 had ended its paper tenure and moved completely to online publication, remarked to me after he had resigned his position that if he had wanted to be a movie director, he'd have gone to Hollywood in the first place rather than working in magazines. The resurgence of audio-visual images in media – they of course were never really gone, christening the twentieth century with motion pictures, dominating its second half in TV, only eclipsed recently if at all by text on computers – raises questions that both pertain to and go beyond censorship, and include an old friend, the relationship of abstract and literal media to the cognitive process. We look at these and others as we enter our next chapter, and the age of the screen.

15

TWENTIETH-CENTURY SCREENS

Notwithstanding radio, the photocopy, desktop publishing, and the fax, the twentieth century can indeed be characterized as the century of the screen. It has been that all along. It started with the silent silver screen, competing with novels and plays for the narrative audience. Radio didn't hit its first full stride in entertainment and news until the 1930s, and by then, the screens of talking motion pictures were already also in high gear. By the 1950s, television had in effect subsumed motion pictures and radio on its new kind of screen — and although radio, as we also saw, amply thrived in the aftermath, television has no doubt been since then the medium of ratification for our culture. The advent of computers brought to the convocation yet another screen, one that displays text authored by its users, and text by other authors, interconnected worldwide with the radically new capacities, possibilities, and implications we have been exploring in the past four chapters. But the computer screen also brought forth a new kind of image, the icon, and then another, in the virtual reality cartoonish graphic, and now a battery of more "traditional" images, such as we're accustomed to seeing on television. These are the stars of this chapter.

We know that our culture has both fed, and been vividly shaped by, things on the screen. We also know that screens are not monolithic in their cultural import, and different kinds of things go on different kinds of screens, and engage different kinds of cognitive and emotional processes. Our question, then, is what kinds of things have appeared on what kinds of screens — especially computer screens — and to what effect. To find an answer, to start building a taxonomy of screens, we first need to make a fundamental distinction often overlooked by critics of the computer, eager to pin on it the overstated sins of television.

A COMPUTER SCREEN IS NOT A TELEVISION

Analogies that help us understand disparate events or things by showing us a bridge between them (metaphor, as McLuhan liked to point out, comes from the Greek *metapherein* — to bridge, or bear a transfer in meaning) always operate by selecting a common factor, usually one of many, to serve as the anchors at each end of the bridge. One could well look at the text upon computer screens, and explore them, as we have in this book, as new kinds of books. Computer screens are books whose readers might converse, in the manner yearned for by Socrates, with their authors, if the authors and their readers are in an online community. Computer screens are also books created by authors free of the yoke of negotiating about changes with the typewritten page, books literally connected to an unlimited number of other books via hypertext, and books in the other revolutionary ways we have discussed in preceding chapters. Yet Neil Postman (e.g., 1992, 1994), perhaps to make his indictment of twentieth-century technology as an underminer of literacy and even rationality more comprehensive, looked at the computer screen and concluded that, since it has a screen, which it indeed does, it is really just another form of television, via which we "amuse ourselves to death."

A list of similarities and dissimilarities between TV and computer screens may be instructive.

Here are the similarities:

1 Both screens have the refreshability that distinguishes all screens — movie, television, and computer — from other modes of presentation, such as paper.

Here are some of the most significant dissimilarities:

1 TV, with the important exception of home video recorders, is completely programmed by people other than the viewer. Computers, with the important exception of the structure imposed by underlying programs such as word processing and Web hypertext, is programmed only by the proximate user. But note that the content of word processing is supplied solely by the user, and the content of hypertext is for the most part supplied by other people similar to the user — in contrast to TV programming, almost all of which is supplied by professional TV producers, filmmakers, TV network programmers, and so forth (a very minor exception would be community-supplied programming — e.g., announcement of local events — available on some cable TV stations).

2 Each TV station broadcasts exactly the same programming to everyone. The only possibility of variety resides in different channels broadcasting at the same time, or in viewers watching video tapes (which indeed can be construed as an early mode of "personally computerized" television). At present, the maximum number of stations available is in the hundreds. In contrast, each computer screen displays the pinpoint, specifically tailored decision of each user: to word-process, and if so, what to write; to browse the Web, and if so, where; to discuss a topic, asynchronously or synchronously, in whatever online forum; etc. There are by and large as many different events "showing" on computer screens as there are personal computers (the exception would be more than one user reading the same online text at the same time – this, in effect, would be the computer simulating, on a tiny scale, the dynamics of a TV environment).

3 Television is, to a significant degree, an "incidental" medium in its condition of attendance – meaning that people can do other things when the television is on. Radio is much more incidental in this sense, but people nonetheless talk, read, eat, sleep, even make love in front of the flickering television screen. In contrast, users of computer screens are interacting with the computer – they are participants in what is happening on the screen, since they are often its very creators – rather than passive observers. They sit up, faces alert, a few inches from the screen, and constantly control what they see via keyboard or mouse, in sharp distinction to "couch potatoes" who only trouble to change the channel by remote during commercials or between programs. The most significant talking that takes place in the presence of computers is conversation through the computer and modem to another user or users, asynchronously or at the same time. The only reading that takes place when people participate in or via computers is (a) reading documentation, on or off the screen, to better use the computer, or (b) the far more prevalent activity of reading all other text on the screen. When love is made in the presence of a computer screen, it takes place, for better or worse, through the screen, again, in interaction with the human being on the other side of the online connection. McLuhan wrote at apt length (e.g., 1964, Chapter 31) about television as an "involving" medium – his point being that because all that television offers are images that in fact cannot be held, images of people unable to respond to us, TV therefore creates an enormous ache for people to reach out and connect – thus, TV is "involving" in that it creates a great need for it. Computers, in contrast, amply fulfill a lot of this need. They are involving not in the negative, not in the involvement-as-rebound as in McLuhan's description of TV, but in the directly positive sense

of people being interactively connected, absorbed, and focused in the work or play they are doing via the computer screen.

4 TV screens for the most part traffic in images and sounds, with occasional written words. Computer screens, as we have explored in detail, traffic in text, with occasional (but increasing) presences of icons, images, and sounds.

The case for the computer not being a form of television – and not subject to its critiques, be they valid or not for television – is overwhelming. But, as mentioned at the conclusion of the last chapter, the nature of computer traffic, and perhaps hence of computer discourse, is indeed changing on the fourth point above. In the next section, we look at the non-alphabetic computer environment, online and off, and probe what it might mean for the present and the future.

NEW ONLINE FACES – INTER, SMILEY, AND MORE

"Graphics" on computer screens cover a lot of territory. Icons, or stylized little pictures, that help people use their computers – an image-driven command system, in effect, for online and off-line use, usually employed in conjunction with point-and-click, Windows systems – are one kind of graphic. In addition to such hieroglyphics-as-operating-systems, images play an increasing role as content, especially on the Web and in off-line CD-ROM sources. Graphics in that context range from stick-like, two-dimensional renderings that most people associate with computer-generated imagery and art, to digitization of initially off-line photographs, and motion pictures and video with or without sound.

Use of icons for computer navigation and operation commercially arose in the 1980s with the Apple Macintosh, and its highly successful effort to carve out a way of doing things on personal computers both distinct from and wherever possible better than the IBM PC (introduced in 1982), and still flourishing then on older CP/M systems. CP/M – which early Apple computers had used a variant of prior to the Mac – used strings of letters to issue commands. Sometimes the string made a traditional, immediately comprehensible word, as in the CP/M command "erase" to erase; other times the letter strings could be complete gibberish to the neophyte or non-user, as in the CP/M command "pip" for copying and some related tasks like printing. (The command was an acronym for "peripheral inter-change program." I confess to still having a soft spot in my heart for it, since I made good use of it in my very first word-processed texts.) IBM and MS-DOS improved upon this mixed bag of instantly comprehensible and unintuitive commands by rendering all of its lettered commands in plain English words. Thus, the DOS copying command was and still is: copy.

The Macintosh alternative dispensed with letters completely, wherever possible, and called upon a combination of hieroglyphics (icons) and physio-logistics performed on the screen (point-and-click) to control the computer. Instead of typing "erase" or "delete" filename at a command prompt, the Mac user clicked on the name of the unwanted file with a mouse – a device which in effect specified the unwanted file as the object of the computer's attention, and thus rendered the file ready for any of the computer's operations – and then "dragged" or literally moved the specified filename across the computer screen to an icon of a garbage can, upon which the filename was "dropped" or deposited, which had the result of deleting the file. This system thus bypassed both the keyboard and the letters it generated in favor of a different "digital" approach – i.e., one which utilized the finger to point rather than type.

The mouse system had and has a certain non-verbal, actions-speak-louder-than-words eloquence, and its dispensing with the keyboard – at least in part, for files still had to be given lettered names in the first place – has the cachet of doing away with the keyboard as a rear-view mirror holdover from the typewriter, an instrument presumably no more *ipso facto* germane to the future of computing than the television. On the other hand, the icon's re-enlistment of the hieroglyphic for communication service far less peripheral than road-signs partakes of a rear-view mirror reaching so far back into the past for its inspiration as to seem like the Hubble, except quite the reverse of forward and outward in its outlook.

I confess to never much liking the Hubble rear-view mirror of icons in personal computing (see my "Icons and garbage cans," first published online in 1986, and reprinted in my *Electronic Chronicles*, 1992, pp. 78–79). Part of this feeling is no doubt an expression of what I call the "first love effect" – we tend to most enjoy systems which have most in common with those we took our first tentative steps upon; and for me, that was the staunchly lettered and keyboarded CP/M, and then DOS. But there are general, less personal considerations that count against icons as well. Our language – any human language – entails thousands of years of refine-ment in which meanings were assigned, expanded, narrowed, found insufficient in a word or related group of words with the result that a new word was created or drafted into use, etc. How does such a tool compare to pointing-and-clicking in operations we might want to perform on a given computer file? We might want to copy it and leave it in place, or copy it and remove the original ("move"), or just erase it without copying, or rename the file, or print the file, or send the file via e-mail to someone else. All of these operations, and many more, can be implemented simply by typing an obvious word (copy, move, erase, print, mail) at a command prompt, followed by the name of the file. Where is the advantage in having to "drag" that same filename to one or another corner or edge of a screen in order to accomplish the same thing? Moreover, the screen only has a finite amount of space for display of icons at any one time. Although a family of icons could no doubt accommodate the above small series of operations, more extended operations – say, working with a series of chapters in a book, spell-checking some of them, printing out others, e-mailing yet others – require invocation of icons residing in screens at first hidden from view. At that point, the icon becomes no more obviously at hand and thus no easier to use than typing the name of a verbal command – indeed, less so, as we spend our lives speaking and writing verbal commands outside of computers, with no commensurate investment in, and thus knowledge of, icons.

Further, although pointing-and-clicking and icons seem to go together like a horse and carriage, the former need not be wedded to the latter in order for the mouse to pull its physio-logistic weight. Online services, for example, display in their graphic interfaces the names of files to be clicked upon. This replaces verbal syntax as a command structure – point-and-click instead of typing "get" or "read" or specifying the pre-assigned number of the online text to be read – but retains the benefits of language as a label for each of the files. Indeed, in the above garbage-can example, the file to be eliminated became the mouse's object of attention when the mouse clicked upon the name of the file, not an icon. The file could then just as well have been dragged into the arms of a series of words awaiting it in on the border – erase, copy and then erase, whatever – as to the garbage can. And, again, words are more easily displayed and convey a far greater range and subtlety of meaning.

But if the disadvantages of icons can be eliminated by dissolving the marriage of mice and icons, and linking mice only to words, why use mice – or other pointing-and-clicking devices like track balls – at all? Why not retain the power of language in command as well as label, in prescription as well as description? Speaking from my own experience once more, I can see at least one significant advantage in mouse above verbal navigation as follows: pointing-and-clicking seems to call upon a somewhat different part of the cognitive apparatus in the brain, something more entwined with motor functions, than the specification of commands via words. Somehow, the non-linguistic route allows me to think about, write, read the linguistic content more quickly – click on a file, then read it or write it – than having to write the command to open the file and the name of it first, which on some level seems to push slightly ahead of, preempt for a moment, the linguistic content – the text in the file – on my cognitive queue. An analogy that comes to mind is the automobile. Driving, thinking, and conversing is no problem at all, as long as my hands and feet are doing the driving; but if I had to drive my car via verbal command – "speed up," "slow down," "turn left," and so forth – this would no doubt greatly interfere with my capacity to speak other things, and even to some extent to think of other things at the same time. In the online mouse environment, command via motor function – pointing, clicking, dragging – frees the verbal/linguistic part of the brain for immediate function.

Or so it seems to me. But this also seems a good place to point out that, in addition to personal preferences flowing from past experience (as in the "first love effect" syndrome) versus general considerations that flow from the objective nature of the communication tools (such as the far greater range and specification power of language), there is a third factor – in between the two – that plays a role in any consideration of the advantages and disadvantages of a communications medium, including different approaches within a medium. This third factor is the obvious but often overlooked fact that different people have different cognitive styles, or different ways of best processing information. Some people work best with words, as both generators and describers of ideas. It will come as no surprise, I hope, to readers of this book, nor to my many students over the years, that I am one of these people, who indeed relishes language both spoken and written. On the other hand, though I appreciate a nice piece of Impressionist and even abstract art from time to time, and love as a viewer the fluid narrative of motion pictures, I clearly have not much if any talent in the visual arts. (Our daughter, however, does, and helped design our Web page.) I would guess that people who have such talent are more congenial to icons than am I. And perhaps preference for more mixed arrangements of mice and words – rather than fully iconic or fully linguistic – similarly reflects the hard-wired cognitive ratios of the user.

In the next chapter, in which we consider the future of paper, we look more carefully at, and try to disentangle where possible, the nexus of nostalgia, cognitive style, and objective communication function that governs the comfort we have with various media.

But, for now, we can stipulate that in order for a diversity of cognitive styles to best be served, we need a diversity of media possibilities. With this desideratum in mind, we return to the issue of images on the Web – not as icons for navigation, as we have been examining above – but as still and motion photography, with and without sounds, for content. We look at what is conjured upon the hypertext screen after the clicking takes place.

THE WORLD ON DEMAND

When last we looked at television in detail, we discussed how the VCR had revolutionized TV by allowing viewers to specify exactly when they watched its programs. In short, the VCR allowed viewers to replace television's schedule with their own. If the photograph had rescued the image from its proper corruption in time, the VCR performed the far more superficial but still satisfying function of rescuing the TV program from its artificial installation at a set time in the broadcast schedule.

But the VCR, of course, can only rescue that which is already imprisoned in the TV line-up. Three factors in the past two decades have served to greatly expand the range of VCR programming beyond the recording of broadcast TV, its initially intended task in the 1970s. The combination of all three still leaves the VCR with but a fraction of the Web's reach and diversity.

The playing of home video recordings made by owners of "camcorders" or home video cameras offers an option most like the Web's in terms of giving viewers the capacity to create their own content, but is the least significant of the three VCR-extenders in accounting for actual viewing. Rental and purchase of video tapes of movies, concerts, and even old television shows burgeoned through the 1980s and into the 1990s; they are expected to generate some $17 billion in revenue in 1997, more than twice the amount anticipated for motion pictures shown in movie theaters (Dizard, 1997, p. 146). But these pictures are of course always created by people other than their audiences, and the number of options that video rental and sales afford their viewers are, for all their numbers, still few in comparison to other modes of TV watching. This is due, in large part, not only to the different programs offered day after day, week after week, on broadcast TV, but the enormous growth of the third kind of VCR-extender: cable television. This development has been of considerable import not only to the growth of television, but of media in general, and warrants a bit of further discussion.

Cable began in the 1950s as a way of getting TV to parts of the United States that were beyond the range of TV broadcasts. That state of affairs was in turn due to the underlying broadcast technology of television, which uses an FM carrier wave that broadcasts more clearly than AM (the first mode of radio broadcast), but much shorter distances. So cable constitutes another example of a remedial medium – a mode remedying the shortfall of conventional television broadcast power. But cables, which can in principle be laid down in any amounts, were also far less immediately limited in their growth potential than electro-magnetic carrier waves, which were confined to a few handfuls of stations on radio and a handful on television. As we saw, this initial scarcity of the broadcast resource led to the creation of the FCC. Cable from its outset thus differed from broadcast TV in two important ways: (a) it was physically not limited in its growth possibilities, i.e., its capacity to add new programming, and (b) it was not limited legally by the strictures of the FCC. Both of these characteristics – classic unintended consequences of a medium designed to improve the physical range of broadcasts – would work to all but unseat network broadcast television from its prime media position by the mid-1990s (down to 57 per cent of TV viewers in 1995; see Chapter 14). At the same time, as we'll discuss in more detail below, the Web and slightly before it the personal computer have slowly begun to supplant, co-opt, combine with, and otherwise transform television altogether into a different medium from the one we have known.

In the 1980s and 1990s, cable expanded its programming to as much as five to ten times that of broadcast TV. Cable offerings in America now include stations devoted twenty-four hours a day to news; all-movie channels; stations devoted entirely to re-runs of popular old programming; stations for children; comedy stations; channels devoted to science, or history, or science fiction. Just as magazines had evolved from broad-appeal media like newspapers to narrow-cast publications that cater to specialized tastes (cooking, gardening, fashions, popular mechanics, automobile culture, etc.) – and radio from all-purpose entertainment to stations that broadcast just rock (indeed, classic rock, alternative rock, etc.), country, classical, jazz – so the cabling of television turned it into a medium more able to suit personalized interests (see Gumpert, 1970, for discussion of this development in magazines and radio). Moreover, freedom from the FCC's provisions for broadcasters enabled cable to do what mainstream motion pictures had already been doing since the late 1960s, but television networks were unable or unwilling to do: show films with all manner of nudity and love-making, to wit, what most societies define as pornography. Here another characteristic of cable in contrast to broadcast TV – their respective economic bases – served to stoke the furnace: whereas broadcast TV, as we have seen, was and is dependent on advertisers, who could presumably decline to have their commercials broadcast next to content they thought objectionable, some cable TV stations show no commercials, and instead make their money completely from viewer subscriptions. Thus, HBO, Showtime, and Cinemax in the US are all supported via viewers, not advertisers, and make these viewers happy by presenting "R"-rated movies ("restricted" – because of sex, violence, nudity, language, or some combination) as a major part of their programming. (Such stations usually come into homes via a "scrambled" signal that parents can keep scrambled at any given time, if they like, and thus out of the reach of children – another reason that the V-chip is unnecessary.)

Everything on cable is of course available for VCR recording and playback. Thus, the one-two punch of video rental and cable has expanded the range of the VCR far beyond the precincts of broadcast TV. And these options are themselves expanding almost daily, as video rental "superstores" spring up across America, and cable adds new stations, some showing movies that have just finished their theatrical showings, for an additional fee (see Dizard, 1997, pp. 158–159).

And yet: this plethora of programming still fails to give people the information they want, when they want it. With all the viewer-option riches of TV plus VCR plus video rental plus cable, the result is still poor in choices in comparison to point-and-click choosing of effectively endless possibilities on the hypertext Web.

In the weeks after the tragic explosion of flight TWA 800 in July 1996, I was eager for any news as to what caused the plane to go down. Occasionally, I would see extended reports, usually on one of the cable news stations, that would provide some partial explanations. More often, I would hear and see "news bites," of a minute or two, on various newscasts. Some provided intriguing hints as to progress being made in the investigations – a few quick words about possible new evidence or a new hypothesis about what had happened on that terrible evening in New York. I'd search the other channels for more. Usually I'd find nothing, except maybe a repeat of the same small news report I had seen in the first place. I wanted more. Sometimes, I'd log on to the Web, and find more detailed reports of these stories. But even these were little more than what I'd be able to read in *The New York Times* the very next day. For the hypertext Web, as we have emphasized here many times, is still predominantly made of print.

But what of the advent of pictures, sounds, and even motion pictures on the Web? In the abstract, these might indeed seem like a threat to the resurgence of text – its electronic resurgence in an electronic age otherwise carrying sounds and images everywhere on its buoyant shoulders. In practice, however: I very much would have liked to have seen full audio-video coverage on the Web of the new evidence and FBI hunches and briefings regarding TWA 800 that I caught such brief, tantalizing reports of on cable television. I would have appreciated being able to access such Web reports anytime I wanted – as is the way of the Web. And, put in such real rather than abstract media-theory terms, I cannot see how access to such full audio-visual reports – full in terms of its pictures and images, qualities it shares with TV, but full also in terms of its availability all the time, and its capacity to be linked to other relevant stories, a myriad of other relevant stories, in principle – could in any way hurt the new literacy on the Web.

In fact, a new cable network – MSNBC, a joint venture of Microsoft (the Windows corporation) and NBC (the oldest broadcast network) – began its operation the very week of the TWA calamity. It, like CNN, has a significant Web presence, with Web pages for further reference advertised after many stories. Thus far its Web content has still been little more than the equivalent of newspaper stories and replays of audio-visual clips. But it points to a hybrid of television and the Web, a convergence of the two media that offers much more than either does now. Indeed, in December 1996, web-browsing devices designed to work with TVs (with phone connections) – to connect to the Web, to click, write, and read on it via mouse, keyboard, and TV screen – were offered for sale across America. Initial reports by its users posted on various Internet discussion groups give this new embodiment of Web–TV convergence high marks.

There is no doubt that media compete with one another for the very finite amount of time and attention we can give them. But just as the addition of a new medium to an information environment is, as we have seen, transformative not additive (blue dye plus water makes blue water), so too is the subtraction of time profoundly transformative not just simply reductive in our lives. What this means for any subtraction of time we might otherwise spend reading when we look at video clips on the Web is that it may well result in a net *increase* in reading – a net gain for text after we see pictures on the Web because, by very virtue of being on the Web, we have instant access to more text to satisfy our curiosity piqued by pictures, more text than we can possibly encounter except in the biggest libraries, and even then, far less efficiently.

Indeed, contra the decades of criticism of television as a detractor from reading (see Schreiber, 1953, for an early hue and cry), the evidence shows books being a bigger business than ever before (see statistics in Chapter 10; see also Chapter 7). The game of information and media competition for human subscription seems clearly win/win – as long as each of the players, as we saw with radio, has a legitimate stake in the human ecology of communication.

I would predict, then, that the growth of images on the Web – the conclusion of this century with yet another show on the screen – will serve, like motion pictures and TV before it, and contrary to the scholarly attacks on those media that turned out groundless, to greatly increase the habit of literacy. Indeed, I suspect this increase will be comparable to that engendered by the printing press and the electric light in their own different ways. A rising informational tide, as we have seen so often in this volume, indeed lifts all books.

But this moves us from the realm of explanation to the far more tenuous one of prediction. Indeed, beginning with our consideration of word processing, we have been entering the waters of prediction for longer and longer dips. Much that pertains to computers and especially their online functions is yet in its infancies of application.

In the next and ensuing chapters, we take that plunge completely, and look at the media futures of paper, intellectual property, artificial intelligence, and – to return to the beginnings of media, literally – at us, and what aspects of human communication and information processing are likely to survive and transcend the foreseeable evolution of media. We begin first with paper, and an assessment of our attachments to it.

1 6

PAPER FUTURES

When I was growing up in the 1950s, nearly everyone had an old uncle, an odd friend, maybe even a parent, who lovingly clung to a fountain pen in that clean new age of the ball-point. Perhaps the signature of the fountain pen had more personality than the ball-point's output, but the flow of the fountain was in just about every other way less reliable and efficient. It required constant refilling from bottles or cartridges that were always in some real danger of tipping over or breaking open; its inscriptions, even though advertised as "quick-drying," always threatened to smear on a humid day. Its devotees freely acknowledged these and other drawbacks, such as its greater expense, but such logic was no match for an attachment not so much to a cherished specific instrument as to a mode of written expression.

We have seen similar attachments to outmoded media in the past few decades: the writer who, with real or figurative cigarette dangling from a corner of the mouth, pounds obsessively away on an Underwood manual typewriter; the hardy few who, incredibly, still use carbon paper rather than xerox for their copies; the academic department that relies on the sweet-smelling purple mimeograph rather than plain-paper photocopies (my course outlines were mimeographed by the Communications Department at Hofstra University in Hempstead, New York, as recently as the fall of 1994).

Is paper itself now becoming such an outmoded medium?

Is the increasing facility of words on screens that we have seen in the past five chapters the equivalent of ball-point pens, computers, Xerox machines for a stubborn, romantic band who will cling to paper along with their fountain pens, typewriters, and carbons?

To address this question, we need to consult again the lesson of radio's success in an age of television, and the eradication of silent movies by talkies – the lesson that media survive by attaining a niche of consonance with some fundamental process of human communication, a process that they perform better than their competition, as discussed in Chapter 9. But the niche for paper is complex and multiple, not one niche but many, because paper conveys so much of what we do. It serves in single sheets for note-taking by hand, and letter-writing by hand, typewriter, or computer printout. It serves in groups of sheets for documents – as in school reports and scholarly papers – and of course in sheets bound together in one way or another to form newspapers, magazines, and books, hardcover and paperback, by a variety of printing and production methods which, like desktop publishing, now enlist the aid of digital technology in one or more parts of the process.

Indeed, so ubiquitous is paper to recording and communication of our thoughts, that it is obviously essential to ball-point and photocopying technologies, two of the successful new twentieth-century media instanced above. The computer as word-processor also relies on paper for its printouts, though it also provides a non-paper option for output. The investigation of that option, more precisely what it bodes for the future of paper, is the subject of this chapter. But it entails a consideration of paper *media* – not as the word is often misused to mean a single medium (as in, "the media of television"), but as the very much more than one medium that paper is in its many applications. We might well conclude, for example, that the likelihood of the survival of paper in books is less than that of paper in note-taking.

One strategy for approaching this problem is to look for analogies in other media appropriate to paper's different roles. Radio, motion pictures, and television are, like books and newspapers, mass media, and thus their life-stories seem pertinent to the question of paper's survival as a mass medium. But what about paper as a very personal, individual medium? Here we might find better testimony in a device more literally at hand. The analog watch, for example, has apparently well survived the onslaught of sleeker, digital models. Is this just more nostalgia? I would say not: the moving hands on a clock face provide a sense of past and future, of context, very basic to the human psyche's narration (see, again, Marshack, 1972) and absent in digital read-outs. So, as a one-on-one medium, we might ask if paper is more like the fountain pen or the analog watch in its survival potential. Is its strongest suit nostalgia, with a longevity not likely to far exceed the people who grew up with it, or attainment of a far more profound and enduring human ecological niche?

At the same time, we can look at certain characteristics of paper common to all of its uses – words are inextricably wed to its pages, except in the marginal case of pencil; paper is subject to physical deterioration, both immediately via tearing and over time via yellowing; etc. We can then ask whether these common properties of paper make it more or less fit to compete with screen writing-and-reading in its sundry tasks. We can ask, in other words, if paper in its many roles and common denominators is a better servant of words, and therein of deep human communicative needs, than computer screens. It will survive only to the extent that the answer is yes in any area.

We begin with the fax, which posted an impressive early victory for paper in the digital age.

DRAWING CONCLUSIONS FROM THE FAX

There is a style of narrative, of which a natural history (and future) is certainly a constituent, that attains much effect by presenting its conclusion at the beginning. We see the dead body, as it were, perhaps even the murderer, and then in the rest of the story find out just how that came to be. In that spirit, I offer the following about the fax: if the province of paper were the Roman Empire, then fax could well be regarded as its Justinian – surmounting many of its shortcomings, recapturing some of its former glories and giving courage to its most devoted adherents, yet fated to fall in the end to the exigencies of a more modern age.

Among the many drawbacks intrinsic to all paper prior to the fax – words fixed to pages, perishability, as mentioned above – the most immediately frustrating, I would say, was the reliance of paper on physical transport for consummation of communication, and the inevitable delay entailed. I certainly felt and still feel that way – and not just about errors in the transport, such as mail taking much longer to be delivered than expected, although such episodes are of course annoying too. But there is something intrinsically excruciating in the very proposition that words, and the quickness of thought they convey, be hostage for any length of time to muscle power, motor transport, even air travel. All seem so slow to the task of carrying our ideas and emotions to our intended audiences, be they the receivers of our personal or business correspondence, or, in the case of professional authors, of their essays, articles, stories, and books. Of course, professional authors suffer other kinds of delay – such as editorial gatekeeping – but physical transport nonetheless lurks as a frequent source of frustration at the end of this queue also, and afflicts not only authors but readers, as in students awaiting the arrival of their required texts at the college bookstore.

The telegraph, as we have seen, demonstrated more than one hundred and fifty years ago the advantages of instant communication of text. But its venue was the short, clipped missive, and anything the length of a book, usually even a long letter, going great distances was obliged to travel at the speed not of light but of airmail well into the early 1980s. By that time, the parents of today's Internet – Bitnet, Usenet, and the like – were already in various phases of operation. Commercial online services like CompuServe and The Source were also up and running. A few people had already tasted the power of e-mail (see Quarterman, 1990, for online network history; Townsend, 1984, for e-mail). But to use e-mail, one had to learn both word processing and telecommunication, and the series of arbitrary commands required for such tasks was more than most secretaries were willing to learn and most bosses apt to insist upon. So the business world, in those early digital days, for the most part settled for word processing – the results of which were printed out on paper, and mailed by air or other suitable physical modes of transport. Net gain in speed of communication: zero.

Then into the breach came the fax.

Lengthy documents, short of books, could now be communicated in their entirety in minutes; even a book-length manuscript could be sent by the fastest fax machines in an hour. The results of word processing – or, for that matter, hand-writing or manual or electric typing – could now be on the other side of the world as quickly as a telephone call. And there was really nothing complicated to learn.

I remember thinking sometime in 1988 that our organization – Connected Education – would soon have to purchase a fax machine. More and more people were asking for our fax number, or if we could fax whatever document (usually a list of our online courses) to them; and reliance on our local fax outlet, a camera store, was being stretched beyond convenience. We purchased a fax machine in 1989. By the end of that year, certainly by the next, there was no one we were doing business with who lacked a fax. By 1992, I decided as Editor-in-Chief of the *Journal of Social and Evolutionary Systems* that page proofs would be provided to authors only by fax. And soon there were few correspondents of any sort without fax capabilities. As Dizard (1997, p. 53) remarks, "the fax machine has been consumerized. It is the fastest-growing service in the new telemedia environment."

Thus, fax in the 1990s is nearly as universal in business and academia as paper itself, and increasing in personal use as well. But e-mail's use has grown too, borne on the surge of some 50 million Web denizens, each of whose Internet providers – the local or central (such as CompuServe) system via which people connect to the Web – provides an e-mail option. Part of e-mail's new appeal is that it now utilizes the same easy point-and-click technology as the Web; part of e-mail's new appeal is the advantage it always has had as a comprehensively digital process. Its messages remain digital at all stages, in creation via word processing, in transmission via modem, in receipt on the destination's screen. In contrast, the fax's intended destiny is an analogic piece of paper. It may be word-processed or digitally scanned from a document, transmitted via digital media, and even received at first on a computer screen (as in computers with fax/modems). But its *raison d'être* nonetheless remains subtly but significantly different from that of e-mail – to transmit not just information, but literal copies. Its very name – facsimile – announces what fax is about: "exact copy," "duplicate," *The American Heritage Dictionary* (1991, p. 484) says, from the Latin "*fac simile*, make similar."

Literal copying of course has its benefits, notably in situations such as legally binding signatures, where authenticity not only of information (name) but rendition (what the signature of the name looks like) is crucial. But the price we pay for such authentication of rendition is a clumsiness in the communication of the information. Digital communication, precisely because the units of information look nothing like what is being communicated about, is far more flexible and effective – as we saw with the "digital," atomistic alphabet versus analogic hiero-glyphics, and with DNA, the communication system of life. The recipe for my grandmother's apple strudel can be communicated much further than facsimiles, re-renditions, of her pastry. Recipes can be carried in the head, on tiny pieces of paper, in books, on radio, via telephone, speech, and indeed any kind of medium. In contrast, a literal, analogic copy would entail a new baking of the cake itself – the results of which would of course not travel very well, nor likely last beyond the watering mouths in its immediate vicinity. (A faxed or otherwise communicated photograph of the cake would convey neither information about how to make it, nor its taste – it would thus in this case not really be a literal copy of the original, or at best it would be a literal copy only of a generally inconsequential character-istic of the original, the physical appearancce of a cake.)

The paper resolutions of fax no doubt have more endurance than any piece of apple strudel, but they partake of similar shortcomings in communication, in comparison to texts that remain digital. The fixation of words on a faxed page causes them to drop out of their electronic transmission stream like fish turning into pebbles. Such titration of text pulls it off-line, out of Socratic play, a party neither to the burgeoning interactive commentary going on worldwide on Usenet lists and commercial online meeting halls, nor the automated hypertext links of the Web that provide answers to questions that the author of the originating text never dreamed of. Instead, words printed on fax serve as trophies of events wrested from the scene of the action, snapshots to be filed in pendaflex folders, mementos of an intellectual engagement once removed.

Assessed, then, in terms of extension across space and time, dissemination and preservation, that we have seen performed either one or the other, or in some combination, in all media, fax seems to have an advantage over e-mail and online text only on a narrow "authentication" segment of the preserving end. It is similarly less useful than digital text in each Darwinian stage in the growth of knowledge discussed by Campbell (e.g., 1974b) – generation of ideas, criticism and selection, dissemination and preservation – with the partial exception, again, of preservation. The thinness of this ecological niche suggests that the fax for all its current success may be a transitional medium, like hand-tinted photographs and Méliès' artificially arranged scenes, a sheet with one edge in the digital world, on its way to an online environment in which paper for business and personal correspondence will be dispensed with almost altogether.

But what about the many other functions of paper? It once of course covered better than any other medium all of the above extensions and stages, certainly in the period between the employment of the printing press in the fifteenth century, as we saw in Chapter 3, and the emergence of alternatives to paper communication in telephone, phonograph, motion photography, radio, and television at the end of the nineteenth and into the twentieth century. Indeed, with the exception of the phonograph and motion pictures, none of paper's rivals allowed for retrievability until telephone answering machines and VCRs in the second half of our century. Their forté rather was, and is, in dissemination, and paper continues to service the human need for preservation and retrieval of most kinds of information far better than these media.

It thus should be no surprise that the still prevailing advantage of paper in general over electronic text, although under attack, resides in its preservational convenience. As a cauldron for the emergence of ideas – for their debate, critique, hammering out, and selection – the worldwide online environment has no equal. For their consultation and pondering, for their most comfortable retrieval, we reach for the newspaper, journal, or book. Indeed, I am writing this text as a book, not of course to preclude its online publication, but to insure that the ideas herein have that level of convenient durability.

The Roman Empire may have collapsed as an ongoing, total system, but significant grains of its culture animate our affairs to this day. In the next two sections, we consider two such potentially enduring grains for paper.

PAPER AS A FRAMABLE CERTIFICATE OF EXPERIENCE

"'Proof' of sanity," McLuhan wrote, "is available only to those discharged from mental institutions" (McLuhan and Nevitt, 1972, p. 8). Yet all of us want it. Or, to take a less extreme case, consider our craving for diplomas as proof that we can hang on a wall regarding our completion of an education. Having gone through a course of study, we are demonstrably different people. Any conversation or written exchange would usually show this. And we obviously know that we have participated in a learning process, and are aware of it amply in our daily thoughts. Yet none of this is enough. We want certification – not only to others, for whom certification can be demonstrated via transmission of a transcript – but for ourselves.

Certainly paper is a very convenient vehicle for satisfying such certifiable needs. And if satisfaction of such needs, clearly superfluous to the growth of knowledge described above, were the sum of paper's preservational import, then we could easily imagine a world without paper – a world in which we accepted sanity, education, and like conditions without cut-and-dried authentication, or as authenticated via action rather than certification.

But preservation runs far deeper in human relationships and organization of information. Indeed, the ephemerality of speech, its disappearance from the perceived world the very instant it is spoken, was no doubt the stimulus that led to the invention and development of writing in the first place. The price we paid for its preservation, as we saw, was its unresponsiveness and non-connectivity – its capacity to give but "one unvarying answer" lamented by Socrates – but the benefit it bestowed was civilization itself, including science, law, and democracy. Electronic text renders writing "intelligent," as we also have seen, retrieving the interactive capacities of speech, and adding some, such as hypertext, that it never had. But does electronic text improve upon, or even equal, the fundamental preservational capacity of words on a page that was and is its primary occasion for existence?

The very fixation of text on a page that removes it like a filtration from electronic currents swirling at the speed of light enhances its function as a vehicle of authentication, in which stability, not flexibility, is key, and indeed in which malleability works against the goal. One of the great advantages of word-processed text is its facility for revision. For obvious reasons, such facility makes word-processed text a not very reliable document, until it has been printed upon paper.

Our common-sense insecurity about the authenticity of words on a screen finds legal expression in problems currently encountered in EDI, or electronic data interchange, in which the transmission of purchase orders, bills of lading, contracts, and other paper documents that form the lifeblood of commerce is conducted electronically, via personal computers. On the one hand, as attorney Benjamin Wright (1989, p. xiii) points out, "paper shuffling is cumbersome and expensive"; on the other hand, "EDI is evolving so rapidly that there are no well-tested models for handling legal issues" (p. xxi). Wright is confident that

EDI is inherently capable of achieving the legal goals that paper communication achieves . . . EDI messages can be written, authenticated, proven delivered, secured from corruption and stored as evidence, all to a degree comparable to what paper-based communication achieves.

(p. 1)

But the complicated procedures he enumerates and discusses in the balance of his book – e.g., "schemes agreed between partners for secret codes (such as personal identification numbers) to be built into messages" (p. 5) – suggest that the replacement of paper by digital media in the legal/commercial realm is not likely to be imminent.

This is not to say that such a replacement will never occur. But unlike the obvious clear-cut advantages of hypertext over indices and bibliographies on paper, or the instant communication of a text to thousands of widely dispersed people in comparison to the fastest modes of physical-paper transport, the benefits of digital text for legally binding documents are neither entire nor clear-cut. Thus, paper may have some lease on life as a medium of documentation and authentication – not only as a bearer of legal arrangements, but in a wide array of human activities encompassing everything from money to diplomas, where the superior (if still fallible) proof paper provides against forgery of information seems well worth the inconvenience, for most people.

The pressure against this lease indeed comes, again, from the greater convenience of digital communication. As indicated above, the physical difference between paper and electricity – in particular, the fact that the latter travels at the speed of light – means that most things on paper will be less at hand than most things online. We might not trust electronic text – for good reason, or because of simple nostalgia, or whatever – but we cannot doubt that, for anyone who can afford the cost of a second-hand computer, it is more convenient than paper.

But is it always more convenient, in all cases?

We turn now to a consideration of the enduring convenience of that oldest mode of paper expression: the book.

BOOKS, NEWSPAPERS, AND THE SPINNING CALCULUS OF CONVENIENCE

Stated as basically as possible, the central principle governing media survival runs as follows: an information technology will survive to the extent that it satisfies human needs better than its rivals. But at least two factors, as we have seen, complicate the operation. First, the ongoing evolution of new media, usually with profound unintended consequences, means that the rivals of any given medium are often in flux. Second, a given medium usually performs a variety of tasks, with the result that it may well best its rivals in one area, and fail against the same or a different set of rivals in another area. Radio thrives in an age of television because it no longer performs at the center of attention in the evening living room – where it was easily surpassed by television – and instead plays to our inherent capacity to hear and do something else. Books and newspapers, as we saw above and throughout this volume, were for hundreds of years better than their competitors at not only preserving but spreading information, until electronic media in the twentieth century successively dulled their disseminative edge.

How vulnerable are these venerable print media now as vehicles of retrieval?

The following two-part example – of online versus in-person education, and online versus bound printed books – shows that books, at least at present, might yet have a niche.

How does online education – conducted via personal computers and modems, as discussed in Chapter 12 – compare to its competition of in-person education? Any in-person environment, including the classroom, comes replete with thousands of years of subtle and not-so-subtle advantages and drawbacks. Clearly, getting a full sensory repertoire of one's teacher and colleague students is a big plus; equally clearly, having to be in a given physical place at an appointed time every day or week can be a disadvantage, especially for students with special needs, ranging from working adults, to people with physical disabilities, to people who live far away from the classroom. Online education has likely survived, and will likely continue, because going to one's computer, whether on a desk or on one's lap, is almost always more convenient than going to a physical classroom. Other advantages of online education include the permanent record of all discussions, the capacity to take part in the class any time day or night, etc. But the key reason for its success no doubt resides in the fact that its convenience outweighs the disadvantages of online students and faculty not being in close physical proximity (see Chapter 19, as well as Levinson, 1995 and 1997b; for some shy people, of course, not being in physical proximity may also be an advantage).

Now let's look at the relative advantages of online versus off-line books. I noticed early on in Connected Education that students who repeatedly took online courses, and thereby demonstrated their preference at least in that regard for online versus in-person education, eagerly read papers and other postings that were exclusively online, but when given the choice of reading a book-length text that was both online and off-line in traditional book form, they would almost always choose the book. Indeed, since the paperback publication in 1992 of my *Electronic Chronicles*, more than 90 per cent of students in my courses in which that text is required have opted to purchase the book for $14.95, even though the exact text has been available in its entirety, for free, online.

The reason is not difficult to fathom. Picking up a book is easier, almost all of the time, than turning on a computer: the book can be in any room, requires neither batteries nor wire connections, can be easily taken out of the house, and so forth. The fact that its words are wedded to its pages is undoubtedly a drawback, but not strong enough to outweigh its literally palpable advantages. Thus, although electronic stand-alone books (in contrast to texts on the Web, which with hypertext connections are something very different) are beginning to generate public interest via disk-book publishers such as Voyager, we can well understand Dizard's (1997, p. 187) report that "many industry observers still doubt whether there is a significant market for computer-based books in the near future, beyond reference works and other professional publications."

So books seem secure at present, at least as textbooks in university courses, and likely fiction as well, more apt than even textbooks to be read on the beach. But the last part of Dizard's observation suggests that the calculus may break otherwise in different specific cases. An encyclopedia on a CD-ROM is almost always more convenient than a dozen or more books as a unit, which are more difficult to lug out of the house or from room to room than most computers. And a CD-ROM usually is laced with hypertext internal links, and the possibility of external links, which makes it into a tool that no book can touch, a device that is really like no traditional book at all — or as much like a book as a book is like speech.

Newspapers present yet a different situation. Since speed is presumably of the essence in delivery of news, we might expect the online newspaper to easily exceed the sometimes soggy mess of print delivered on our doorstep only in the morning. But since television and radio already satisfy our need for instantaneous news, the paper newspaper turns out to serve another purpose: a more leisurely reflection of events, served further by the still successful weekly newsmagazines, such as *Time* and *Newsweek*. The result is that the print newspaper may have found a niche that the online newspaper does not really attempt to serve. It seems likely to survive, at least for now (Dizard, 1997, p. 174, advises that, for print newspapers, at present, "the business remains basically healthy").

But what about the long range?

As we have already seen (Chapter 7), the emergence of the paperback in this century made the book much easier to obtain and carry, and no doubt has been responsible for the book's more than holding its own in an age of motion pictures, radio, and television. Similarly, convenient photocopying, desktop publishing, and fax have greatly strengthened paper's hand in the past half century. Print on paper has thus done well at least in part because it has continued to evolve. Can it be expected to in the future – and at the pace of its digital rivals?

A device weighing less than a pound, charged on tiny batteries that last for years, able to pull in any book off the Net via telecom connections that operate over the airways rather than through phone wires, would be a formidable competitor of the book indeed. It is all but here – though, if we bear in mind the decades that videophone has waited as the unrequited heir-apparent of telephone, almost here and here can be two very different states.

Nonetheless: books as a medium of convenient reading, much like paper as a vehicle of easy authentication, have a deep vulnerability in their competition with digital media. The older media enjoy an advantage based largely on the digital media's being in an early phase of development, not on characteristics and limitations fundamentally intrinsic to the digital media. In other words, although books online are less easy to read and paper documents online less easy to authenticate than their off-line analogs, there is nothing inherent in the online forms to prevent their eventually reversing the tables and becoming more easy to read and authenticate than their paper forebears (see Chapter 10 for discussion of what I call the "Ellulian error," or judging the butterfly of a medium by its caterpillar). In contrast, consider, yet again, the survival of radio in an age of television: radio thrives because it plays to the fundamental human perception of hearing without seeing, eavesdropping on the world. No conceivable development in the evolution of television, short of its deliberately eschewing pictures and becoming radio again, could make it better able to do radio's job of providing accompaniment while one's eyes are elsewhere. Radio is thus effectively invulnerable to co-option by television in radio's niche as a multi-tasking, background medium.

Still photography is not quite as secure: we can imagine a motion picture process that provided still shots of personal events for home viewing, and indeed camcorders with freeze-frames are already beginning to do so. Ultimately, the convenience of paper snapshot photography may give way to the same featherweight universal screens that may undermine the book. (Still photography has lasted so long, maintaining an almost unique hold on its ecological niche, because the motion picture process – in contrast to videotaping, and now video in conjunction with computers – was never able to easily provide the home motion-photographer with still shots or freeze-frames.)

But precisely because these are yet very early days in the evolution of digital media, projections of the future are tenuous, especially timetables. Photocopying and faxing, as we have seen, are still very much in the ascendancy. The advent of computer desktop publishing is everywhere making printing easier and more efficient – including in China, where 20,000 different ideograms can now at last be rapidly typeset via computer (Jones, 1987). If paper is a medium of the past through which we look at the future, it is a rear-view mirror as wide as the sky. We will be a long time yet under it.

But when we do move more fully beyond paper, we will take with us that which we most prized in it, that which always was and remains its reason for being: text. There are, after all, many things in our society made from wood, paper, and its derivatives. A book or newspaper is differentiated from a toothpick or a piece of tissue paper by the words on its pages. And these words, as we have amply seen, are as much the lifeblood of electronic as printed text. Thus, although the book is already being transformed online – and the dislocations set off by such trans-formations are of profound importance – there is no doubt that the book – that which makes a book a book, a newspaper a newspaper – will live on in the digital, online environment, and in many respects live better.

BUT WHO WILL OWN WHAT USED TO BE ON PAPER?

Among the many dislocations engendered by the shift of text from paper to screen is the apparent disruption of intellectual property. Prior to the advent of print on paper, words and ideas had an economic fluidity commensurate with their fleeting situation in minds and speech. Their fixation in mass-produced paper allowed these expressions to be treated as property – possessable, saleable, rentable, exploitable in various private and public interests, just like land – for to possess the physical piece of paper was to have some (usually non-exclusive) claim to the words upon it. Written words freed from paper – available, technically, to anyone and everyone, anywhere and everywhere in the world, in a matter of seconds or minutes – seem unamenable to such economic claims. The obvious conclusion, in fact being proffered by many observers, is that copyright can no longer work as it has until now, and is indeed dead.

In the next chapter, we pursue the un-obvious proposition that, although the nature and application of copyright and other markers of intellectual property are no doubt in a state of change, they are far from dead, are still very much needed, and indeed can be serviced as never before by some of the very properties of electronic text and digital technology.

17

ELECTRONIC WATERMARKS

A high profile for intellectual property in the digital age

Intellectual property was never easy. Unlike property you can walk upon or hold in your hand, information has no physical existence other than in its material containers or embodiments. And although purchase of a material container of information can be straightforward, the impact of that economic transaction on the information within is usually quite the opposite. The price you pay for the purchase of a book or CD or computer disk entitles you only to use the information — you have in effect paid to rent that information for as long as you like — and not to sell it to someone else, as you might with a piece of land or a car or even a suit of clothes. This is because you do not own the information — only its container.

In some cases, such as books, you can indeed sell the information along with its container. This is because the information in a book is fixed to its pages — software is wedded to hardware — which means the seller usually has no access to the information after the book is sold. Thus the book is almost as straightforward to re-sell as the car. In other cases, such as computer disks, information can be easily detached and copied from the container. Here you could have the benefit of continuing access to the information, as well as the remuneration of re-selling it. And since the customs and laws of most societies frown on people having their cake and eating it, re-selling these types of information packages is generally not permitted. Computer software, both because of, and despite, its easy detachability from its initial container, is usually intended to be used by the first purchaser only.

The above brings home one of the underlying lessons of this entire volume: although new information technologies can complicate the relations of human beings to each other and the external world, the new technologies rarely, if ever, create such problems in the first place. Rather, the problems arise from characteristics of human beings and the external world that existed prior to the introduction of any given device. And although technology, as we have seen, inevitably shapes and even re-makes its makers — so that the relation of human being to external world to technology is mutually catalytic — the egg of the human being in physical reality clearly came first in this hypercycle.

In the case of intellectual property, the radical differences between information and physical objects generated a whole nexus of problems centuries before the first personal computer was ever produced. Can an idea ever be really owned? The laws of the United States say: yes, if the idea is embodied in a material object (you can patent your idea for a better mousetrap if you have in fact constructed one); no, if the idea is merely written or communicated about (you can copyright the explicit words on a page, but not the ideas described in those words). Does the creator of an idea have any inalienable rights to the idea, *after* he or she has explicitly sold it to another party? France insists on inalienable "moral" rights: Leonardo might have sold the *Mona Lisa* to me, but he can haul me into court and likely win if I dare paint a moustache on her.

Today, the rendering of words, images, and sounds into digital format has quickened their dissemination, blurred author and publisher and reader distinctions to the point that fine differentiations between patent and copyright, between economic and moral rights of the creator, seem more difficult to comprehend, let alone enforce, than ever.

One popular response to this complication has been to propose that we do away with intellectual property altogether. Information never fitted comfortably into the notion of property anyway; since it's really out of the bag digitally, why not let it follow its natural inclination, and let it go its way? As Stewart Brand has observed (Barlow, 1994, p. 89): information wants to be free. Giving it such freedom, Brand and Barlow contend, will result in more and better information.

I will argue to the contrary that (a) dissolution of intellectual property rights will result in a reduction of worthwhile information, and (b) new information technology contains within it modes of greatly strengthening the notion and enforcement of intellectual property. Indeed, in this chapter, I go beyond the description, analysis, criticism, and prediction that comprises this book to advocate the development of a specific new technology to work on behalf of intellectual property.

But to lay the groundwork for such a proposal, we first must consider in further detail the various economic, legal, and moral concepts of intellectual property now and in history; the electronic complication of intellectual property; the main responses to that complication; and in what ways those responses are seriously lacking.

A SHORT HISTORY OF INTELLECTUAL PROPERTY – ITS ORIGINS, MANIFESTATIONS, AND DIFFICULTIES

McLuhan (1967, p. 122) notes that the notion of copyright was a consequence of the printing press. The right, literally, to copy an intellectual work became significant only when copying became easy and automatic – when the press replaced the human hand as the vehicle of copying. The advent of machine over muscle thus brought to the fore, ironically, the notion that property could pertain to something manifestly non-physical. On the other hand, inasmuch as intellectual property is an abstraction or extension of physical property, its championship by the machine, itself an extension of muscle, makes perfect sense.

Once unleashed by the press, intellectual property took on a momentum, an intensity of protection, all its own. The theft of one author's work by another is called plagiarism – from the Latin, *plagiarius*, a kidnapper – used in jest in the first century AD by comic poet Marcus Valerius Martialis to refer to a literary thief, but no laughing matter since the Renaissance. Indeed, theft of physical property carries no such opprobrium, no implication that the crime partakes of any of the heinousness of the kidnapping of one's life's blood, one's ideas, one's words, one's child.

Physical property, to be sure – property *per se* – has an antiquity that clearly predates humanity. Rodents urinate to mark their territory, some smear glandular secretions to tag clumps of grass and stones as their own, and indeed the defense of "mine," be it territory, members of a family, the physical self, is fundamental throughout all forms of life. Thus, ethologist Eibl-Eibesfeldt (1970, p. 311) quotes F. Goethe that "scent marks are chemical property signs," and disputes Rousseau's observation that the builder of the first fence founded civilization. Rather, fences, modes of demarcating possession, seem to be everywhere there is life.

But if civilization did not invent the enforcement of property, it certainly has attempted to codify it, and eventually sought to extend such codification to products of the intellect. Benjamin Kaplan (1966) offers an excellent summary of the genesis of copyright and notions of intellectual property in the modern age. As we saw in Chapter 3, monarchs both benefited from and feared the disseminative powers of new printing presses in Europe, and strove to bring them under control. A Royal Printer commenced operations in England in 1485, just nine years after William Caxton's first press in Westminster, and printing in the following century was regulated by a series of royal grants authorizing the exclusive publication of specified books. Such early "copy-rights" were thus a kind of censorship – designed to protect neither author nor publisher but monarch – a circumstance of birth not lost on Thomas Jefferson, as we'll see below. Furthermore, since the majority of early publications were reprints of classic texts by original creators long dead, the author had little to do with copyright at this stage in any case: it was a relation primarily between monarch and publisher. Copyright, in other words, was a creature not of the creation but the dissemination of text, and this continued well after publishers had gained significant autonomy from the central government. Indeed, authors had to wait until 1710 for the first legal protection of their rights in England, in the Statute of Anne and its vestment of copyright with authors of new books for a period of fourteen years (further clarified by the House of Lords in 1774; see Tedford, 1997, pp. 326–327).

In the newly formed United States, Article 1, section 8, clause 8 of the Constitution gave Congress the power to secure "for limited times to Authors and Inventors the exclusive rights to their respective writings and discoveries" – a power actualized in the Copyright Act of 1790, much like the Statute of Anne. Washington signed the Act into law, but Jefferson was less than sanguine. He was an opponent of both strong central government and property. He had changed "the enjoyment of life and liberty, with the means of acquiring and possessing property, and pursuing and obtaining happiness and safety" in George Mason's draft of the Virginia Declaration of Rights, to "life, liberty, and the pursuit of happiness" in the Declaration of Independence (see Cunningham, 1987, pp. 48–49). He regarded censorship as the worst evil and opposed it in every form, and thus unsurprisingly held that "ideas should be freely spread from one to another over the globe . . . inventions then cannot, in nature, be a subject of property" (quoted in Barlow, 1994, p. 85; see also Cunningham, 1987, p. 58, for more on Jefferson's advocacy of "more general diffusion of knowledge").

The crux of Jefferson's view is that human betterment can be most served by a maximum dissemination of information and ideas (a view which all parties to the current debates about intellectual property in the digital age vigorously share), and the protection of authors' and inventors' rights, certainly by government, gets in the way of such dissemination (this is the issue I will dispute below). Jefferson's election to the Presidency in 1800 thus put into the highest American executive office someone with the most profound reservations about the role of government in enforcement of copyright. No wonder, then, that the subsequent two hundred years have been marked by persistent ambivalence, sometimes bordering on outright confusion, in the meaning and administration of copyright. Text can be copyright, but not titles. A song's copyright holder can control who makes the first recording of a song; thereafter anyone can make a recording, as long as the copyright holder is compensated. Professors can distribute small parts of photocopied text in a classroom (under "Fair Use" doctrines), but placement of these in a binder with other photocopied texts may be illegal (Jay Rosen and eight other New York University faculty were sued over this practice by a consortium of eight publishers in 1982; the case was settled out of court to the publishers' satisfaction; see Margolick, 1983). The net result has been that promulgation of authorship – the public identification of "author" as the paramount factor responsible for text – has gone far beyond the promulgation of income to authors.

Meanwhile, the Industrial Revolution, and its mass production of ideas that could be remunerable if embodied in material form, has created an opposite type of problem: patents abound for just about every device we use; names are on file of the inventors and their assigns; they are usually compensated; but in most cases almost no one knows their names. Do you know who invented the rear-view mirror in your car? Whose idea is embodied in the safety belt that you use, the tie or hairclip that you wear? Of course not. Almost no one does. When we look at the material world, we see the obverse of the problem we encountered in the intellectual: compensation is usually *de rigueur*, attribution is generally nil.

Thus, the twentieth century has brought us known authors of texts, songs, works of art, subject to highly uneven compensation; and well-compensated creators of material objects who remain essentially anonymous.

Such was the blurry state of copyright and patents in this century.

And then communication became digital and information began moving almost everywhere at the speed of light.

THE DIGITAL COMPLICATION

Barlow (1994, p. 85) observes that "copyright worked well because, Gutenberg notwithstanding, it was hard to make a book." The statement is flawed in its first premise – as we have just seen, copyright has been working nothing like well – but it is on target in pointing to the sensitive relationship between amount of intellectual property at hand and conception/enforcement of intellectual property rights. Too little intellectual property, and copyright is unnecessary; too much, and copyright seems impossible to enforce. Thus, if the unprecedented mass production of books by the printing press made copyright necessary, the equally unprecedented increase in text and related forms of information via digital means seems to be making intellectual property impracticable. It is almost as if intellectual property, like the intelligent life from which it arose, flourishes in a very narrow band of copy availability, a limited range of environmental conditions, below and above which other forces reign.

The issue of just what is a copy is also pertinent. Home photocopiers, slower than commercial machines but of equivalent quality, have been available for several years at costs lower than that of most new personal computers. Thus, photocopying the pages of a book is relatively easy and inexpensive. But with the minor exception mentioned above of professors who photocopied sections of disparate books and therein produced "new" textbooks of readings, the Xerox has by and large posed no threat to the commercial hegemony of the book. This is because the book, though essentially comprised of words, is nevertheless more than the words on its pages – the paper, the pages, the feel and heft of the book itself contribute to our experience of reading – and these non-textual aspects still defy easy and inexpensive reproduction. (But photocopiers operated by individuals have threatened political hegemonies, notably totalitarian societies like Nazi Germany and the Soviet Union. See Dumbach and Newborn, 1986, for an account of "The White Rose," a group of six people who worked against Nazi Germany from the inside with the help of a photocopier, and Levinson, 1992, pp. 195–197, for discussion of samizdat media in Nazi Germany and the USSR. The reason such media can have significant political, but not economic, impact is that affairs of state can be influenced by even a single critical text in the right hands.)

The intangible tangibles of books, to return to the theme of our last chapter, are what would be lost by a complete replacement of print with digital "books" – more of an emotional than a cognitive or functional loss – which flows from the fact that electronic text, in itself, is completely intangible, its very appearance entirely dependent on the configuration of the reader's computer. And, because electronic text is so radically less realized than the hardcopy book, because digital code looks like nothing off the screen, it is commensurately easier to copy and distribute. The most palpable part of the electronic book – the reader's personal computer – is usually on the reader's desk or lap long before the text is received.

Telephone, radio, and television, the first media to separate software from hardware, and place in-principle ever-refreshable hardware in consumers' hands, encountered similar problems, although their messages come to the receiver far better formed than electronic text. Telephone was able to charge for the time spent in gaining the new information, because that information was newly created in every transaction – in the words generated in the conversation. Broadcast media were able to deal with, and indeed in some countries profit mightily from, the new flow of untethered information by providing it free to the user – and making a profit from advertisers.

These approaches are less than ideal. In the United States, where most free radio and TV has been supported by commercial advertisers, critics have pointed out that the advertiser can influence program decisions (see Shanks, 1976, Chapter 5, for a discussion of the complexity of that relationship), and the consumer is paying anyway in the higher prices charged for goods and services so advertised (Hiebert *et al.*, 1982, p. 493). Thus far the main viable alternative in other parts of the world has been media controlled by government, an invitation to censorship even in democratic societies. Cable stations such as HBO in the US thrive on viewer subscriptions – a sort of magazine of movies, on television – although most cable operations continue to rely on commercials. And a comparative handful of "public educational" stations get by on a combination of audience contributions and corporate grants (a kind of genteel advertising, since such underwriters get thanked after every program). But imperfect as such solutions have been to the problem of compensation for intellectual property disseminated without the ballast of paper, they obviously have worked to the extent of providing broadcasting to a majority of the world's population during this century (see Head and Sterling, 1987, for a full discussion of the economics of broadcasting and cable, including p. 452 for discussion of the Supreme Court's controversial 1984 decision that videotape recording of programs broadcast on TV was not an infringement of copyright).

None, however, seem very applicable to online digital media. And telephone's solution of charging for time engaged rather than content conveyed has become less useful for online communication as modem speeds have increased a hundredfold in the past decade, and the content of cyberspace, never much like a telephone conversation in the first place, has undergone rapid evolution on the Web.

It was clear even in the now-distant 1980s, when word processing and data management were as much buzzwords of the new digital revolution as telecommunication, that personal computers spelled extraordinary difficulties for intellectual property. Computer manufacturers and retailers who provide software packages with the equipment they sell are in effect giving this informational tool free to the purchaser. And computer software moves so quickly up the scale of versions, into new software entirely, that the purchaser may within a year or two be using programs that are no longer on the coveted cutting edge. Updates may or may not be available, and may or may not work well on the now two-year-old equipment. Thus the temptation to not want to pay for a new program, if it can be had for the copying from a friend or colleague, is great. And the technical capacity to copy is commonplace, indeed among the most fundamental of any computer's abilities. Software manufacturers could sell programs that defied or inhibited copying, but such restrictions would apply when the purchaser wished to make further copies for his or her own use, and the public has quite understandably rejected early copy protection schemes in that direction (see Brand, 1987, p. 202).

Online services faced a different, though related, set of problems. CompuServe and The Source (see Chapter 12; also Quarterman, 1990) began by emulating the telephone's economic "time metering" model, but time online differed from time on the phone from the very beginning. The telephone, as indicated above, offers unique and original content with every use, in the conversation that takes place; in contrast, online communication, with the exception of live text "chats," offers previously recorded, and therefore more static, content. Next, modem speeds drastically increased, as also mentioned above; online services at first tried to keep their revenues constant by levying surcharges for higher-speed modem connections, but they gave up this strategy as unworkable when speeds exceeded 9600 bps. Further, with the content of any online computer connection now poised in hypertext principle to comprise every text ever written in history of which there is a scannable copy extant, not to mention any image, any sound, any computer program, the amount of time that an online user spends online will soon outstrip any purchasing capacity predicated on charge-by-the-minute. No wonder that America OnLine, currently the biggest central online service with nearly seven million users at the end of 1996, finally bowed to the inevitable and offered a flat-fee, "all you can eat," rate (Zuckerman, 1996); it was then nearly overwhelmed with users.

Of course, the most significant part of this inevitability is its implementation in the Internet, with users numbering in the tens of millions, and where information that "wants to be free" finds its apotheosis — because the Internet is indeed, in a highly significant manner of sorts, just that: free.

But freedom in media, as we should now well know, always comes with strings attached. Local access points to the Internet may charge for their access; commercial systems charge for admission if they are accessible via the Internet, and of course tout their outgoing connections to the Internet as among their most important features (Zuckerman, 1996, reports new executives at America OnLine as seeing its task as bringing "the Internet to the masses"); and of course the computer equipment itself can cost anywhere from several hundred dollars for serviceable second-hand machines to thousands of dollars for tools with fastest speeds, brightest colors and sounds, and biggest storage capacities.

But once you get to it, the Internet including the Web is nonetheless free in a way that no online systems, with the exception of local "bulletin boards" with usually very limited informational resources, have been heretofore. The Internet is thus in one sense the equivalent of free public libraries. But since the partakers of its information can keep this information permanently, it is really an equivalent, and perhaps usurper, of the bookstore as well (see Chapter 12). And the Internet in its growing audio-visual content is beginning to become the equivalent of radio and television. But since its information is usually producible on personal computers, it entails no great production costs (as records on radio and programs on television do), and thus can bypass the economic structures – the Scylla and Charybdis of advertising and government control – of those two now traditional media.

So the Internet offers highly copyable information, if not absolutely free of charge, if not free of sometimes costly underpinnings, nonetheless usually free of production costs, free of sponsor costs, free of even most promotion costs – because hypertext links in effect promote themselves – and thus not subject to qualifications that render broadcasts less than free, and palpable realities of paper and print that always entailed a price-tag to the consumer.

No wonder that online communication has been cited as an unprecedented liberator of information (see Levinson, 1989b). No wonder it has been hailed as a fulfillment of the natural metaphysical and economic properties of information, seen to be bottled up in the temporary way station of print for far too long now. In the next section, we'll summarize some of these arguments.

And we'll also see where they fail – that metaphysical liberation of information need not, should not, entail total economic liberation – and look at a way in which new information capacities can be brought to work on behalf of, not against, the operation of intellectual property.

THE ARGUMENTS FOR NO-COST INFORMATION

The logic of severing information from its traditional economic moorings follows from one of its most recognized, signal capacities: unlike physical property, the use of which diminishes its existence (or, in the case of agriculture, diminishes the useful parts of its existence: can deplete the arable soil), information is never immediately diminished by its use. Indeed, its use by someone other than its initial possessor usually leaves it intact, untouched, in its initial form. (Inasmuch as what makes intellectual property different from other property resides in the physical characteristics of information, in contrast to other kinds of reality, Schulman, 1992, contends that we would do better to dispense with the term "intellectual property" in favor of "informational property"; the point is well taken, but I still prefer "intellectual property," since it calls attention to the creative engine of the property, the intellect).

I put the capacity of information to be untouched by its transaction in qualified rather than unconditional form — never "immediately" diminished, "usually" left intact — because significant exceptions to this trajectory are known, and even common. If an enemy has access to my information in war time, he may kill me and destroy both my copy of his/my information, and, for that matter, my copy of any other information. (And if I should possess unique information, this loss could be an absolute one in the universe.) Similar situations can and do arise in the commercial world, where the sharing (authorized or not) of information with a competitor could result in the corporate death of the original repository. Biologically, parents pass their DNA on to offspring, with the parental DNA still very much in place and operation; but should the offspring do something destructive to the parent, then the result could be a dissemination of information destructive to its original.

Champions of economic informational freedom fail to address these qualifications, and focus instead on the undeniable metaphysical fact that whereas a physical object can only be in one place at one time, information can be in an infinity of places. Edmund Carpenter (1973, p. 3), McLuhan's colleague in the 1950s, captured this well when he observed that "electricity has made angels of us all" — by which he meant not that we all have become good, but omnipresent by virtue of our electronic disseminations. An economic ramification of this state can be easily supposed. (a) The economics of information dissemination in the pre-electronic (post-oral) age were based on the most intractable aspect of the informational transaction — that being the physical object in which the information is embedded or conveyed. Thus, the economics of physical property prevailed — the economics of containers rather than contents. (b) Now that electronics, digital in particular, have made information easily detachable from its containers, we need be bound no longer by the metaphysics of physical objects and its economic consequences when transacting with information. In a phrase, information can be free. (c) It follows that those who still want to charge for information are guilty of "rear-view mirrorism," moving into the future looking backward, perceiving the present and future through lenses of the past. On this allegation, anyone who expects to receive payment for information is mistaking the limitless information for the limited physical containers in which it once was obliged to dwell.

Barlow (1994, p. 88) makes this point as follows:

Since it is now possible to convey ideas from one mind to another without ever making them physical, we are now claiming to own ideas themselves and not merely their expression. And since it is likewise now possible to create useful tools that never take physical form, we have taken to patenting abstractions, sequences of virtual events, and mathematical formulae – the most un-real estate imaginable.

But the point is somewhat in error. Not in its historical observation that expressions of ideas, not ideas themselves, were always the subject of copyright and patent, which is entirely correct. But wrong in its assumption that there can ever be a presentation, an availability, of information on any level absent some type of physical conveyance or embodiment. Even speech, to start at the beginning, depends upon the action of the vocal chords upon air for conveyance, and upon the physical structure of brains for creation and understanding (see Levinson, 1988, for more on the necessity of material: I argue that mind and information are "transmaterial," in that they can and do leap from one material base to another, but are never immaterial). And at the other, current end of the human techno-evolutionary scale, we clearly have electronic carriers of information in computer disks, online networks which have an undeniable material substrate, etc.

So Barlow and the above analysis overstate the case. But putting aside these problems for the sake of argument, let us assume that, (i) although dissemination of information can lead to a reduction of information in some instances such as putting a company out of business as discussed above, and (ii) although information is never totally without some sort of significant material accompaniment, (iii) nonetheless, the relationship of digital information to its containers is so different from that of earlier information to its containers that a new economic regime for information is still in order.

If that were the case, and I agree that for the most part it is, I would still very much disagree with Barlow that the nature of this new regime should reflect Jefferson's claim that inventions cannot be property. Rather, I would say that the digitization of information, which indeed has helped fulfill Jefferson's wish that ideas be "freely spread from one to another over the globe," requires that inventions cannot be property in the way they were before – but must be property in some way, if they are to continue their essential role as embodiments of our new ideas. And, further: that the digital revolution, far from making intellectual property *ipso facto* impossible, has within it the means for greatly clarifying and calling our attention to it.

But why should we take such pains to safeguard intellectual property, now that it has broken free of its wooden confines, a splinter or scratch here and there, scars of the past, but vibrant as never before? The answer is: the freeing of information from economic constraints would likely have the very reverse of the effect Jefferson wanted: it would result in a lessening of dissemination, not only because it would weaken current modes of conveyance (including the Internet), but for the far more important reason that it would dry up our sources of information by depriving its creators of compensation.

INFORMATION MAY WANT TO BE FREE – BUT CREATORS OF INFORMATION STILL NEED TO EAT

To be fair to Barlow, he goes beyond the usual musings that information "wants to be free" or is inherently "leaky" (Cleveland, 1985), and indeed proposes a mode of compensation for information in the digital age: pay for performance of tasks involving information, not for information itself. We undoubtedly already rely heavily on such a model, in the economic structures that govern our relationships with doctors, lawyers, and other kinds of consultants, in which we pay people not for their creation of information, but for their capacity to bring information to bear, whatever its sources of creation, to our needs.

The problem with such a model is that it works only if information is already available for such "performances." But if no one writes the song for the singer to perform, if no one does the research which results in knowledge that guides the doctor in the treatment of patients, then there will be no songs or knowledge of this sort in the first place. Information may want to be free – but it doesn't grow on trees. It is created by people, who need to be compensated for their creation. Barlow's schema would work only if creation and performance of information always came hand in hand, which clearly they do not. And of the two, creation is the far more rare.

Of course, creators can be paid in various, sometimes highly indirect modes for their creations. One of the most indirect is the one that holds sway in most scholarly and scientific circles, in which the writer or researcher is compensated primarily not from the creative work *per se*, but from the university or research institution that hires, promotes, and gives job security to faculty and researchers in accordance with their creative output. Thus, a college teacher may earn literally nothing in direct compensation for the publication of articles in academic journals (indeed, some European journals expect scholars to pay for the pleasure of seeing their work published), but may earn in indirect compensation a tenured, life-time, prestigious professorship at an income far more lucrative than all but a series of best-selling books could provide. Problems can arise from such an indirect system – as in pressure on people to write and publish for the sake of job security rather than pursuit of knowledge, or in older faculty insisting for the sake of their reputations that their names be attached to articles written by younger colleagues or graduate students – but the point here is that creative output continues because there is compensation for intellectual property, however indirect.

Common sense and ample evidence agree that creation is jeopardized when compensation is not available. Fiction writers obliged to get day jobs to support their writing obviously have less time to do their work (for example, in the online Science Fiction Round Table on GEnie, 1991–1995, science fiction writers often complained about how the need for other employment due to poor compensation in their chosen writing field reduced their capacity to write and publish). Karl Popper wrote his pathbreaking *Logik der Forschung* after putting in long hours as a high school teacher, and Bartley (1982a) describes how arduous was the task. What possible advantage could there be in setting in motion an economic system that brought creators of works even further from direct compensation than they are now? It would likely serve in the long run to make the Internet and other conduits more accessible to fewer ideas – precisely the reverse of the result intended.

Indeed, the Internet itself is the result of a variety of very traditional kinds of economic sustenance. It arose in the first place as a network of the US military; its creators were compensated for their work and their ideas about networks. And it now flies atop numerous university systems, each supported by complex tuition and funding structures, and through telephone networks supported for the most part by tolls on length of conversation. But suppose the Internet could exist now solely or even mostly in a new environment of free information, with payment for performance rather than property in the traditional sense. Since the Internet is a product of the older, propertied environment, we have no reason to think that this new hypothetical environment, where compensation for property was scorned, would have within it the economic wherewithal necessary to give rise to a successor. By taking the Internet and its informational exchange out of the context of compensation for creation and property from which it arose, we might be scotching the prospects for its future evolution and improvement. Money moved the development of every remedial medium we have considered in this book. Indeed, beginning with the alphabet itself, apparently created under the commercial pressures of Phoenician maritime transactions (see Chapter 2), all media have been cast sooner or later — usually from the outset — in lucre. The only real point at issue on this was whose money: government, church, patron, corporation, investors, some combination.

Of course, remuneration is by no means the only compensation creators seek — the joy of self-expression, the thrill of possible fame, are major players in the drive to create. And pursuit of these profound psychological rewards is no doubt facilitated by the Internet and the Web, where writers can easily publish their own work and make it available to millions of people.

This heightening of authorial presence (the complexities and contradictions of which we explored in Chapters 12 and 13) is usually taken as an argument against the need for intellectual property: the new digital regime pays its participants in self-fulfillment and reputation, so who needs money? But money, not self-fulfillment, pays the rent, gets one fed, buys the clothes on your back; and neither does reputation, except insofar as it can be translated into compensation for further intellectual work. Thus, the separation of the psychological from the economic, the exaltation of the first and the denigration of the second, only begs the question of how creators can be expected to labor over long periods of time absent adequate compensation.

The error here is to assume that the psychological aspects of creation can be separated from the economic at all, to be used as a *de facto* compensation in lieu of money. Once we recognize the way these two impulses necessarily operate hand in hand, we discover something new about the digital revolution. To the extent that it catapults the author into prominence (which, again, is not complete or uncomplicated, since, as we saw in Chapter 13, author/reader distinctions can be unclear in hypertext), it works not against but strongly in support of intellectual property rights.

The creator, as we have seen, received short shrift even after the introduction of the printing press and the onset of copyright protection. We now look at how digital communication, with all of its complications, may be the most important torch-bearer of intellectual property since Gutenberg.

INTELLECTUAL PROPERTY AND THE END
OF ANONYMITY

Anonymity can be a pernicious business. Who knows the names of the people at IBM who developed the first PC, the specific minds at Apple that engendered the first Macintosh, the workers at Xerox's PARC facility (see Rheingold, 1994) who can claim precedence, to some extent, for both forks now re-merging in the personal computer revolution? These creators are on the other side of the coin of self-published digital writers with names available to millions but no money: they were likely well compensated for their labors in salaries and stipends, but their names are known to almost no one. Indeed, this has been the way of most technology, now and through history. Who invented the chairs, paper clips, fabrics that we use? Few, if any, of us know. And although these faceless creators may indeed have been compensated at the time of their initial creation, their anonymity works to dissolve any continuing claim they or their heirs may have to their intellectual property – indeed, dissolves the very notion of intellectual property itself, in a quiet, incessant erosion much more destructive than the high-profile winds of vast dissemination on the Internet. For we as consumers feel we have some right to that which is anonymously created. We feel that it in some way belongs to everyone, like a song or a story or an invention as old as the alphabet that has come down to us. The anonymous plays like public domain, whether it has been newly created or not.

Publishers and monarchs, as we have seen, worked at the dawn of copyright with the author out of the picture – since in most cases the author was indeed already long out of the picture (deceased) at the time of publication. This situation was at last corrected in the eighteenth century. But technologies – inventions which embody human ideas, as distinct from texts which describe and explain them – have yet to undergo such correction. So the name of the manufacturer, IBM, Ford Motor Company, whatever – the equivalent of the publisher – is universally affixed in some way to every product sold, but nowhere on these items can we find the names of their creators.

Manufacturers obviously had the wherewithal to affix the names of creators to their products prior to the digital age, and indeed at all times in history, especially when the product was the result of one or a few minds. On the other hand, most technologies in today's world are embodiments of ideas from a myriad of people – certainly all the human ideas that are embodied in the construction of your automobile number in the thousands, and came from hundreds or more people. A list of their names rendered pre-digitally, in print or engraving, would certainly get in the way of decor, unless it were a deliberate pop art creation à la Andy Warhol's soup can.

But consider, now, the possibilities of a simple, small, read-only computer chip, affixed to every piece of technology manufactured, which could display not only the corporate label but the names of every individual whose ideas and inventions helped bring this technology into being. Such "smart patent numbers" could even be teleconnected to a central international patent office online file, which could be easily updated to include new links to other relevant inventors and inventions. Such windows on invention, such electronic watermarks, could be the size of a thumbnail, and they could be attached to every car, computer, and chair, even to every box of paper clips sold. They are already potentially present everywhere in bar codes.

Clearly, this connection of a product to its human inventors would not in itself do anything directly to stop the pirating of software, the explosion of available data without strings which critics of copyright and intellectual property are saying makes the notion of copyright useless. But it would counter the ennui of anonymity, bring the human being back into this important aspect of the technological picture, and in so doing quite naturally strengthen the notion across the board that people who create need compensation.

The truth, I think, is that the public, the average person on the street (or online information avenue), has no trouble with the notion that people are entitled to be paid not only for their performances, but their creations and their property, intellectual as well as physical. To return to the opening of this chapter, property is more than a human notion, more than a concept or idea: it is a biological behavior, a property, in more ways than one, of life in the natural world. Granted that the emergence in this natural world of intellectual property – of human ideas suffused by humans into letters and books, carriages and cars – has complicated the reality of property, in much the same way that the Golden Gate Bridge carries vastly more ideational and social cargo than a beaver's dam. But that does not obviate the existence of the bridge as an evolutionary extension of the beaver's dam. And if a new technology were to come along which made construction of bridges much easier, to the point of being low-cost individual rather than expensive societal creations, then that might well change some significant aspects of the bridge as well, but not its fundamental nature as that which originates with beavers and ants and non-human life and at the same time is uniquely furthered by the human being.

This biological antiquity of property, the likely propensity for it in our very genes, is no doubt what led to the development of provisions for intellectual property when the printing press for the first time put such property in the form of books on everyone's shelf. The press did not create the concept of intellectual property – it rather stimulated and began to fulfill it, much as the press created the wherewithal, not the initial idea, for Luther's heresy that people should read the Bible for themselves. To suppose that the digital revolution, because it has set into motion many new currents that run in directions different from the press (almost all beneficial, as I have discussed throughout this book), has obsolesced the notion and applicability of copyright and intellectual property is to miss this essential point: the digital world, in replacing the press, is not likely to erase what the press did not create in the first place.

But calls for repeal of intellectual property laws and customs based on misconceptions of the digital revolution and its impact can do much damage nonetheless. They can weaken our social structures precisely at a time of speed-of-light technological change when we need them most – precisely at a time when at least some of these changes, such as feasibility of inventors' identification chips or "smart" patent numbers as per my proposal, can work on behalf of our longstanding biological impulses for property and compensation.

And the countering of anonymity is not the only way digital communication can serve intellectual property. Electronic fund transfer, credit and debit cards, and the digitization of money all work to facilitate payment for property in cyber-space. Had the copy shop been electronically connected at the time the NYU professors put together their textbooks comprised of photocopied chapters from other books, payment to the authors and publishers via electronic fund transfer could well have been automatic and unavoidable. (Nelson, 1990, suggests that every document in a hypertext linkage should come packaged with an electronic "cash register" which pays the copyright holder a royalty, via electronic fund transfer from the reader's account, for each reading or time the document is invoked in a link. Although such a plan would require a re-education of Web browsers currently accustomed to paying nothing for the myriad of links they engage, one wonders why something along the lines of this idea from the father of hypertext receives no attention at all from Barlow and others in their brief on the impossibility of intellectual property.)

Thus, powerful aspects of digital communication can strengthen the conception and enforcement of intellectual property, can clarify and tie together aspects of attribution and payment that were at loose ends prior to computers, even as the plethora of texts, images, and sounds disseminated by the Internet and its adjuncts undoubtedly clouds a copyright picture already unclear before the first vacuum tube was ever deployed. Neither result – the buttressing nor the dissolution of intellectual property – is inevitable or foretold. The technology has propensities for both. And, contrary to Jacques Ellul and the vision of technology as autonomous and out of our control, the choice is ours.

WHAT PROPERTY OUGHT NEVER TO EMBRACE

Complex and difficult as the notion and practice of intellectual property in the digital age has become, it at least has had the virtue, thus far, of applying to entities which themselves are non-intelligent in the active, old-fashioned sense of the word – that is, not yet capable of generating independent thought. But this may change someday, and if and when it does, we will encounter a series of ethical problems the likes of which will make the above seem like child's play.

The notion of non-intelligent life as property is of course as old as the human notion of property itself – my horse, your dog, his flowers, her goldfish – and unsurprisingly has its antecedents in the biological world with ants that "enslave" other insects, etc. More recently, the principle that new configurations of DNA created via genetic engineering could be exploitable property was confirmed by the US Supreme Court in 1979 (see Adler, 1984).

Intelligent life, though, is quite another matter. Here the instinct towards property – towards making one human being, the only intelligent life we thus far know, the property of another – has quite rightly been curbed. Indeed, its eradication is one of the clear indices in support of the proposition that human progress has been real, if uneven, not relative – a reality to which I very much subscribe (see Hays, 1995).

But what happens when we invent entities – be they organisms that arose naturally and were implanted with chips, organisms that we manipulated or created genetically, computers and robots constructed from silicon, artificial life programs that are entirely creatures of virtuality – that evince intelligence to our satisfaction?

Whose property, if anyone's, can they reasonably be supposed to be? We address these issues, our furthest reach into both ethics and the future, in our next chapter.

18

ARTIFICIAL INTELLIGENCE IN
REAL LIFE

Every medium whose effects, intended and unintended, we have thus far encountered in this book could be considered an auxiliary to, or amplification of, intelligence – to wit, ours. From speech itself to its early expressions in writing in various forms and mechanizations, through the revolution in photo-chemical reproduction of images and electronic transmission of information beginning in the nineteenth century and proceeding through the personal computer and all of its links and possibilities on our verge of the twenty-first century, each and every mode of communication has served as an amanuensis of the human brain, a third, extended hand for helping its dreams come true, for shaping its thoughts and launching them out and far and deep into the world where they can have the most impact.

In these many millennia of media as auxiliary intelligence, the only option we humans have had for creating any other intelligences like ours – not augmenters of our intelligence, but intelligences on their own – was by the pleasurable expedient of creating other humans. Our DNA, it seemed, had provided us with but two options: create wondrous technologies which extended our intelligence mightily, but could not think on their own, or create wondrous children, who grew up with, by and large, the same sets of cognitive capacities as their parents. Deliberate breeding of intelligence in our animal assistants, such as dogs, is perhaps a partial exception. But the exception is slight indeed, as even dogs were bred not to exercise independent judgement and thought, but to more intelligently follow orders – that is, be better assistants.

Science fiction and even legend before it, often ahead of the technological curve in indicating what we humans most want from life and technology, filled in the gap – often with dire warnings – prior to and throughout the twentieth century. The medieval story of the Golem made by the Rabbi of Prague tells of the creation of what we would today call an intelligent clay robot, and the eventual deadly consequences (again, unintended) for its creator. Mary Shelley's *Frankenstein* told this same story in a somewhat different way in 1818, as did Karel Čapek's *RUR* (*Rossum's Universal Robots*) one hundred and three years later. In both stories, which were otherwise not much alike, the destruction of us the human creators who took it upon ourselves to try to behave like gods was significantly retained.

Isaac Asimov, whose eleven-book "Foundation" and robot series we looked at in Chapter 13 as an example of hypertext off-line, ahead of its time, was also out front and even more revolutionary in the way he treated robots. Beginning in 1940, he published a series of short stories — culminating in seven of the novels in the eleven-book series — in which robots were programmed to operate both on behalf of humanity and, in many cases, with genuine independent judgement. That they did not always succeed in the first prong of the design but often did in the second is what makes the Asimov narratives such good reading; but the robots also often succeeded in the first, and in such original ways as to make Asimov's stories not only explorations of "AI" defined as autonomous, stand-alone intelligence, but intelligence that broke the Golem's mold of our own creations turning against us.

The 1940s were also the years in which Turing and von Neumann were putting the finishing touches on the theoretical groundwork for the first computers — in effect, picking up the loose, unimplemented ends left by Babbage a century earlier, and refining and weaving them into twentieth-century technological possibility. The astonishing practical results, explored here in the past seven chapters, grew from the vision of Bush, Englebart, Nelson, and others about the use of computers for word processing, text communication, and linkage to texts, sounds, and images online all over the world — all of these accomplishments, again, being instances of computers as auxiliary to our intelligence (see Levinson, 1988, Chapter 6, for more on augmented or auxiliary intelligence via computers verses autonomous intelligence; and Skagestad, 1993, 1996, for more on the pioneers and philosophical implications of the former).

But theorists during that same time, either after reading Asimov and other science fiction writers (Minsky, 1986, p. 325, says he was influenced "most of all by Isaac Asimov"), or independently, did lots of hypothesizing and thought-experimentation about computers as autonomous human-like intelligences. The famous Turing test for distinguishing human from artificial intelligence is the best known, and we will discuss it below. Indeed, an inverse relationship of sorts arose between science fiction and which AI possibilities — auxiliary or autonomous intelligence — were in fact realized. Personal computers and their auxiliary-intelligence applications received little attention from science fiction writers in the 1940s and 1950s. Asimov (1984, p. 197) admits that he was late in seeing these possibilities – writing instead about "computers that were so large as to be immobile and existed only in order to solve enormously complex problems" (see also Asimov, 1986b, p. xv) – and says (in Asimov *et al.*, 1984, p. 129) that the first "home computer story" was "A Logic Named Joe" by Murray Leinster, published in *Astounding Science Fiction* in March 1946, and now all but unknown. In contrast, robots and computers that thought like us – though always with intriguing differences – captured the center stage of science fiction and public attention from Asimov's robot stories in the 1940s and 1950s through Arthur C. Clarke's "HAL" in *2001* in 1969. And not a single one of their dramatic possibilities has come to be in reality.

But this does not mean that artificial intelligence as a genuine, autonomous intelligence – in a robot or a stationary computer – is for any reason or principle impossible. Nor does it mean that some very interesting first steps in that direction have not been taken on several fronts. In this chapter, we explore some of these issues, including the ethics of artificial intelligence – for us, and for them. We begin with a brief consideration of what is impossible, and why autonomous artificial intelligence seems not.

THE PERILS OF PROTEIN CHAUVINISM

I often cite time travel as a clear-cut example of what is impossible. If I travelled to the past and accidentally killed my younger self, how could I have travelled to the past and done that in the first place? Variants of this grandfather paradox – named after the presumably less terrible act of preventing one's grandfather from reproducing, by whatever means, than one's parents or grandmother – abound in science fiction. One can even depersonalize it by positing a machine that sent a signal to its immediate past to destroy the machine. And travel to the future is no better, for it is utterly incompatible with everyone's free will. If I travel to the future and see you doing anything, you have no choice but to do just that. One can come up with twistings of reality that might somehow permit such absurdities. For example, we might posit that every act of time travel brings into being an alternate time line or reality, after the time travel takes place – so the destruction of my earlier self after I travel back in time brings into being a new, parallel reality, different from the one in which I arose and time-traveled in the first place, which allows me to both kill myself (time-line two: I'm dead) and live long enough to kill my earlier self (time-line one: the place we started). But these "solutions," though exquisite fun in fiction, seem far too tangled to make any sense at all in the lives we in fact live (see Kaku, 1994, for summary and discussion; Thorne, 1994, for argument on behalf of time travel; and Levinson, 1994a, 1994b, 1995b, for critique).

The good news about autonomous artificial intelligences — as in Asimov's robots — is that they require nothing like such eschewal of our very sense of reality to exist. Their operation poses no paradox at all. This of course means neither that such robots do exist nor will exist, merely that they can exist. In the next section, we'll look at weaknesses in claims that forms of genuine autonomous AI in fact are in operation today. Here we consider what reasonable grounds people claim for insisting that autonomous intelligence in machines can never exist — reasonable, that is, after we acknowledge that such AI entails no logical impossibilities like those invoked by time travel.

Our consideration of such reasonable grounds can be very brief, because such grounds do not exist. In the absence of logical proscriptions, the only grounds for insisting that some entity or process can "never" exist is some species of dogmatic assumption.

Some dogmatic assumptions are necessary for any life of the mind, indeed any life at all. A new-born organism survives only because it acts immediately on its dogmatic assumptions — in the case of the offspring of mammals, for example, to suckle for food. In the case of human beings, most of us hold a belief that the world is real — a dogmatic assumption, incapable of logical refutation, that we assert and act upon in the face of the possible contrary assumption, equally irrefutable by logic and evidence, that the world is my dream. (Johnson's kicking a big stone to prove that the world was no one's dream was, alas, to no avail: he and Boswell could well have been dreaming the entire event.) Further, rationality can only reasonably — rationally — explain its efficacy by presenting a rational argument, or calling upon precisely the process, rationality, which is at issue. Bertrand Russell, George Santayana, and Karl Popper all recognized or acknowledged this in one way or another, speaking of a necessary "animal faith" (Santayana) or "irrational" faith (Popper) at the root of reason. Bartley's attempt to substitute an ever criticizable process of criticism for the core of reason failed (see Chapter 11), because some mode of criticism is always essential, and hence indispensable and in that sense beyond criticism, if we are to employ criticism as the universal process. In *Mind at Large* (1988, Chapter 2), I argued that we could at least save this core from the label "irrational" by recognizing the roots of reason as pre-rational, in much the same relation to irrationality (the negation of rationality when it is possible) as a non-living stone has to a dead organism. But although this shift may remove us from the path of the irrationalist's worst weapon – that there is no difference between rationality and irrationality – it does not remove the requirement of a non-negotiable assumption at the core (see also Popper, 1963/1965, p. 49; Munz, 1985, p. 85; and Cleveland, 1985, p. 72).

What, then, are the origins of dogmatic assumptions about the impossibility of autonomous artificial intelligence – and what needs do they serve? If we roughly define intelligence as a capacity of the brain needed to generate and effectively use the universal human communication mode discussed in this book – some kind of speech – then we can make at least two pertinent observations about where we find intelligence in our world. First, we find it in humans. Second, we find it in what may be the rudiments of speech in other organisms, such as dolphins. Do we find it in parrots? Most people would say definitely not. I would agree: parrots are mimicking speech, an activity very different from speaking. Do computers demonstrate autonomous intelligence when they speak, or are they glorified parrots? Turing argued that if a computer's performance were such that a human being could not tell the difference between the computer and another human, then the first human would have no good reason – only prejudice – for denying the intelligence of that computer. But would this protect us from identifying such a computer as an intelligence when all it did was spew forth a very effective simulation of intelligence, like a parrot behind a curtain? Joseph Weizenbaum (1976) sought to highlight this weakness of the Turing test with a computer program, "Eliza," that fooled human patients into believing they were conversing, via computer, to their (human) Rogerian psychotherapist. In view of this and similar "parrot" problems, I have been offering to my students, for the past decade or more, "Levinson's addendum" to the Turing test: if a computer's performance were such that a human being could not tell the difference between the computer and another human being, *forever*, then the first and all other humans would have no good reason – only prejudice – for denying the intelligence of that computer. The situation of the Turing test in such a time frame should easily smoke out both the parrot and the computerized Rogerian behind the curtain. (Though the Rogerian case is a bit complicated by the fact that human Rogerians apparently conduct a therapy which is computer-like to begin with – answering the patient's question with a rephrasing of the question, as in the patient saying, "I have trouble with my job, what should I do?", and the Rogerian answering, "You have trouble with your job?") And, in encounters with a questionable entity that are substantially shorter than forever, my addendum would advise that the longer the encounter, the more confident we can be in our assertion of the other entity's intelligence.

So, computers seem to fail the intelligence test on the speech criterion. Again, this does not mean that tomorrow, or the next century, or further in the future, a computer won't be invented that will demonstrate something closer to autonomous intelligence. But at present, when we look at entities that have intelligence – as evidenced, in some way, by the universal human communication process of speech – we find that humans have it (we have it by definition here, since human intelligence, and the invocation of speech, is our assumptive starting point), some animals may have something like it, and computers do not, just non-intelligent speech in the parrot–Eliza sense.

Well, perhaps speech is not the best criterion. Let's try another, very different from any given communication mode: intelligence operates in its own self-interest. Of course, humans daily do things that are destructive to themselves as individuals and the species. But the gist of this nonetheless holds. We by and large constantly apply our intelligence to the task of making impacts on the world, however small, for our benefit. That we sometimes, maybe even often, fail, is an expression of ubiquitous noise in this system, not of the fundamental orientation of intelligence to the rest of the world. Animals, too, often take wrong and deadly turns; but they too seem undeniably in the business of getting food, reproducing, manipulating the world in whatever ways they can in their favor. Indeed, the same is true of plants. Can we say the same about artificial intelligence programs?

At this juncture, I would offer two propositions. One is that we could likely come up with numerous additional criteria for human intelligence – sense of humor is one that comes to mind – and the lines of demarcation would likely come out the same: humans have more in common, on the characteristics of intelligence, with the living things from which we emerged than with the technological things which we construct. Intelligence, at least up until now, and based on what we know about it here on Earth, seems an emergent property of life – a property that apparently emerged, thus far, in its most fully developed form in humans. Indeed, its development is so far advanced in humans that there seems as profound a breakpoint between thinking (human) life and non-thinking (all other) life, as between life and non-life. But our intelligence, at present, seems nonetheless an exclusively living property.

My second proposition is both an acknowledgement and a proposition. The acknowledgement is that there are no doubt many examples of artificial intelligence, neural networks, expert systems, "bottom-up" configurations, and artificial life today whose performances may in part satisfy some of the above criteria and others for intelligence. My proposition about these, which we look at in more detail in the next section, is that individual performance similarities – even if these discrete points hold over long periods of time and in that sense come closer to passing the addendum I suggested for the Turing test – constitute neither intelligence nor something necessarily on the way to intelligence. Though, once again, this does not mean that human-like intelligence, created by human beings, will never autonomously exist in entities outside of our skulls.

Since human intelligence is the standard, and since humans are alive, we should not be surprised to find intelligence so implicated in life. We look around us and see intelligence, our intelligence, the only intelligence we know, arising in the natural world – even to the extent of noticing prefaces to our intelligence, comprehensive systematic expressions of intelligence of sorts, in other living organisms, to some degree in all living organisms. This seems at least as likely a basis for the dogmatic assumption that we will never create a genuinely autonomous artificial intelligence as the theistic insistence that only the Deity can create a soul. But both are prejudices. The natural "protein" chauvinism that holds that because intelligence emerged from DNA it cannot emerge without it, no less than the supernatural religious chauvinism that sees intelligence as a gift bestowed only upon us, or other living things, from on high, is a position that goes way beyond logic in its jump from description and explanation to prediction and fore-closure of possibilities.

We do not yet know enough about life – or intelligence – to even know much more than that the second emerged from the first. But how? And we do not yet understand enough about technology, even though it is our creation, to be clear that our technologies may not already have some of the properties of life. For these and many other reasons, the claim that we will never create entities in our silicon or similar programmed circuitry with autonomous intelligence the same, greater, or less than ours is unwarranted. We cannot even be sure, notwithstanding the connections between life and intelligence all around us, that life is a necessary plat-form for the operation of intelligence. There may be other routes, other substrates, other foundations. And if life is indeed an indispensable milieu for generation of thought, we cannot be sure that silicon or some other inorganic circuitry might on some other very powerful criteria be judged alive.

Of course, serious consideration of such possibilities, outside of science fiction, can complicate rather than satisfy our constant need to clarify for ourselves what it means to be alive. To the oft-mentioned triad of the Copernican revolution that dethroned us from the center of the universe, the Darwinian revolution that removed us as the ideal being on this planet, and the Freudian revolution that toppled our rational selves as always or at least usually in real control, we may need to add the Asimovian revolution that renders our intelligence perhaps not so unique. That this last partner in the new tetrad has not yet come to any real fruition may be no more than a consequence of the still unspectacular technological performance of the would-be new silicon thinkers. Or, it may be a consequence of some profound aspects of life and intelligence we do not at present understand, or even realize we do not understand.

It is in any case a consequence about which most of us, deep down, are more comfortable than not.

CHIMPS, PROGRAMS, AND COMPUTERS

Once we get beyond protein chauvinism, and admit the possibility in principle of autonomous intelligence performing in non-DNA, non-naturally selected entities – as in those designed by humans – we can ask: are there then any examples extant of computers in fact "thinking" autonomously? To answer this question – I hesitate to say, "answer this question intelligently," for danger of begging the question – we need in turn to further inquire just what we mean by autonomous thinking or intelligence.

This question can best be addressed, I would suggest, by subtracting what we have discussed throughout this book as auxiliary intelligence – in particular, the auxiliary intelligence of computers – and seeing what if anything remains. Popper (1972, pp. 225, 239) approvingly quotes Einstein's observation that his pencil was smarter than he, and adds that computers are just the latest pencils. This provides a quintessential definition of auxiliary or augmented intelligence. Einstein's pencil was smarter than he in that he was able to do work in writing – say, mathematical computation – that he could not do just thinking or speaking. Moreover, such written expressions when refined and published were able to reach far more people than Einstein's unextended mind or voice. Thus, in that sense too was his pencil a better communicator. But no pencil – not Einstein's, not anyone else's – has ever written or communicated anything on its own, anything absent a human hand and mind behind that to direct it.

Has any computer?

As is recognized by both common sense and philosophy of science, the more provocative the claim, the more vivid, comprehensive, reliable, overwhelming the kind of evidence required. If someone says that chimpanzees and apes evince human intelligence, is it enough to show an ape who, under painstaking human training and supervision, apparently learns a few symbolic signs – is that sufficient to support such a claim? I would want more. I would want to see an ape who, under painstaking human training and supervision, apparently learned to appreciate the controversy about whether apes share human intelligence – an ape who, if not able to write a discourse on such a topic, could at least be educated to read it. Otherwise, all we have with the barely symbol-using ape is demonstration of a given cognitive module, capable of being elicited to function in apes by humans, that humans also have. When we consider that the rest of human cognition, whatever exactly it is, has invented technologies that have re-made this planet, lifted us off it, shuffled the elements of life – and, yes, has at least written about the possibilities of autonomous artificial intelligence – and we compare these to what chimps and apes have done, either on their own or under human guidance, the finding of some common given components of even abstract intelligence looks more like finding that all three species have lungs or eyes than anything remotely like a shared capacity of overall intelligence.

What, then, about computers? They of course process symbols far better than chimps – even better, in some respects, than humans. But that's just Einstein's pencil again. Has a computer ever come up with a theory – not necessarily one like Einstein's, let's be fair, but any kind of theory? Has it ever written or indeed done anything it was not first programmed by humans to do? Other than the ubiquity of noise which leads all processes, biological as well as technological, to err on many occasions, what do computers in performance of their programs exhibit that is spontaneous?

On this score, computers seem worse off than chimps, who at least demonstrate a kind of technological intelligence, unprogrammed by humans, in the use of sticks as tools to serve up tasty termites in the wild. Indeed, genuinely new, learned behavior – not just in an isolated odd-ball individual organism but in groups that have continued and expanded over decades – is well known in other primates, such as Japanese macaque monkeys on Koshima Island, who were fed sweet potatoes for the first time in 1952, and soon developed a complex process of washing the potatoes, sometimes in fresh water, sometimes in salt, passed on from mother to children, and within ten years practiced by three-quarters of the monkeys on the island (Eibl-Eibesfeldt, 1970, p. 222). Life itself is on all levels a knowledge or "intelligence" process, in its generation, testing, and dissemination of strategies for survival, though of course only humans are apparently aware of it. This fundamental recognition of evolutionary epistemology (Popper, 1972; Campbell, 1974a, 1974b; see also Wuketits, 1991, for a brief explicit rendition, and Levinson, 1988, for the three-way equation of life, knowledge, and technology) is what leads me to group the amoeba and Einstein – to use another favorite Popperian riff on

Einstein – as much closer together on the capacity of intelligence than either is to any current computer or computer program.

But we must be careful, in invoking the criterion of programming, not to render our argument against the demonstration of autonomous intelligence in computers into a tautology: all computers are programmed, therefore anything a computer does is the consequence of programming and therefore not autonomous. That sort of reasoning is scarcely preferable to protein chauvinism.

The better question, then, is not whether computers have written a theory which they were not programmed by humans in some first instance to do – we already know the answer to that question before we ask it, to wit, no – but whether computers have written a theory which is original in content, whatever the programming that may have led to it. The theory of course need not be as original – or brilliant – as Einstein's in order for us to move the computer ahead of the amoeba, closer to Einstein, in the above grouping. Even a crackpot, incorrect, patently dumb theory would do. The key criterion is that the intellectual work not appear to be the result of programming even though it in fact may be.

What do we mean by "not appear to be" in this context? We actually want a demonstration that goes deeper than mere appearances – that avoids the pitfalls of a shortform Turing test, the parrot's mimicry, the Eliza program, painting by numbers, laughter at a joke due to politeness rather than finding it genuinely humorous. We want an ideational product that appears to be less the result of programming than any of those provocative but dead-end examples.

In effect acknowledging the difficulty of finding such a product or performance, some of the boldest champions of autonomous AI have questioned to what extent any human work, including Einstein's, is really unprogrammed. This is of course the old Skinnerian behaviorist proposition that there is no such thing as truly spontaneous, unconditioned thought or action – only behavior whose roots may be unavailable to our conscious scrutiny, and which we in our need to believe in freedom and dignity mythologize as being original, generated in the most significant sense by us rather than others. In the hands of AI advocate Marvin Minsky, the behaviorist claim provides an ingenious occasion for reversing the tables on human critics of AI. Right, he argues, computers never satisfy the requirement for productions that survive a search for programs at their roots – but, then again, neither do we. Human mentality is but a bundle of "brain machines" (Minsky, 1986, p. 163).

This line of argument thus seeks to demonstrate the claim that the computer and human intelligence are analogous not by showing how computers think like humans, but the reverse. The argument can be defeated in at least three ways. One is the failure of the behaviorist proposition on its own terms. Humans do lots of things we're not asked or supposed or conditioned to do, and to assert that all such cases are just examples of conditioning too recondite to identify is an attempt to win the argument not by evidence but expansive re-definition – everything is conditioned, including things which do not seem to be, which are classes of conditioned behaviors in which the antecedent may be hidden but nonetheless in operation. Two, even were all human thought and action in some way the result of conditioning, such "programming" comes from such a diversity of interacting sources as to have little meaningful resemblance to even the most complex computer program source code. And three: let us assume for the sake of argument that most human thought and behavior – say, the whoppingly high percentage of more than 98 – is indeed programmed in exactly the same way as the most sophisticated known computer's. I picked the number 98 deliberately, because genome mapping has disclosed that human and chimp DNA patterns are more than 98 per cent the same (see Brown, 1990, p. 127). And somewhere in that little more than 1 per cent of difference, Shakespeare, spaceships to the moon, genetic engineering, and AI – at the least, in the auxiliary sense – arise. Applying this chimp criterion to the problem at hand, we would be reasonable in expecting that even were computer and human "programming" 98 per cent the same – not in content, but in partaking of a same programming structure – a world of difference, a chasm of accomplishment, could emerge from that other tiny per cent.

As indeed it has, from whatever percentage of difference in underlying structure. The most brilliant expert systems function more like exaggerated idiot savants, who can do just a few things wonderfully and not much else in the way of intellectual performance, than like normal human multi-variate intelligence. Indeed, even the autistic can do a myriad more things than the expert system. Neural networks, in which programs compete and survive in a Darwinian fashion, on the basis on their success, are more promising – as are "artificial life" programs, whose virtual reality representations left to run on their own simulate cycles of life – because these approaches recognize the living prerequisites of intelligence in the real world. But promises and performance, as any programmer no doubt knows, are two very different computer kettles of fish.

Yet what if all of the above promises, and other AI and AL projects now under way or yet to begin, were to fulfill their expectations? What if one or more indeed produced a theory original in the sense that its programmed antecedents were unapparent? Such an accomplishment would be remarkable – as is, for that matter, the current work actually being done in these areas. But would it bespeak an autonomous human intelligence *in toto* any more than the chimp is human by virtue of the common body structure we share, the result of our 98 per cent similar genomes?

Behaviorists are prone to regard such constructs as "self" and "mind" as "superstitions" that we conjure and impose upon our palpable brain machines in our quest for meaning and order (Minsky, 1986, p. 232). But spaceships are no longer imaginary – they are now as palpable as brains – and the text of Shakespeare, and Einstein, and indeed every text ever written became at the instant of its writing as visible as any machine. The real challenge of AI, then, is not to produce a single text or toothpick which might impress us with its seeming spontaneity, not some isolated piece of the process – 98 per cent of which pieces, on the genetic level, are the same for chimps and humans – but some continuing, representative fraction of the immense and varied aggregate of human mental production. That aggregate is eminently observable and external, the consequence of multidimensional human intelligence in action in every doctor, carpenter, witchdoctor, and farmer, the technological world around us. To ask that AI demonstrate some equivalent capacity for this is only to request what AI advocates and behavioral psychologists have been demanding in debates concerning the nature of human mentality all along: move it from the imaginary into the tangible, from the hypothetical and projected into the obvious and real. Until then, AI still seems closer to Einstein's pencil than Einstein – more indeed like any pencil than any person, Asimovian robot, or chimpanzee, which at least has its own termite-hunting stick to show for itself.

But that's today. And one thing our survey of the information revolution has shown is how unreliable injunctions about future developments, including time-tables, can be. Thus, given that we cannot rule out the possibility of autonomous artificial intelligence, we conclude this chapter with a classic "what if?" science fiction question: if we do someday create machines which think so much like us that we must acknowledge that they are thinking machines, or perhaps machines that are alive, what ethical problems will ensue?

Contrary to most science fiction until recently – except, to a significant extent, Asimov's – we may find that the most likely ethical quandary to arise will concern not the way they treat us, but vice versa.

AI AND THE GOLDEN RULE

As we saw at the beginning of this chapter, Isaac Asimov reversed a centuries-long tradition of looking at robots and other artificial sentiences as undoers of human life, and instead posited that robots could be programmed to work on behalf of humans. The loci of this programming were three "laws" of robotics, now famous, that Asimov developed after they were suggested and spelled out to him in essence by his editor, John Campbell, in 1940 (Asimov, 1979, p. 286). They were installed in the hard circuitry of Asimov's robots – their "positronic" brains – to insure that (1) no robot would act ever to harm a human, or allow, by inaction, any harm to befall a human; (2) no robot could disobey an order given by a human – except if that contradicted the First Law; and (3) no robot could fail to act on behalf of its own survival – except if such actions contradicted the First and Second Laws. Clever humans were of course able on occasion to surmount even the First Law, and manipulate robots into not operating in the best interests of other humans, but these were exceptions that were provocative precisely because they were threats to the regime of robot as trusted assistant that Asimov had constructed so well. By the 1980s, difficulties in robotic fulfillment of the First Law – which human being, or group of humans, to save, or side with, when there was more than one choice, or competing human interests – led Asimov (1985) to promulgate a new utilitarian-derived "Zeroth" Law, which held that robots could do harm to a few human beings on behalf of the many, or the good of humanity as a whole. Although this new law obviously – and, again, from the perspective of good fiction, deliciously – complicated the application of the First Law, the result was nonetheless still very much in accordance with robots operating to the benefit of humans.

Indeed, by the late 1980s and 1990s, robots in science fiction were not only working for the human weal, but even being regularly depicted as victims of human conduct – thus reversing even further the *Frankenstein* theme, though a few elements of sympathy for the monster's plight were present all along, especially in the Boris Karloff movies of the 1930s. A classic *Twilight Zone* TV episode first broadcast in 1959, "The Lonely," tells of an innocent man sentenced to solitary life imprisonment on a barren asteroid for a crime he did not commit, and a captain who, taking pity on him, brings him a beautiful female android for company. A year later, the captain returns in a tiny ship with good news: the real criminal has confessed, and the prisoner can come back home with the captain. But there's a problem: the prisoner has fallen deeply in love with the android, and there's no room on the ship for the android. The prisoner refuses to leave, time's of the essence, and the captain, to bring the prisoner to his senses, blasts the android's lovely head off. In a more recent television series (1987–1994), "Star Trek: The Next Generation," the android character Lieutenant Commander Data often faces situations in which his existence is jeopardized by humans who consider "him" something less than alive. The Arnold Schwarzenegger model of android in the second Terminator movie (*Terminator 2 – Judgement Day*, 1991; see Castell, 1996, p. 1118) has been constructed anew and reprogrammed to help the good cause, and in the end has acquired enough autonomous wisdom to sacrifice himself in the interests of humanity.

Such dramatizations have an intrinsic drawback when applied to the questions we were grappling with above about whether robots and AI programs are capable of autonomous human thought, are in some sense alive, etc., because the portrayal of the androids by human beings confuses our feelings as human viewers about whether we are in fact seeing a living being, or an artificial creation, and whether there is some meaningful difference between the two. I call this the paradox of human portrayal of androids, and it flows from the very device of androids in science fiction, entities with computer brains and human or human-like bodies, as distinct from robots which are usually given gleaming metallic bodies (Asimov, however, uses the term "humaniform" robot for android). But the evocation of our human feelings for androids by human actors and actresses portraying androids nonetheless has the good result of bringing to our attention the question of what fundamental respect we might owe our artificial, intelligent creations.

One might well wonder, to begin with, why AI ethics ever arose and flourished in pursuit of the opposite, the robot as our grim comeuppance. The answer probably resides in the wide intellectual appeal of critics of technology – such as Mumford, Ellul, and Postman, whose work we have encountered throughout this book – and their claim that auxiliary technologies, out of control by virtue of their unintended consequences, go on to enslave or severely damage us. If television and automobiles – autonomous only by the most extreme metaphorical writ, and one which ignores our rational development of remedial media – can enslave us, then is it not reasonable and indeed necessary to assume that artificial entities designed to be autonomous could bury our species?

Of course, there is ample evidence that auxiliary technologies of many sorts can be extremely destructive. But that result derives entirely from the fact that they are auxiliary – that is, that they are under human control, not independent of it. Nor is what I am saying here in any way an argument that all technologies are equal, all worthy of retention and development. To the contrary, some – like guns and nuclear weapons – ought to be destroyed wholesale precisely because of the wholesale destruction they inflict upon humans at the behest, under the wielding, of other humans. Once this human origin of all that is negative in technology is recognized (see "Guns, knives, and pillows" in Levinson, 1996, for more) – though, as the thrust of this volume attempts to demonstrate, so much throughout history, now, and likely in the future is positive – the prospect of a genuine autonomous, thinking technology, free of our control, should be cause for celebration.

But, were autonomous AI to be a major achievement in getting technology out of the loop of humans hurting humans – of humans using technology against humans – it would engender the new set of problems pointed at by Asimov, dramatized in "The Twilight Zone" and "Star Trek: The Next Generation" episodes, of humans doing harm to technologies. When a television is thrown out of a window by a technophobe seeking to make some point about the media, no one else much cares – or should care, assuming no other people are in the path of the falling TV. But deliberate destruction of an entity thought to be autonomously intelligent, and therefore perhaps alive, is a very different proposition. Equally troubling is an autonomous AI's decision to end its own existence: Schwarzenegger's sacrifice in *Terminator 2* touches us most because it is self-sacrifice, not programmed.

But if we did develop artificial intelligences capable of independent thought and judgement, would not one primary reason for such development be to have the AIs or robots do work at once too complex and dangerous for humans – say, work in outer space, or even here on Earth in chemical facilities such as that in Bhopal, or in nuclear reactors, or in areas rent by earthquakes? The very appeal of this, it seems, would be that such entities could do intelligent work without risk of human life.

This problem presents itself as early as Asimov's three laws. A robot must operate on its own behalf, yes – but that is the Third Law, and meant to be overridden not only by the First Law (a robot must always act to prevent harm to humans) but the Second Law as well (a robot must follow all human orders, except when they are contradicted by the First Law). So, under these laws, any robot can be ordered by any human to commit suicide, presumably just for the sheer perverse human pleasure of it. And such a hapless robot, if its positronic circuits were operating properly, would have no choice but to obey. Even the most enslaved humans in history were not subject to such indignity.

Of course, if robots, androids, autonomous AI programs are not alive, then the indignity would be less, perhaps non-existent. But since the two phenomena – life and intelligence – are so closely entwined as we saw above, might not the more ethical route be to assume that we might be bringing life into being with our AI creations, and in view of that possibility aim for partnership rather than slavery in the relationship? How about at least a Second Law which says a robot must obey all commands issued by humans, except when such commands contradict the First Law, and except when such commands might result in harm to the robot, with the further exception that such harm must be risked if the First Law is at issue: i.e., if the robot is attempting to prevent harm befalling a human?

Such an approach might eliminate the worst of our AI ethical quandaries – ordering an independently intelligent, quasi-living entity to its death – but would still leave a host of painful ethical issues revolving around whether we are right to make a slave of any sentient entity, of our creation or otherwise. The obvious strategy for avoiding such problems entirely would be to deliberately "dumb down" our robots – design them so that they were not autonomously intelligent in the first place, in no sense alive, not even ambiguously, and thus no more warranting of ethical treatment than the desktop computer I am typing this upon.

The ethical coupling of sentience and freedom – and the dilemma of sentience and slavery in machines – of course derives from our experience with humans. And this in turn derives from, and points to, yet a deeper paradox concerning technology, and one which is epistemological as well as ethical. We invent and deploy technologies in the very areas where our unaided senses, our naked coordinates, are least effective. But this means that we have the least means of non-technological, direct eye-witness corroboration, in precisely those areas where technology stands to do us the most good by telling us what we do not already know. We see, or think we see, new planets around distant stars via the Hubble Telescope. By what else, other than the Hubble or its technological equivalent, can we corroborate those findings, get better bearings on them? Least of all – not at all – by our naked vision (here we encounter the end of the line for Aristotle's advice that we should trust the testimony of our naked senses over that of our artificial devices). And so we face the prospect of bringing into existence artificial entities that/who may be autonomously intelligent and alive, to do things, one hopes, that we have never done before, and we face this with no sound ethical bearings, since the only intelligent and alive beings we have ever behaved ethically towards, and even then not most of the time, were beings quite different from machines – namely, human beings – we who are already indisputably intelligent (if not always wise) and alive.

Yet, in the end, we have no bearings at all – neither epistemological nor ethical – other than our own, those we derive from our biological heritage and our technological extensions. This Kantian standard cannot be waived, only worked through and around by bringing as many disparate human lessons as possible to bear on the other-than-human, more-than-human realms we investigate and bring into being. Somehow, if autonomous artificial intelligences are ever created, we will   need to bring lessons to our relationship from partnerships, even employer–worker dynamics, absurd as this sounds when speaking of machines. But they will be needed, precisely because any entity with a capacity to think will be as a consequence unlike any machine – or auxiliary mode of intelligence – heretofore.

Indeed, our emphasis on the lessons of natural selection and evolution throughout this volume, on the analogies and implications of DNA and its workings to the processing of information via technology, is part of this Kantian recognition that we can only see what will be via the lenses of what we are. And part of this recognition entails an acknowledgement that part of what we are, part of the way we have been doing business via biology and technologies that augment it, will likely endure and inform whatever new relationships we devise with our technology, whatever radical ways we may continue to transform ourselves via our embodiment of our ideas in a myriad of external forms – just as we carry within us the stamp and spark of DNA that in one program or another animates all life.

We thus conclude our tour, in the next chapter, with a survey and assessment of what parts of our biological nature and information processing seem likely to hold sway, stand inviolate, in a world in which the vicarious pursuits and extensions of cyberspace limn the infinite.

19

YOU CAN'T TOUCH THAT IN CYBERSPACE

The same DNA that gives rise to the brains which develop and utilize the many information technologies considered in this book creates flesh and brains that have needs unmet by information technology. Some needs – such as nutrition on the individual level, and procreation on the species level – are intrinsically incapable of satisfaction by just information, in any known meaning of the term. They require not the representations or re-presentations that are information, but the presentation of physical originals – not communication, but the physical, living processes which so much communication is about. Other pleasures, such as feeling the breeze upon one's face, might someday be provided by some clever electronic stimulation or simulation that is so realistic as to be all but indistinguishable from the original, and in that sense not quite a simulation either. But at the end of the twentieth century, such satisfactions are as incapable of provision by information technology as the more tangible hungers.

We might, of course, someday work on our very DNA to create versions of humans who can thrive without food, who can survive without sperm and egg unions, who can feel no advantage in a cool autumn breeze upon their faces. Such alterations would address the very Kantian condition we discussed at the end of the last chapter. But even these would be unlikely to totally replace it – rather, being guided by human cognition in the first place, as ideas for presumable "improvement" that arose from us, they would almost certainly leave in their products at least some significant human needs unrequited by information technology.

A good way of assessing, if not precisely measuring, the nature and extent of the irreducible, irremediable component of human communication – that which cannot be accomplished in the present state of electronic communication, and perhaps never will be – is to re-trace the hierarchy of vicariousness that characterizes the emergence first of modes of perception, and then of communications media. Donald T. Campbell, as we saw in the Introduction to this book, noted that the most primitive forms of life, such as amoebas, only know of their world what they bump into. This form of total engagement and embracement, evolutionarily preceding the less involving process of touch, is extremely accurate as a vehicle of knowledge. The amoeba, as far as we know, suffers no illusions – not optical, nor the cognitive and emotional kind that we humans at the other end of the evolutionary spectrum with our advanced brains and schemes are so prone to spin and ingest. But the amoeba pays a high price for such environmental honesty: it dies with every noxious external state it encounters so fully.

And thus is the impetus for vicarious modes of perception engendered. Touch is safer than complete immersion, because it allows the touching organism to withdraw. Taste is preferable to immediate – unmediated – ingestion for the same reason. Smell, hearing, and vision are safer still, for they allow its bearers to learn about aspects of the external world without any direct physical encounter at all. In human beings, the upward spiral of vicariousness continues on two profound, more or less simultaneous tracks. One, which was the terminus of Campbell's evolutionary epistemology, is the mode of abstract thought – we humans can replay, anticipate, contemplate much of the world in the total remove of the mind's theater. The other, explored at length by me in *Mind at Large* (1988), and in this book as well, is technologies. Some devices, like telescopes and microscopes, literally allow us to see things without being there, when "there" is either too far away or too close at hand for organisms of our size to otherwise cognitively encounter. A camera brings us into contact with another kind of inaccessible "there" – the "there" of yesterday and before. Other technologies, such as books and computers, enhance abstract thought directly, by in effect allowing us to think across vast distances and vast epochs of time (and in the case of computers, also allowing us to perform mathematical operations on these thoughts at much faster speeds).

But in each of these developments, the price that the amoeba paid is translated, transferred, not eliminated. In place of death as a consequence of a wrong turn, we get at each stage a commensurately greater likelihood of making a wrong, albeit not necessarily fatal, turn. To see is indeed to be open to the possibility of optical illusion – of false reports about the external environment. To think is indeed to be open to deception – whether of oneself or from others – and to misinterpretation of what the eyes report. And, of course, technologies are imperfect in their extensions. This does not mean that they cannot be improved but, rather, that their improvements are ever subject to noise.

Nonetheless, the transfiguration of the amoeba's death into the ever-increasing organic and human propensity for error is obviously well worth it. We can live with most error – we can let our ideas "die in our stead," in the apt words, again, of Karl Popper (1972, p. 248) – and we can apply our vicarious means of perceiving and knowing to correcting such error, if never completely. And part of that correction should entail consideration of what aspects of amoebic, full-contact existence we still very much need, and would be in serious error to think could be satisfactorily accommodated in cyberspace, or any vicarious media environment. The illusion that we have taken leave of the amoeba and its world of total immersion in its entirety is itself the error – a consequence of the vicarious spiral – that we will focus on in this chapter.

Before looking at the role of physical presence in our social and emotional lives, we begin with the need for hands-on, direct observation and experience in the pursuit of human knowledge.

THE FEEL OF KNOWLEDGE: ON EARTH, MARS, AND BEYOND

One of my longstanding jokes about online education, found all too often in my talks and articles on the subject, is that were I to need brain surgery – and usually for an additional chuckle I ruefully add here that some people in the educational establishment no doubt think that I do – I would not want to be operated upon by a graduate of any of my Connected Education online programs. In addition to the minor truth that some educators no doubt think online education is an oxymoron (and its practitioners therefore in some leave of their good senses), the major truth contained in the above is that some subjects indeed cannot be taught well, or at all, online. Clearly, topics which thrive in an environment of text and discussion – what have been known as the humanities, liberal arts, social sciences, including the subject of this very volume – are ideal for educational fora operating via electronic text. And, equally clearly, areas that require any degree of physical dexterity and direct observation – medicine in general, and brain surgery even more in particular – do not seem amenable to any kind of complete teaching in an entirely online mode.

The expansion of the online purview to full audio-visual communication of course increases the roster of subjects that could be successfully taught and studied online. Surely all manner of art and music courses are now becoming appropriate denizens of the online curriculum. Many more aspects of medicine would work in such a venue too, though I would still want my brain surgeon educated in the old-fashioned hands-on way, thank you.

I think most people, even the rare champion of online education more radical and passionate than I (and I have yet to meet one), would agree on the brain surgery exclusion. Virtual reality immersions, in which surgery were taught much like learning to drive a car or fly a plane, could conceivably be valuable in training surgeons in the future (see also Longan and Scarrow, 1996, for successful practice of telemedicine – via remote video – for some kinds of medical care). But even here I would imagine that, given the potentially fatal consequences of a surgeon not fully trained, our society would insist that all surgeons receive some actual training with tissue and blood – just as our society currently and aptly insists that no one can get a license to drive or fly purely on the basis of virtual simulation training.

What is at stake here, then, is the necessity of tactile experience for education in tactile skills and professions. But such training and jobs comprise only a part of the overall growth of knowledge of our species. What of less applied forms of knowledge? These, as indicated above, might be successfully taught and studied – communicated, disseminated – entirely online.

But what of their initial generation and discovery?

Critics of the personned part of the space program (I find the word "personned" preferable to "manned" on sexist grounds, and preferable to "crewed" for the purely acoustic reason that it sounds like "crude") argue that robotic exploration of space is more reliable, less expensive, and of course less endangering of human lives (see, e.g., Roland, 1994). The last point is undoubtedly true, though it overlooks the potential problem we discussed in the last chapter about the ethics of consigning intelligent, and perhaps therefore alive, machines to dangerous missions. But let us assume, for the sake of this discussion, that any intelligent robots who risked their lives on harrowing missions volunteered in a knowledgeable way to do so – that is, by the same standards of risk-taking that pertain to humans. And let us also grant, for the moment, the claim that robotic exploration would be less expensive – even though the cost of building such a robot seems far higher, at this time in our technological knowledge, than training a human.

What, then, about the first claim? What about the assertion that knowledge obtained by either remote or robotic investigation is any way more reliable than or superior to knowledge flowing from first-hand human observation and experience?

The announcement in August 1996 that life may have been discovered on Mars, on the basis of a rock discovered in Antarctica on Earth, provides a dramatic occasion for assessing our relative confidence in indirect, technological versus direct human observation. Missions to Mars to further investigate the Antarctic discovery are already under way or being planned (see Kargel and Strom, 1996, p. 86). Which kind of mission would carry the most weight: (a) expedition to Mars with just robots, which do all the analysis of rock samples there, and telecommunicate the results back to Earth; (b) expedition to Mars with just robots, which scoop up good-looking samples and return with them to Earth; (c) expedition to Mars with humans, who do all the analysis there, and telecommunicate the results back to Earth; (d) expedition to Mars with humans, who scoop up good-looking samples and return with them to Earth?

The first is the clearly the weakest, and for good reason. We are totally reliant on proxies for the choice and analysis of suitable samples, and being notified about the results. Errors in the robotic function on Mars, or noise in the telecommunication of the results, could create a false negative: the choice of a poor sample, a mistake in the analysis, or garble in the transmission could distort the findings enough to tell us there was no evidence of fossilized micro-organisms on Mars, when in fact there are. The second and third mission configurations are each in their own way preferable to the first. The second provides no defense against poor proxy choice of samples, but at least brings them back to Earth. The third gives us much better on-site initial work, but is still subject to error in the initial transmission of results, and limits in the number of humans who can re-test the findings. The fourth is obviously the most preferable, in that it puts humans directly into contact with the source of knowledge at both crucial places – in the choice of samples on Mars, and in the analysis back on Earth. And because the analysis is done on Earth, telecommunication of the results to others on Earth becomes a trivial part of the knowledge discovery process.

Alas, all but the last currently planned missions are in category "a" (robots telecommunicate findings from Mars); and the last planned mission – a US Mars Surveyor in 2005 – is category "b" (robots return to Earth with samples from Mars). (A mission to Mars with people is being discussed for 2009; see WNBC-TV, 1997.)

Direct human involvement is preferable to remote technologies not because humans are incapable of making mistakes or even less likely to err. On the contrary, our technologies in any given situation are usually designed to make fewer errors than humans performing the same tasks. The problem rather arises in technology's far more limited capacity than ours to detect error and recover. Let's say the telecommunication of results from initial laboratory or laboratories on Earth was all in error. The scientists involved would know almost immediately of the error – as soon as reporters called to confirm the findings. But let's say the same error was committed in the telecommunication of results from the Mars site, where the work was done solely by robots. Unless the robots had been programmed to monitor the results of the transmission to Earth, and watch for error, who or what would correct the error? And, given the obviously inherently unpredictable nature of error, what confidence could we have in a program designed to detect error in transmission of results from an environment as little known to us as Mars?

Of course, many kinds and levels of technological safeguards can be built in. More than one probe will be sent to Mars. This would help with a random noise, transient problem; but it would not help much if at all with some sort of systematic malfunction accidentally programmed into the overall operation. The only expedient for reducing that kind of error is the presence of human beings.

This is not a throwback to Aristotle's advice to always trust the testimony of naked senses over technology – which, as we saw in Chapter 3, was taken up by the Church in its argument against Galileo and his support of Copernican theory via telescopic observation. Without highly sophisticated technological modes of analysis, including extremely powerful microscopy, we would have known nothing about possible life on Mars in the first place. Rather, the need for human presence in learning about radically unknown environments beyond Earth reflects the reality that technologies are not able to do everything – that the best mode is one in which humans, as much as possible, are present during the technological work.

This irreducible need for direct human involvement in knowledge acquisition – writ large in the case of Mars, but a factor to some degree in all other cases – is but the other side of the coin of auxiliary technology that we examined in the previous chapter. To be an extension of an eye is to be radically less than the eye, unless accompanied by the eye – certainly the extension unaccompanied is drastically less than the eye unaccompanied, and, from the point of view of actual perception, does really nothing at all when not in tandem with its extendee. Eyeglasses, telescopes, and microscopes see nothing on their own. Only our anthropocentric imagination makes us think today's computers do anything like thinking on their own. They are really – to peel yet another analogy off their screens – nothing more than eyeglasses with a myriad of retinal images projected from the inside out. They have no brains, save the enormously powerful ones of the humans who program and use them.

It is not that we design our technological extensions to be deliberately in need of human involvement to work. It is rather that in creating technologies to extend our perception and thinking, we cannot help but make them dependent upon us to operate. Of course, we leave an immense discretion and flexibility as to when and how we become involved with our cognitive media. Even in the first category of new missions to Mars – the one in which robots do the on-site work, and tele-communicate the findings back to Earth – the ultimate receivers and interpreters of the information are we humans. But recognition of our essential presence in some part of the knowledge process should entail awareness of the danger of keeping us too far or long out of the equation. The only completely satisfactory technological alternative would be development of the autonomous artificial intelligences which were discussed in the previous chapter. And certainly a crucial characteristic of these, at least if they were programmed or chose to pursue the acquisition of knowledge, would be their capability of recognizing a range of possible error as broad as that which can be recognized by humans.

But we, of course, do not live by scientific knowledge alone. There is obviously more to the information which flows through our lives than analyses of possible life on other planets, however pre-eminently important; and indeed more than all the knowledge conveyed by formal education, online and otherwise. If the information revolution is insufficient, in the absence of tangible, direct human presence, as a generator and even conveyor of formal knowledge – if we need more than cyberspace and robots for knowledge and exploration of deep space (see Levinson, 1994c) – how do other human transactions in information fare in the digital world?

INSTANT COFFEE AND INFORMATION

The difficulty of dining on fine food and spirits not in a restaurant but online, of making love with procreative possibility not in bed with a flesh-and-blood partner but in cyberspace, is obvious. They are patent examples of what cannot be done in cyberspace, of basic aspects of the human condition simply not satisfiable by information technology as we now know it.

On one level, they are workaday, commonplace biological functions. But in their centrality to human existence – indeed, to all life (except sex for unisex organisms, although the amoeba's splitting could be construed as a form of making love, to itself, which might be done by humans online) – they are of the most profound philosophic import. Thus, Popper (1972, p. 37) suggested that our most fundamental individual contact with the external world comes through ingestion of foodstuffs. Recalling the amoeba's process of knowledge-by-engulfment, we can see the merit of Popper's thought: when we eat, we are at our most amoebic *vis-à-vis* the ingested part of the external world. We have a fundamental "knowledge" in the eating process more direct than even touching and tasting – a knowledge which apparently defies transmission by any information technology.

I invoked instant coffee as a metaphor in Chapter 2 to explain how the phonetic alphabet breaks down the external world into a series of granules – letters – to be sent somewhere and reconstituted into external reality in the eyes and brains of the people who read it. Instant coffee – not as metaphor but the powder it is – can also help highlight how even the simplest physical material can be transported but not communicated. Instant coffee starts, of course, with some quantity of full, liquid, drinkable (if not necessarily tasty) coffee. Not only can it not be communicated, it cannot even be transported very easily, very far, in that form either. But when rendered into a powder – encoded, to now borrow a metaphor the other way, from information theory – the coffee can now be easily sent anywhere in the world, and can also stay potentially fresh for a very long time. All the receiver need do to decode the message – to recover the coffee as a drinkable form, much as readers of alphabetic text recover its meaning – is add hot water to the powder. The result, in terms of in effect moving a steaming cup of coffee from any place in the world to any other, is miraculous. But the result is a wonder entirely of transportation, not communication.

One of course can communicate lots of information *about* coffee. Endless texts describing its rich aroma could be e-mailed or linked in hypertext documents about beverages; some enterprising company could no doubt start a successful cable television station which displayed nothing but steaming cups of coffee all day – this would likely be especially successful in the winter. Indeed, coffee – instant or liquid – could be purchased online. Arrangements could be made to deliver it, either in instant form from far away, or even in a steaming cup of some sort if the local coffee shop was online with its own interactive Web page. Purchasers could have their checking accounts or credit cards billed for such transactions. All of this information about coffee, concerning coffee, pertinent to coffee, could be easily processed on the Internet. But not a drop of coffee – in either liquid or powder form – could be sent online.

On one level – that of common sense – the un-e-mailability of instant coffee is so plain as to be absurd to even mention, let alone discourse upon. On another level, however, the evolution of media has so integrated the modes of communication and transportation as to make us expect any device that does the first to be able just as easily to do the second. In the beginning of our human existence, of course, there was no difference between the two: in order to communicate, one person had to walk, run, or swim into another person's physical presence and hearing distance. Talking and walking, to revive a phrase I used in my Ph.D. dissertation years ago ("Human replay: A theory of the evolution of media," 1979), were one and the same. Writing immediately severed that relationship, serving as the "voice of an absent person," as Freud observed and we noted in Chapter 2. The person continued to be absent — communication had no elements of transportation — through the alphabet and the printing press. Neither of these had any residue of the physical human being. Their replacement of walking and talking with *sedere et legere* transformed the full-bodied interactive community into a virtual, one-way, uni-dimensional flat service (see, again, McLuhan, 1962). This was the price paid for their enormous powers of extension across space and time — and well worth it, as we have seen many times in this book.

But this profound decoupling of talking and walking in the hegemony of print created a deep need for media that repaired the breach, while maintaining the benefits of print's extension. Photography began part of the repair. When a photograph is sent from one place to another, from one time to another, a literal physical image is sent. This is still just a representation of the original — not the original itself, of course, and not at all interactive — but it obviously bears a much more immediate resemblance to the original than written description, whose resemblance to anything physical is always radically indirect and second-hand. Meanwhile, telegraph began to address the loss of interaction in print. Later media such as the phonograph, motion pictures, radio, and television provided successively fuller representations of physical reality, while the telephone literally reinstated the voice to the instant, human-paced interactivity of the telegraph.

The irony of the computer and all of its cyberspatial interconnections is that, even in the full audio-visual modes now being developed and implemented, it is no more advanced in reuniting talking and walking, communication and transportation, than the video-telephone — or interactive television — that has been technically possible if not commercially practicable for more than half a century. To be sure, such online images, when fully integrated in the on-demand hypertext of the Web and its myriad individual connections, will be far more powerful in both their accessibility and their impact than most images on television. And their interactivity will be more potent, because of the information conveyed in a moving image, than the telephone's. But they will be no less representational — and no more able to convey a cup of coffee, a kiss on the lips, or any physical thing or process — than the television screen.

Freud (1930, pp. 38–39) observed, in a passage close to his thoughts about writing, that when we don our technologies we feel omnipotent, like gods.

Working on a computer connected to so much knowledge, so much emotion, can make us feel omnipotent indeed – can make us imagine a truly new Java hypertext program, some hot feature, that can deliver a foodstuff, a cup of coffee, a whole person, through the digital line.

But that's not telecommunication. That's teleportation. And though it may seem like the next logical step, and though we can see how easily it might work in *Star Trek*'s transporters, that mode of transport is probably even further away than the development of autonomous artificial intelligences.

A PARTING CUP OF CHEER FOR THE ROAD AHEAD

In the meantime, consider a very modest, decidedly low-tech development in many of the big new bookstores – "superstores" – in the New York City area, and, I assume, in other areas as well. Right there amongst the bookshelves crowded with colorful new hardcover, trade paperback, and mass paperback releases are tables and chairs, to which browsers can bring over coffee and a danish from a nearby dispensary with smiling service, and the conversation of either a new-found acquaintance or a friend brought along from the outside. Or, if conversation is not their wont, browsers can bring over a copy of a book they might want to buy, or read just a few pages of, right on the spot, or maybe a copy of a newspaper – from a wide out-of-town selection – also close at hand.

The bookstore, of course, created this environment, mixed together print on fixed pages with coffee, danish, and conversation, as a way of making the process of selecting and buying books more appealing, in some significant way, than ordering books online, or reading texts that are altogether available, in hypertext or straight plain ascii, online. The coffee not only is utterly untransmissible online, but it symbolizes, in the tangible pleasure it affords, the heat of its cup upon the fingers and lips, the physical enjoyment that some people very much feel in the actual touching and reading of books. The strategy – and it of course works just as well with tea, hot or cold, with milk or lemon, or any stronger kind of cheer – is thus a satisfying and clever one.

Whether it will be enough to enable bookstores to survive is another story. As we saw in Chapters 10 and 16, that question, like issues concerning the survival of any medium, depends upon whether the bookstore does enough unique service to human needs. Computer "cafes" have also been opening around the US –

giving people personal computers to log on with, while providing opportunities for conversation with people sitting right next to them. What advantage, other than the books themselves, do bookstore cafes have over the computer kind, when the latter are not only digital but personal? And stores that rent videos are beginning to encounter similar problems, as cable stations show movies closer and closer to just after theatrical release, directly into the home. Will coffee and danish soon be served along with the videotapes in Blockbuster Video and similar outlets?

Whatever the results, coffee in bookstores, computer cafes, and videostores speaks to the central point of this chapter, and, indeed, by extension, of the entire book: until our DNA and bodies themselves are changed to make us a species very different from what we are today, the soft edge of information technology is best wielded when attached in some way to a hilt of life in the flesh, material in the tangible round, from which we human beings who invent and apply the keenest parts of the edge arose in the first place.

But that still leaves us and our information revolution the whole wide universe to explore.

BIBLIOGRAPHY

Adler, R.G. (1984) "Bio-technology as intellectual property," *Science*, 224: 357–363.

Agassi, J. (1968) *The Continuing Revolution*, New York: McGraw-Hill.

—— (1982) "In search of rationality – a personal report," in P. Levinson (ed.) *In Pursuit of Truth: Essays on the Philosophy of Karl Popper*, Atlantic Highlands, NJ: Humanities Press.

American Heritage Dictionary, The (1991) Boston, MA: Houghton Mifflin.

Appleton, V. (1914) *Tom Swift and his Photo Telephone*, New York: Grosset & Dunlap.

Aristotle (n.d.) *De Anima*, trans. J.A. Smith, in R. McKeon (ed.) *Introduction to Aristotle*, New York: Modern Library.

—— (n.d.) *Physica*, trans. R.P. Hardie and R.K. Gaye, in R. McKeon (ed.) *Introduction to Aristotle*, New York: Modern Library.

Asimov, I. (1951) *Foundation*, New York: Gnome.

—— (1952) *Foundation and Empire*, New York: Gnome.

—— (1953a) *Second Foundation*, New York: Gnome.

—— (1953b) *The Caves of Steel*, New York: Doubleday.

—— (1956) *The Naked Sun*, New York: Doubleday.

—— (1957) *The End of Eternity*, New York: Doubleday.

—— (1979) *In Memory Yet Green*, New York: Avon.

—— (1982) *Foundation's Edge*, New York: Doubleday.

—— (1983) *The Robots of Dawn*, New York: Doubleday.

—— (1984) *Opus 300*, Boston: Houghton Mifflin.

—— (1985) *Robots and Empire*, New York: Doubleday.

—— (1986a) *Foundation and Earth*, New York: Doubleday.

—— (1986b) *Robot Dreams*, New York: Ace.

—— (1988) *Prelude to Foundation*, New York: Doubleday.

—— (1993) *Forward the Foundation*, New York: Doubleday.

—— (1995) *Gold*, New York: HarperPrism.

——, Waugh, C., and Greenberg, M.H. (eds.) (1984) *Isaac Asimov Presents the Best Science Fiction Firsts*, New York: Barnes & Noble.

Bardeche, M. and Brasillach, R. (1938) *The History of Motion Pictures*, New York: Norton.

Barlow, J.P. (1994) "The economy of ideas," *Wired*, 2.03: 84–90, 126–129.

Bartley, W.W., III (1982a) "A Popperian

harvest," in P. Levinson (ed.) *In Pursuit of Truth: Essays on the Philosophy of Karl Popper*, Atlantic Highlands, NJ: Humanities Press.

—— (1982b) "Rationality, criticism, and logic," *Philosophia*, 11, 1–2: 121–221.

Bazin, A. (1967) *What Is Cinema?*, trans. H. Gray, Berkeley, CA: University of California Press.

Bell, A.G. (1922) "Prehistoric telephone days," *The National Geographic*, XLI, 3: 223–241.

Benzon, W. (1993) "The United States of the blues," *Journal of Social and Evolutionary Systems*, 16, 4: 401–438.

Birkerts, S. (1994) *Gutenberg Elegies: The Fate of Reading in an Electronic Age*, Boston: Faber and Faber.

Bohm, D. (1980) *Wholeness and the Implicate Order*, London: Routledge & Kegan Paul.

Bolter, J.D. (1984) *Turing's Man*, Chapel Hill, NC: University of North Carolina Press.

Brand, S. (1987) *The Media Lab*, New York: Viking.

Brodie, R. (1996) *Virus of the Mind: The New Science of the Meme*, Seattle, WA: Integral.

Brooks, J. (1976) *Telephone: The First Hundred Years*, New York: Harper & Row.

Brown, M.H. (1990) *The Search for Eve*, New York: Harper & Row.

Burlingame, R. (1959) "The hardware of culture," *Technology and Culture*, 1, 1: 11–28.

Bush, V. (1945) "As we may think," *The Atlantic Monthly*, July: 101–108.

—— (1970) *Pieces of the Action*, New York: Morrow.

Butler, S. (1910) *Life and Habit*, New York: Dutton.

Campbell, D.T. (1974a) "Evolutionary epistemology," in P. Schilpp (ed.) *The Philosophy of Karl Popper*, La Salle, IL: Open Court.

—— (1974b) "Unjustified variation and selective retention in scientific discovery," in F.J. Ayala and T. Dobzhansky (eds.) *Studies in the Philosophy of Biology*, Berkeley, CA: University of California Press.

Carpenter, E.H. (1973) *Oh, What a Blow that Phantom Gave Me!*, New York: Bantam.

Carr, J. (1995) "Pleasant 'ride' drives interactive movies forward," *Boston Globe*, 5 May: 62.

Castell, R. (ed.) (1995) *Blockbuster Video Guide to Movies and Videos, 1996*, New York: Island.

Chapman, R.L. (ed.) (1987) *American Slang*, New York: Harper & Row.

Cherry, C. (1985) *The Age of Access: Posthumous Papers of Colin Cherry*, ed. W. Edmondson, London: Croom Helm.

Chester, G., Garrison, G.R., and Willis, E.E. (1971) *Television and Radio*, 4th edn, Englewood Cliffs, NJ: Prentice Hall.

Chew, V.K. (1981) *Talking Machines*, London: HMSO.

Chomsky, N. (1975) *Reflections on Language*, New York: Pantheon.

Cleveland, H. (1985) *The Knowledge Executive*, New York: Dutton.

Communications Decency Act of 1996 – *see* Telecommunications Act of 1996.

Conquest, R. (1991) *Stalin: Breaker of Nations*, New York: Viking.

Cunningham, N.E., Jr. (1987) *In Pursuit of Reason: The Life of Thomas Jefferson*, New York: Ballantine.

Curtis, J. (1978) *Culture as Polyphony*, Columbia, MO: University of Missouri Press.

—— (1987) *Rock Eras: Interpretations of Music & Society 1954–1984*, Bowling Green, OH: Bowling Green State University Popular Press.

Dampier, W.C. (1929/1942) *A History of Science*, 3rd edn, New York: Macmillan.

Dawkins, R. (1976) *The Selfish Gene*, New York: Oxford University Press.

—— (1993) "Viruses of the mind," in B. Dahlbom (ed.) *Dennett and His Critics: Demystifying the Mind*, London: Blackwell.

de Haan, D. (1977) *Antique Household Gadgets and Appliances*, Woodbury, NY: Barron's.

Deutscher, I. (1949) *Stalin: A Political Biography*, New York: Oxford University Press.

Dipboye, M. (1977) "Wallace Nutting, photographer," *American Collector*, November: 27, 30.

Dizard, W., Jr. (1997) *Old Media, New Media*, 2nd edn, White Plains, NY: Longman.

Dornsife, R. (1978) *The Ticket Book*, La Jolla, CA: Ticket Book.

Dubie, W. (1994) "Networds: The impact of electronic text-processing utilities on writing," *Journal of Social and Evolutionary Systems*, 17, 2: 127–166.

Dumbach, A.E. and Newborn, J. (1986) *Shattering the German Night*, Boston: Little, Brown.

Dunlap, O.E., Jr. (1951) *Dunlap's Radio and Television Almanac*, New York: Harper & Brothers.

Dyson, F. (1971) "Energy in the universe," *Scientific American*, September: 50–59.

Eder, J.M. (1945) *History of Photography*, trans. E. Epstean, New York: Dover.

Eibl-Eibesfeldt, I. (1970) *Ethology: The Biology of Behavior*, trans. E. Klinghammer, New York: Holt, Rinehart and Winston.

Eisenstein, E. (1979) *The Printing Press as an Agent of Change*, New York: Cambridge University Press.

Eisenstein, S. (1957) *Film Form and The Film Sense*, ed. and trans. J. Leyda, New York: Meridian. (*Film Form* originally published in 1949; *The Film Sense* originally published in 1942.)

Ellul, J. (1962/1965) *Propaganda: The Formation of Men's Attitudes*, trans. K. Kellen and J. Lerner, New York: Vintage.

—— (1964) *The Technological Society*, trans. J. Wilkinson, New York: Vintage.

Emery, M. and Emery, E. (1992) *The Press and America*, 7th edn, Englewood Cliffs, NJ: Prentice Hall.

Encyclopedia Britannica, vol. 5 (1954) Chicago, IL: Encyclopedia Britannica, Inc.

Feenberg, A. (1984) "Utopia and dystopia," online seminar conducted for the Western Behavioral Sciences Institute, June.

Ferrell, K. (1996) Personal conversation about *Omni* magazine, White Plains, NY, 12 July.

Fest, J.C. (1973) *Hitler*, trans. R. Winston and C. Winston, New York: Harcourt Brace Jovanovich.

Fleming, M. (1992) "Stars and scenes that got lost on the way to the screen," *Cosmopolitan*, 213, 4: 198–203.

Florman, S. (1976) *The Existential Pleasures of Engineering*, New York: St. Martin's Press.

Fornatale, P. and Mills, J. (1980) *Radio in the Television Age*, Woodstock, NY: Overlook Press.

Freud, S. (1908) "The relation of the poet to daydreaming," trans. I.F.G. Duff, in B. Nelson (ed.) *On Creativity and the Unconscious: Papers on the Psychology of Art, Literature, Love, Religion by Sigmund Freud*, New York: Harper & Row, 1958.

—— (1918) *Totem and Taboo*, trans. A.A. Brill, New York: Vintage.

—— (1930) *Civilization and its Discontents*, trans. J. Riviere, New York: Cape and Smith.

Fuller, B. (1938) *Nine Chains to the Moon*, Carbondale, IL: Southern Illinois University Press.

Gans, H.J. (1974) *Popular Culture and High Culture*, New York: Basic.

Garratt, G.R.M. (1958) "Telegraphy," in C. Singer, E.J. Holmyard, A.R. Hall, and T.I. Williams (eds.) *A History of Technology, Vol. IV, The Industrial Revolution*, New York: Oxford.

General Electric Network for Information Exchange ("GEnie") (1991–1995) Online discussion in the Science Fiction Round Table.

Gernsheim, H. and Gernsheim, A. (1968) *L.J.M. Daguerre*, New York: Dover.

Gibson, C.R. (n.d.) *The Wonders of Modern Electricity*, Philadelphia, PA: McKay.

Goertzel, B. (1992) "Self-organizing evolution," *Journal of Social and Evolutionary Systems*, 15, 1: 7–54.

Gordon, C. (1971) *Before Columbus: Links Between the Old World and Ancient America*, New York: Crown.

Green, P. (1990) *Alexander to Actium: The Historical Evolution of the Hellenistic Age*, Berkeley, CA: University of California Press.

Greenhouse, L. (1996) "Statute on Internet indecency draws high court's review," *The New York Times*, 7 December: 1, 10.

Greenstein, M.A. (1996) Review of *Truths and Fictions: A Journey from Documentary to Digital Photography* by P. Meyer, *Afterimage*, 23, 5: 23.

Gumpert, G. (1970) "The rise of the mini-comm," *Journal of Communication*, 20: 280–290.

Haile, H.G. (1980) *Luther: An Experiment in Biography*, Garden City, NY: Doubleday.

Hall, E.T. (1966) *The Hidden Dimension*, New York: Anchor.

Halstead, M. (1892) *The Life of Jay Gould*, New York: Edgewood.

Hawthorne, N. (1851/1962) *The House of the Seven Gables*, New York: Collier.

Hays, D. (1995) "Relativism and progress," *Journal of Social and Evolutionary Systems*, 18, 1: 9–32.

Head, S.W. (1976) *Broadcasting in America*, 3rd edn, Boston: Houghton Mifflin.

—— and Sterling, C.H. (1982) *Broadcasting in America*, 4th edn, Boston: Houghton Mifflin.

—— and Sterling, C.H. (1987) *Broadcasting in America*, 5th edn, Boston: Houghton Mifflin.

Heim, M. (1987) *Electric Language*, New Haven, CT: Yale University Press.

Heppner, R. (1993) "Electronic information technologies and the Gulf War," *Journal of Social and Evolutionary Systems*, 16, 1: 45–97.

Hiebert, R.E., Ungurait, D.F., and Bohn, T.W. (1982) *Mass Media: An Introduction to Mass Communication*, 3rd edn, New York: Longman.

Hitler, A. (1924/1971) *Mein Kampf*, trans. R. Manheim, Boston: Houghton Mifflin.

Hogarth, S.W. (1926) "Three great mistakes," *Blue Bell*, November.

Hogan, J.V.L. (1923) *The Outline of Radio*, Boston: Little, Brown.

Information Please Almanac (1994) New York: Houghton Mifflin.

Innis, H. (1950) *Empire and Communications*, Toronto: University of Toronto Press.

—— (1951) *The Bias of Communication*, Toronto: University of Toronto Press.

Jacobs, L. (1969) *The Emergence of Film Art*, New York: Hopkinson and Blake.

Jaspers, K. (1931/1951) *Man in the Modern Age*, trans. E. Paul and C. Paul, London: Routledge & Kegan Paul.

Jones, S.V. (1987) "Chinese characters encoded for computers," *The New York Times*, 8 August: 18, 34.

Josephson, M. (1959) *Edison*, New York: McGraw-Hill.

Kaku, M. (1994) *Hyperspace*, New York: Oxford University Press.

Kantor, A. and Neubarth, M. (1996) "How big is the Internet?" *Internet World*, December: 44–51.

Kaplan, B. (1966) *An Unhurried View of Copyright*, New York: Columbia University Press.

Kargel, J.S. and Strom, R.G. (1996) "Global climatic change on Mars," *Scientific American*, November: 80–88.

Koestler, A. (1959) *The Sleepwalkers*, New York: Grosset & Dunlap.

Levinson, P. (1977) "Toy, mirror, and art: The metamorphosis of technological culture," *et cetera*, 34, 2: 151–167. (Reprinted in Levinson, 1995a.)

—— (1979) "Human replay: A theory of the evolution of media," Ph.D. diss., New York University.

—— (1979/1980) Review of *Four Arguments for the Elimination of Television* by J. Mander, *The Structurist*, 19/20: 107–114.

—— (1981) "McLuhan and rationality," *Journal of Communication*, 31, 3: 179–188.

—— (1985a) "Basics of computer conferencing, and thoughts on its applicability to education," excerpted from unpublished report, "The New School online," January. (Reprinted in Levinson, 1995a.)

—— (1985b) "Impact of personal information technologies on American education, interpersonal relationships, and business, 1985–2010," report prepared for the US Army Research Institute, February. (Reprinted in Levinson, 1995a.)

—— (1987) "The technological determination of philosophy," in S. Thomas (ed.) *Culture and Communication*, Norwood, NJ: Ablex.

—— (1988) *Mind at Large: Knowing in the Technological Age*, Greenwich, CT: JAI Press.

—— (1989a) "Cosmos helps those who help themselves: Historical patterns of technological fulfillment, and their applicability to the human development of space," in C. Mitcham (ed.) *Research in Philosophy and Technology, Vol. 9*, Greenwich, CT: JAI Press. (Reprinted in Levinson, 1995a.)

—— (1989b) "Intelligent writing: The electronic liberation of text," *Technology in Society*, 11, 3: 387–400. (Reprinted in Levinson, 1995a.)

—— (1989c) "Media relations," in R. Mason and T. Kaye (eds.) *MindWeave*, London: Pergamon. (Reprinted in Levinson, 1995a.)

—— (1990) "McLuhan's space," *Journal of Communication*, 40, 2: 169–173.

—— (1992) *Electronic Chronicles: Columns of the Changes in our Time*, San Francisco, CA: Anamnesis.

—— (1994a) "The case against time travel," unpublished manuscript.

—— (1994b) "Telnet to the future?" *Wired*, 2.07: 74.

—— (1994c) "Will the Delta Clipper turn deep space into cyberspace?" *Wired*, 2.02: 68.

—— (1995a) *Learning Cyberspace: Essays on the Evolution of Media and the New Education*, San Francisco, CA: Anamnesis Press.

—— (1995b) "The real thing," *Tangent*, Winter: 48–49.

—— (1995c) "Web of weeds," *Wired*, 3.11: 138.

—— (1996) "On behalf of humanity: The technological edge," *The World and I*, March: 305–313.

—— (1997a) "Innovation in media and the decentralization of authority: The view from here, there, and everywhere," in G. Radnitzky (ed.) *Values and the Social Order, Vol. 3*, Aldershot, UK: Avebury.

—— (1997b) "Learning unbound: Online education and the mind's academy," *Analog*, March: 48–57.

Levinson, P. (ed.) (1982) *In Pursuit of Truth: Essays on the Philosophy of Karl Popper on the Occasion of His 80th Birthday*, Atlantic Highlands, NJ: Humanities Press.

Löfgren, L. (1979) "Goals for human planning," in R. Ericson (ed.) *Proceedings of the Silver Anniversary Meeting of the Society for General Systems Research*, New York: Springer.

—— (1981a) "Knowledge of evolution and evolution of knowledge," in E. Jantsch (ed.) *The Evolutionary Vision*, Boulder, CO: Westview.

—— (1981b) "Life as an autolinguistic phenomenon," in M. Zeleny (ed.) *Autopoiesis*, New York: Oxford University Press.

Lohr, S. (1995) "Reluctant conscripts in the march of technology," *The New York Times*, 17 September: 16.

Longan, R. and Scarrow, L. (1996) "Telemedicine Texas-style cuts prison costs," *Teleconferencing Business*, September/October: 22–23.

Lum, M.-K. (1984) "A study of the impact of

the telephone on human sexuality," M.A. thesis, The New School for Social Research.

Lynch, A. (1996) *Thought Contagion*, New York: Basic.

Maddox, B. (1972) *Beyond Babel*, New York: Simon and Schuster.

Maeroff, G. (1978) "Reading achievement of children in Indiana found as good as in '44," *The New York Times*, 15 April: 10.

Mander, J. (1978) *Four Arguments for the Elimination of Television*, New York: Morrow.

Manguel, A. (1996) *A History of Reading*, New York: Viking.

Margolick, D. (1983) "Publishers and N.Y.U. settle suit on colleges' photocopying rights," *The New York Times*, 15 April: 1.

Marrou, H.I. (1956) *A History of Education in Antiquity*, trans. G. Lamb, New York: Mentor.

Marshack, A. (1972) *The Roots of Civilization*, New York: McGraw-Hill.

Mast, G. (1971) *A Short History of the Movies*, New York: Pegasus.

McCullagh, D. (1996) "DOJ Dodge," *Hotwired*, 21 August.

McDaid, J. (1994) "Luddism, sf, and the aesthetics of electronic fiction," *The New York Review of Science Fiction*, May: 1, 8–11.

McKeever, W.A. (1910) "Motion pictures: a primary school for criminals," *Good Housekeeping*, August: 184–186.

McLuhan, M. (1962) *The Gutenberg Galaxy*, New York: Mentor.

—— (1964) *Understanding Media*, New York: Mentor.

—— (1967) "The relation of environment to anti-environment," in F.W. Matson and A. Montagu (eds.) *The Human Dialogue*, New York: The Free Press.

—— (1976) "Inside on the outside, or the spaced-out American," *Journal of Communication*, 26, 4: 46–53.

—— (1977) "The laws of the media," with a preface by P. Levinson, *et cetera*, 34, 2: 173–179.

—— and Fiore, Q. (1967) *The Medium is the Massage*, New York: Bantam.

—— and McLuhan, E. (1988) *Laws of Media*, Toronto: University of Toronto Press.

—— and Nevitt, B. (1972) *Take Today: The Executive as Dropout*, New York: Harcourt Brace Jovanovich.

—— and Parker, H. (1968) *Through the Vanishing Point*, New York: Harper & Row.

McNeill, W. (1982) *The Pursuit of Power*, Chicago, IL: University of Chicago Press.

Meyer, P. (1994) *Truths and Fictions: A Journey from Documentary to Digital Photography*, New York: Aperture.

Meyrowitz, J. (1985) *No Sense of Place*, New York: Oxford University Press.

Minsky, M. (1986) *The Society of Mind*, New York: Simon and Schuster.

Monaco, J. (1977) *How to Read a Film*, New York: Oxford University Press.

Morrison, S.E. (1942) *Admiral of the Ocean Sea*, Boston: Little, Brown.

Mumford, L. (1934) *Technics and Civilization*, New York: Harcourt Brace & World.

—— (1967) *Technics and Human Development*, New York: Harcourt Brace Jovanovich.

—— (1970) *The Pentagon of Power*, New York: Harcourt Brace Jovanovich.

Munz, P. (1985) *Our Knowledge of the Growth of Knowledge*, London: Routledge & Kegan Paul.

Nayman, I. (1996) "Tell me a story I can live: Electronic interactive narrative and the effacement of the author," M.A. thesis, The New School for Social Research.

Nelson, T.H. (1990) *Literary Machines*, Sausalito, CA: Mindful Press.

Newhall, B. (1964) *The History of Photography*, New York: The Metropolitan Museum of Art.

—— (1976) *The Daguerreotype in America*, 3rd edn, New York: Dover.

Ohmann, R. (1985) "Literacy, technology, and monopoly," *College English*, 47, 7: 657–689.

Pember, D.R. (1981) *Mass Media in America*, 3rd edn, Chicago, IL: Science Research Associates.

Percival, R. (1994) "Dawkins and incurable mind viruses? Memes, rationality, and evolution," *Journal of Social and Evolutionary Systems*, 17, 3: 243–296.

Petroski, H. (1985) *To Engineer Is Human*, New York: St. Martin's Press.

—— (1992) *The Evolution of Useful Things*, New York: Viking.

Phillips, D.C., Grogan, J., and Ryan, E.H. (1954) *Introduction to Radio and Television*, New York: Ronald Press.

Plato (n.d.) *Phaedrus*, in B. Jowett (trans.) *The Dialogues of Plato*, New York: Scribner, Armstrong.

Platt, C. (1995) "Interactive entertainment: Who writes it? Who reads it? Who needs it?" *Wired*, 3.09: 144–149, 195–197.

Popper, K.R. (1963/1965) *Conjectures and Refutations*, London: Routledge & Kegan Paul.

—— (1972) *Objective Knowledge: An Evolutionary Approach*, London: Oxford University Press.

Postman, N. (1979) *Teaching as a Conserving Activity*, New York: Delacorte.

—— (1985) *Amusing Ourselves to Death*, New York: Viking.

—— (1992) *Technopoly: The Surrender of our Culture to Technology*, New York: Knopf.

—— (1994) "John Culkin Memorial Talk," New School for Social Research, New York City, 16 February.

Pribram, K.H. (1971) *Languages of the Brain*, Englewood Cliffs, NJ: Prentice Hall.

Quarterman, J.S. (1990) *The Matrix*, Bedford, MA: Digital.

Read, D. (1992) *The Power of News: The History of Reuters*, New York: Oxford University Press.

Redford, D.B. (1984) *Akhenaten: The Heretic King*, Princeton, NJ: Princeton University Press.

Reif, R. (1977) "Collectors focus on daguerreotypes," *The New York Times*, 9 October, sec. 2: 24.

Rensberger, B. (1978) "The oldest works of art," *The New York Times Magazine*, 27 May: 26–29 ff.

Rheingold, H. (1993) *The Virtual Community*, Reading, MA: Addison-Wesley.

—— (1994) "PARC is back," *Wired*, 2.02: 91–95.

Rhode, E. (1976) *History of the Cinema*, New York: Hill and Wang.

Richards, I.A. (1929) *Practical Criticism*, New York: Harcourt Brace.

Riesman, D. (1950) *The Lonely Crowd*, New Haven, CT: Yale University Press.

Rifkin, J. (1995) *The End of Work: The Decline of the Global Labor Force and the Dawn of the Post-Market Era*, New York: Putnam.

Roberson, J.T. (1988) "The Black Church and technology," unpublished paper, available in the private, online Connected Education Library.

Roland, A. (1994) "How we won the moon," *The New York Times Book Review*, 17 July: 1, 25.

Sale, K. (1995) *Rebels Against the Future*, Reading, MA: Addison-Wesley.

Schreiber, F. (1953) "The battle against print," *The Freeman*, April 20.

Schulman, N. (1992) "Informational property: Logorights," *Journal of Social and Biological Structures*, 13, 2: 93–117.

Schwartz, T. (1973) *The Responsive Chord*, Garden City, NY: Anchor/Doubleday.

Shanks, B. (1976) *The Cool Fire*, New York: Norton.

Shiver, J., Jr. (1995) "Broadcaster and FCC reach settlement on indecency suit," *Los Angeles Times*, 2 September: D1.

Skagestad, P. (1993) "Thinking with machines:

Intelligence augmentation, evolutionary epistemology, and semiotic," *Journal of Social and Evolutionary Systems*, 16, 2: 157–180.

—— (1996) "The mind's machines: The Turing machine, the Memex, and the personal computer," *Semiotica*, 111, 3/4: 217–243.

Socrates – *see* Plato.

Sontag, S. (1977) *On Photography*, New York: Farrar, Straus, and Giroux.

Stearn, G.E. (ed.) (1967) *McLuhan: Hot and Cool*, New York: Dial.

Storey, G. (1951) *Reuters' Century*, London: Parrish.

Tabori, P. (1993) *The Natural History of Stupidity*, New York: Barnes & Noble. (Originally published as *The Natural Science of Stupidity*, Philadelphia, PA: Chilton, 1959.)

Tedford, T.L. (1985) *Freedom of Speech in the United States*, New York: Random House.

—— (1997) *Freedom of Speech in the United States*, 3rd edn, State College, PA: Strata.

Telecommunications Act (US) of 1996 (1996), including Title V, "Obscenity and Violence," Subtitle A, "Obscene, Harassing, and Wrongful Utilization of Telecommunications Facilities" (also known as the "Communications Decency Act of 1996"), and Subtitle B, "Violence," Sec. 551, "Parental Choice in Television Programming".

Tenner, E. (1996) *Why Things Bite Back: Technology and the Revenge of Unintended Consequences*, New York: Knopf.

Thorne, K.P. (1994) *Black Holes and Time Warps*, New York: Norton.

Townsend, C. (1984) *Electronic Mail and Beyond*, Belmont, CA: Wadsworth.

Turner, F. (1996) "An evolutionary/chaotic theory of beauty and meaning," *Journal of Social and Evolutionary Systems*, 19, 2: 103–124.

Vincenti, W.G. (1990) *What Engineers Know and How They Know It*, Baltimore, MD: Johns Hopkins University Press.

Volkogonov, D. (1988) *Stalin: Triumph and Tragedy*, trans. H. Shukman, New York: Grove Weidenfeld.

Wachtel, E. (1977/1978) "The influence of the window on Western art and vision," *The Structurist*, 17/18: 4–10.

Waechtershaeuser, G. (1984) "Light and life: On the nutritional origins of perception and reason," paper presented at the Annual Meeting of the American Association for the Advancement of Science, New York City, 27 May.

WBNC-TV (1997) "News 4 New York", 5 May.

Weizenbaum, J. (1976) *Computer Power and Human Reason*, San Francisco, CA: Freeman.

Whelpley, S. (1826) *Compend of History, from the Earliest Times; Comprehending a General View of the Present State of the World, with Respect to Civilization, Religion, and Government; and a Brief Dissertation of the Importance of Historical Knowledge*, Boston: Richardson & Lord.

Whetmore, E.J. (1979) *Mediamerica*, Belmont, CA: Wadsworth.

—— (1989) *Mediamerica*, 4th edn, Belmont, CA: Wadsworth.

Wiener, N. (1948) *Cybernetics*, New York: MIT Press and John Wiley.

Wilford, J.J.N. (1996) "In Australia, signs of artists who predate homo sapiens," *The New York Times*, 21 September: 1, 5.

Winner, L. (1977) *Autonomous Technology*, Cambridge, MA: MIT Press.

Wright, B. (1989) *EDI and American Law*, Alexandria, VA: Electronic Data Interchange Association.

Wuketits, F. (1991) "Life, cognition, and 'intra-organismic selection,'" *Journal of Social and Biological Structures*, 14, 2: 184–189.

Yoon, C.K. (1996) "Parallel plots in classic of evolution," *The New York Times*, 12 November: C1, C7.

Zimmer, P.E. (1996) Personal conversation about word processing and writing, at "Albacon," Albany, New York, 11 October.

Zuckerman, L. (1996) "America OnLine announces a newer transformation," *The New York Times*, 30 October: D5.

INDEX